THE GROUND HAS SHIFTED

RELIGION, RACE, AND ETHNICITY
General Editor: Peter J. Paris

For a complete list of titles in the series, please visit the New York University Press website at www.nyupress.org.

The Ground Has Shifted

The Future of the Black Church in Post-Racial America

Walter Earl Fluker

NEW YORK UNIVERSITY PRESS

New York

NEW YORK UNIVERSITY PRESS
New York
www.nyupress.org

References to Internet websites (URLs) were accurate at the time of writing. Neither the author nor New York University Press is responsible for URLs that may have expired or changed since the manuscript was prepared.

Library of Congress Cataloging-in-Publication Data
Names: Fluker, Walter E., 1951– author.
Title: The ground has shifted : the future of the Black church in post-racial America / Walter Earl Fluker.
Other titles: Religion, race, and ethnicity.
Description: New York : New York University Press, 2016. |
Series: Religion, race, and ethnicity
Identifiers: LCCN 2016021209 | ISBN 978-1-4798-1038-3 (cl : alk. paper)
Subjects: LCSH: African American churches—21st century. | Race relations—Religious aspects—Christianity. | Church and social problems—United States. | Post-racialism.
Classification: LCC BR563.N4 F58 2016 | DDC 277.3008996073—dc23
LC record available at https://lccn.loc.gov/2016021209

New York University Press books are printed on acid-free paper, and their binding materials are chosen for strength and durability. We strive to use environmentally responsible suppliers and materials to the greatest extent possible in publishing our books.

Manufactured in the United States of America

10 9 8 7 6 5 4 3 2 1

Also available as an ebook

For my children—Clinton Rahman Fluker, Hampton Sterling Fluker, Tiffany Marie Henderson, Wendy Deneen Whitley, and Melvin Très Watson

CONTENTS

ACKNOWLEDGMENTS

I have a lot of people to thank for their support throughout the writing of this book. I begin with Professor Peter J. Paris, who approached me about the project while he was serving as visiting professor at Boston University School of Theology from 2013 to 2015. At first, I was reluctant because of other outstanding projects that were staring me down, but no one can say no to Peter, with the exception of Adrienne, his beloved wife. He has been a colleague over the years and a dear friend who "sticketh closer than a brother." As the series editor, Peter read the manuscript several times and offered excellent advice, which is reflected in these pages. Jennifer Hammer, my editor at New York University Press, has been a constant guide, prodder, encourager, and critic who inspired and challenged me to give a bit more and to find my voice. I owe her an incredible debt of gratitude.

Dean Mary Elizabeth Moore has been a gentle but enthusiastic supporter of my work since coming to Boston University School of Theology in the fall of 2010. I am thankful to her and all my colleagues at the School of Theology. I extend special thanks to Professors Courtney Goto, Pamela Lightsey, and Nimi Wariboko, who advised me or made contributions to my thinking at important junctures in my writing. The teaching fellows Onaje X. Woodbine, Kathryn House, and Derrick Muwina and my research assistant Julian Cook have done much of the nitty-gritty, behind-the-scenes work of finding correct citations and obscurely published documents that hopefully have added to the density and scope of the argument found in this text. I am also grateful to have a son who has chosen a scholarly path. Clinton R. Fluker has listened to and read portions of the book, especially chapter 7, and has offered observations that have kept me on the straight and narrow of black aesthetics and culture. Other scholars whom I acknowledge throughout have provided thoughtful commentary in places where I was treading on shallow ground, especially Herbert Marbury, associate professor of Hebrew Bible at Vanderbilt University; and Shively Smith, assistant professor of New Testament at Wesley Theological Seminary.

The idea for *The Ground Has Shifted* has been germinating for some time, but without the fellowship of colleagues and collaborators, it would not have seen the light of day. My good friend R. Drew Smith, professor of urban ministry at Pittsburgh Theological Seminary, invited me to co-keynote with Alan Boesak at a conference sponsored by the Transnational Roundtable on Religion, Race and Ethnicity in Johannesburg, South Africa, in 2011. The lecture was subsequently published as "Shape-Shifting: Cultural Hauntings, Contested Post-Racialism, the Black Church and Theological Imagination" in *Contesting Post-Racialism: Conflicted Churches in the United States and South Africa*, edited by R. Drew Smith, William Ackah, Anthony Reddie, and Rothney Tshaka (Jackson: University Press of Mississippi, 2015). The following year, 2012, the same organization invited me to keynote at the Birbeck College of London University, where the early seeds of my thinking on the Pentecostal symbolism of "a scattered and scattering peoples" were presented. In February 2014, I was invited to serve as the Distinguished Lecturer for the Paul Allen Lecture Series at McCormick Theological Seminary in Chicago. I presented two lectures that find form in the present text: "Cultural Asylums and the Jungles Planted in Them: The Exilic Condition of African American Males in a Post-Industrial, Post-Modern World" and "Tools of the Spirit: Identity, Otherness, and Human Flourishing and the Exilic Condition of African American Males." I am indebted to these individuals and institutions and so many others who have exhorted, reproved, and rebuked my feeble attempts presented in this book. I bring what I have done back to all of you as an offering, a debt paid to you and to so many ancestors who crowd these pages.

I am also deeply indebted to Silvia Glick, managing editor of the Howard Thurman Papers Project, for her editing of the manuscript. Her careful eye and uncompromising standards have guided me throughout the writing and final production of the book. I am the senior editor and director of the Howard Thurman Papers Project at Boston University, and since I've lived with this work for over twenty years, readers should not be surprised that Howard Thurman speaks often in this text. I have not attempted to quiet him down—he deserves our hearing.

Finally, I have been extraordinarily blessed to have a life companion, Sharon Watson Fluker, who for thirty-five years has shared in my every success and has supported me in my every failure. In my eyes, she continues to be the wisest and most beautiful of all God's creations.

PART I

Memory

Remembering Our Story

Memory believes before knowing remembers. Believes longer than recollects, longer than knowing even wonders.
—William Faulkner, *Light in August*

1

From Frogbottom to a Bucket of Blood

I was born in 1951 in Vaiden, Mississippi, a small town about ten miles from Winona, Mississippi. Winona is about 190 miles northeast of a small town in Louisiana that bears my paternal family's surname. Although Fluker is German, the convoluted history of Africans, Native Americans, Spanish, French, German, and English who were part of the settlement of this area runs through my veins and spills over into the waters of the great Mississippi.[1] Our section of Vaiden was known affectionately as *Frogbottom*, a name that could have come from either the croaking of the frogs or the groaning of the black residents, whose existence was often lower than that of the frogs. Winona is the town where Fannie Lou Hamer, Annelle Ponder, and fourteen-year-old June Johnson were jailed and beaten mercilessly after attending a voters' registration campaign sponsored by the Student Nonviolent Coordinating Committee in the summer of 1963. Hamer suffered permanent kidney damage and loss of sight in her left eye from the beatings. Two black male inmates were forced, while white officers looked on, to pummel her with a blackjack until they were exhausted. "I had been beat 'til I was real hard, just hard like a piece of wood or somethin'," Hamer would later say. "A person don't know what can happen to they body if they beat with something like I was beat with."[2]

About thirty miles down the road from Vaiden is Kosciusko, the birthplace of Oprah Winfrey. The first time I met Ms. Winfrey and shared that I was born in Vaiden, she asked, "How did you get out?" I told her that Daddy left Frogbottom in 1956. He felt like a piece of wood or somethin'. Mr. Joe Hand, his boss-man, used to "make our figgers turn somersets" at the end of the cotton-picking season.[3] My two oldest sisters, Rosetta and Helen, left first. Working in the cotton fields, daily they would hear the City of New Orleans train coming through Winona to collect passengers who were leaving for points north in search of the Promised Land.[4] Rosetta and Helen would prop themselves on their hoes in the middle of the hot fields and swear, "Lord, I'm going to ride that train one of these days!" They eventually left with new husbands, Curtis and Eddie, who had made the journey to Chicago and, like saviors, returned for them.

My father, Clinton, followed. He later sent for my mother, Zettie; my older brother, Clinton; my sister Beatrice; and me. Another sister, Ceonia, had died a few years before from a rheumatic heart. There were four other children who had died before I was born, most at birth. My uncle and namesake used to say to me, "Boy, your daddy and mama seen a hard time, a hard time."

Daddy sent for Mama, Clinton, Bea, and me after locating several piecemeal jobs as a brick cleaner, car wash attendant, and dishwasher. He didn't have the skills necessary to compete in a city like Chicago—social skills, professional skills, and survival skills. His was a journey to a "new world" nearly five hundred years after Columbus sailed, but he simply was not prepared for what he discovered in a compassionless urban society. In fact, I am convinced he never really left Mississippi. *He traded Frogbottom for a Bucket of Blood.*

In the Northern Diaspora, Mama and Daddy missed "home."[5] In a strange, almost ironic twist, Frogbottom became a mythical abode of innocence, a means of return to sanity, a remembering that offered a basis for hope in an alien urban context to which my parents never truly adjusted. Mama found "home" in the church. It was a little storefront located between a barbershop and two houses on Forty-Third Street, infamously known as the "Bucket of Blood" because of the vicious knife fights and shootings in the area. A pool hall and Princess's Restaurant were located farther down the street. Across the street were a rib joint and a tavern. The church was a sanctuary and social center that protected my youth from madness like an old package used to transport fragile cargo to safe quarters. The building originally served as a church, then an animal hospital, and was later refashioned to accommodate black saints: mostly women, mostly migrants from Mississippi.[6] I, too, found *a home in dat' rock*, as the old spiritual goes—in fact, the church *saved* me.

My Mama took me to church. Every Sunday she would dress up in her white usher's uniform with a black handkerchief delicately placed over a badge that read, "Centennial M. B. Church." I never knew why the founders chose the name "Centennial," but my best guess is that the church is still less than a hundred years old. Black storefront churches are known for their quixotic names, misplaced metaphors echoing the journey from *downsouth* to *upsouth*—names with sounds often more prominent than their signification. I've always felt that these sounds represent the primordial search for black identity in the midst of the dissonant sirens of late modernity, where literacy is the agency for salvation. I have heard those sounds many times and in many places, like the time I saw a woman *shout* across the bar in a blues joint to a saxophone bellowing, "I can't stop loving you"; or whenever I hear Sam Cooke's melancholy hymn of hope, "I was born by the river in a little tent / Oh and just like the river I've been running ever since / It's been a long, a long time coming / but I know a change gone come." But the best were the sounds streaming every Sunday morning from that little storefront church challenging all the cultural caricatures of blackness and protecting us from the wiles of the many devils that sought access to our souls; sounds like the choir singing, "Oh, it's a highway to heaven / None can walk up there / but the pure in heart. / Oh, it's a highway to heaven / I'm walking up the King's Highway!"

I remember how Sylvia Thornton's petite body with its elfin features rocked back and forth as her tiny feet hardly touched the pedals while she crouched over the Hammond organ, getting all fired up and playing like it was Judgment Day. We were as clean as the board of health in our double-toned light and dark blue robes, with all of us in the choir belting out the lines as Sylvia, in her chic, elegant outfits, brought a style to the moment that convinced me that God meant for everything we wore to be as beautiful as whatever they were wearing in heaven. "Christ walks beside us, angels to guide us / Walking up the King's Highway!" We did not want to be outdone by the angels while we were walking up the King's Highway! Heaven was a place for styling, laughing, and playing! No sad faces—just pure joy and light!

We needed Christ to walk beside us! Forty-Third Street was a highway to heaven or hell—it all depended on with whom you were walking. Once I was walking with a high school classmate, a block down the street from the church, when Thunder, the leader of the Black Stone Four Corners Rangers, threatened my friend's life if he ever repeated to the authorities details about an assassination that he had witnessed. Or the time on the highway when Richard, the itinerant preacher, whose right arm and leg were lost in a prankish teenage accident while playing on the "L" tracks, met me in one of my frequent states of inebriation and laid his remaining hand on my head in prayer for my future. I remember best the last stanza of the song, "If you're not walking, start while I'm talking / Walking up the King's Highway!"

My memory is a chamber of sounds—black sounds, rich with life, pregnant with hope and possibility rallying against the damning, depressing nihilistic dirge of machine culture and progress Western-style; the rhapsodic rhythm of congo and bongo drums on hot summer nights in the Chicago of my youth calling upon ancient spirits for deliverance from cultural asylums and redlined urban concentration camps; sounds of young black boys "doo-wopping" to the tunes of the Temptations: "I've got sunshine on a cloudy day / and when it's cold outside, I've got the month of May"; sounds like the pistol shot that left a bullet in Romero's neck; sounds like the late-night heavy breathing "up on the roof," rushing and pushing hard, shooting babies that would never know their fathers; sounds of broken windows from home runs off Tony Kelley's bat in the vacant lot across the street from Mrs. Grant's house; sounds like the "epistemologically opposed and existentially tense"[7] moaning I heard on late Saturday night and early Sunday morning at the Centennial Missionary Baptist Church, sounds of lament and rejoicing; gospel choirs and the musical wizardry of the Reverend Hosie Robinson reaching his sermonic climax in the sensual cadence and incantations of horns blowing kisses—*In the beginning was the Sound and the Sound was with God and God was the Sound*—"Somebody, say 'Amen!'"

Mama was the proudest person alive as she greeted the congregants with an extended arm and a swift turn and escorted them to their seats. Those simple movements—*the extended arm* and *swift turn*—were what Milan Kundera called "gestures of immortality."[8] I was my mother's caretaker. This was not my duty alone. I was privileged to share this responsibility with other family members, but since I was the youngest sibling, during my brother Clinton's military tour of duty in Vietnam, the weight of my mother's daytime care fell to my sister Bea and me. Mama's epilepsy and fiery temperament did not make this task easy. The seizures would leave her confused and with loss of memory. She would forget where she was and often not recognize us for some time. In public places, we learned to protect and comfort her while onlookers stared. Under guarded breath, they called her "crazy."

I really don't know much about my mother's childhood except that her father was an abusive man, prone to fits of rage. He died the year before my birth. My grandmother, whom we affectionately called Maugh, was the backbone of the family of four boys and four girls. She was a medicine woman upon whom the community relied for healing and counsel. She was born with a veil over her face, which meant that she could *see*. Maugh was strong, rugged, and free. She rode a horse well into old age. The white folks called her a "crazy nigger," but she wasn't crazy—she was fearless!

My mother inherited Maugh's fearlessness. I remember once when I was eleven years old, Mr. B. C., who lived in the basement apartment in the building where we rented the first-floor, four-room flat, got into an argument with my mother. My mother and I were home alone. In a drunken stupor, he came upstairs, broke the window of our apartment door with a pistol and pointed it in my mother's face. I was crying and pleading with Mr. B. C. not to shoot my mother. My mother stood there

in defiance and told him, "You can shoot me, B. C., but you can't eat me."
Madness.

Early I witnessed the tragic violence that dogs the footsteps of the oppressed: gangs, crimes, drugs, murder—it was all there. Society had already written a nighttime script for the young black men and women of
my neighborhood. But my little Mama knew something about the other
side of *madness*—she possessed a subversive quality of hope. Constantly
in poor health, functionally illiterate, misplaced in a hostile urban environment, Mama still found a place called "hope." Every Tuesday evening, no matter what activity demanded my youthful attention, Mama
required that I go to prayer meeting at our little storefront church on
Forty-Third Street. It was there that I would witness the source of this
"hope." During testimony time, Mama would rise and give her testimony. "I just rose to tell my determination," she began her memorized
litany. "My determination is for heaven. Sometimes it's hard living in
this place. Trials are on every hand. Raising children is hard, but I keep
on keeping on, 'cause I know that the Lord is able to keep them from
falling. I've put my children in the hands of the Lord. Sometimes I want
to give up, but I can't. 'Cause this joy that I have, the world didn't give it
to me and the world can't take it away."

O dear mother of mine! How did she know that sometimes when
daybreak would seem a million nighttimes away, when I could not see
my way for the tears in my eyes, when lonely nights would come way
down in the valley where I couldn't hear nobody pray, that her words
would find a place in my heart that rings even now: "This joy that I have,
the world didn't give it to me and the world can't take it away!"

Once I saw my mother in a vision, seated at a campfire and wrapped
in animal skins, and around her were other elders making preparation
for ritual cleansing. She rose from a crouched posture with a staff in her
hand and walked to the huge pot in the midst of the fire. I shall never
forget the regal beauty and rustic elegance with which she rose—like a
goddess, ancient and holy. She uttered incantations and began to spit

into the flame. As she spat, I felt the roar of the flames in my belly, burning my deep inward parts. I screamed with the voice of a soul possessed, receiving a deep inner healing. I knew instantly that she was making preparation for my becoming—a foretaste of the future that I could not see, a baptism in the Fire that prophesies in many languages to many nations. "See," she says, "I have refined you, though not as silver; I have tested you in the furnace of affliction."[9] *She is like the refiner's fire.*

* * *

My father was a handsome, gentle man who rested in a place that I sometimes call "peace by a waterfall." But long after he left Mississippi for the Promised Land, the ghosts of Mississippi haunted my father. Those *ha'nts*, as he called them, were ever present, working sometimes for evil and sometimes for good. *Hoodoo* was real strong in those parts of the country where he grew up, and people still practice this invisible religion alongside their Christian beliefs.[10] A family story that I heard from my father was about the time he was poisoned close to death and he went to a conjure doctor. The conjure man placed a dime in his mouth and the dime turned greenish black, which was a sign that he had been poisoned. The roots worker gave him a potion and he was healed in several days. It took me a while to realize just how powerfully my father's beliefs in ghosts and ha'nts impacted my own journey into the world of shape-shifting spirits and taught me to observe their different guises, animating mundane things and returning to the silence of memory in old songs.

My best times with Daddy were those kitchen moments before the others rose, watching him bake biscuits.[11] Daddy made the best biscuits. Not those store-bought, spongy Pillsbury doughcakes, but big, thick, Mississippi, hand-sized, mouthwatering, long-lasting, *Heavy D* biscuits that sat awkwardly on the side of the plate to save space for the sausage, eggs, and Alaga (Alabama-Georgia) syrup. Even as a small child I had a sixth sense for great cuisine, but I saved the seventh for Daddy.

Sometimes he would sing a song while brewing his coffee in one of the small tin pots. He said he first heard it from a white woman evangelist in the Delta.

> Me and the Devil had a tussle, but I won.
> Me and the Devil had a tussle, but I won.
> I hate the Devil, he hates me.
> Me and the Devil cannot agree.
> Me and the Devil had a tussle, but I won.

Daddy struggled with many devils: devils from Mississippi, devils in Chicago, devils of fear, devils of hopelessness, and devils he could not name. The greatest of these devils was *hopelessness*. It is only in retrospect, looking back at the horror of those early years in Chicago, that I remember how difficult it was for him to make sense of the deep alienation and harrowing fear of transitioning from *downsouth* to *upsouth*. *Tussling* constantly without jobs, being too old, too unskilled, and too black to make a living for his family, was a veritable hell with many fiendish imps mocking his every effort to remain sane and whole.

In *The Inferno*, Dante placed a sign over the entrance into hell. It read, *Abandon hope all ye who enter here*. Hopelessness reigned on the Southside of Chicago and played itself out in razor fights, shootings, bad whiskey, and fantastic visions of hell that street-corner prophets used with great facility and reward. Daddy didn't have much use for any of these sedatives or for churchgoing. Although he attended church in Mississippi, he started going to church in Chicago only after he was diagnosed with cancer. He would sing to himself—*those old songs*. Yes, how I remember *those old songs* that come when hope has exhausted itself and like angelic guides they lead us into misty wanderings and quiet ways.

Early in the morning, there in the kitchen, between the stove and the table, transitioning back and forth between time and song, between *downsouth* and *upsouth*, between devils he left behind and devils that greeted him in the Promised Land, Daddy established his rhythm, the rhythm that would carry him through the day:

> Me and the Devil had a tussle, but I won.
> Me and the Devil had a tussle, but I won.
> I hate the Devil, he hates me.
> Me and the Devil cannot agree.
> Me and the Devil had a tussle, but I won.

In hell, hope comes with small steps. There are no great eschatological leaps into a heaven where the streets are paved with gold—no, there are only small, calculated, carefully maneuvered steps. I understand *those old songs* better, now. Sometimes as he limped through tight, crooked spaces, *those old songs* were melodic walking sticks that helped Daddy to stand and delicately identify safe places in the dark—he was *negotiating tragedy and transcendence.* He had another song that would follow the first:

> Do you know Him?
> Do you know Him?
> Jesus Christ, God's Son?

After the coffee was made and the biscuits were baked, he would sing that *old song.* Often it was during a morning when Daddy was making decisions about the day. I remember the times when there was no bus fare for my sister and me to go to school. Daddy would sing the song:

> Do you know Him?
> Do you know Him?
> Jesus Christ, God's Son?

He was pondering the next step: "Do you know Him? / Do you know Him? / Jesus Christ, God's Son?" I dare not attempt a hermeneutical exploration of what was going on in Daddy's soul while he pondered these things, but I imagine that Gethsemane would be an appropriate metaphor.

> Do you know Him?
> Do you know Him?
> Jesus Christ, God's Son?

Jesus, God, and the angels never show up when we beg and plead for deliverance. The sheer carnage of black bodies and the titanic loss of black mothers' petitions should teach us this. But it is in remembering, in transitioning, in making and baking fresh things that we make contact with the eternal within us. It is there that the answers are provided: God dons human garments, Jesus becomes a bosom friend, and the angels just show out in the mid-heavens. Somewhere between the stove and the table, between the pouring of the coffee and the *sopping* of the biscuits in Alaga syrup, Daddy received his answer and a new day of hope would spring forth.

Daddy died in 1984, but he still visits me in dreams and songs. In one dream I was in the backyard of my house in Nashville, Tennessee, fearfully approaching two terrible Dobermans chained to a tool shed. In the dream I was a child, innocently walking into the fangs of these vicious predators. Suddenly I felt a lift from two huge arms that gently transported me to safety. They were Daddy's arms. Daddy's arms still come to me at times of crisis when my way is lost and I am walking into dangerous territory without a map.

He also sings to me. Some years ago I was invited to speak at a church, but for some reason the "word" would not come. Nearly an hour before I was to present, an *old song* came to me in Daddy's voice: *I'm going to sit at the Welcome Table one of these days.* The refrain called me back to memory. I remembered my father's flight from Mississippi and his altercation with Mr. Hand and how he had to leave in a hurry and how he later sent for his wife and three children to join him in the Promised

Land. The rest of that story was written in the pain and travail of a displaced black southerner in a hostile urban environment to which he was never reconciled. But his journey marked the meaning of black people in America in search of deliverance from the retribution of Crusoe and acceptance into a land flowing with milk and honey. But there was never enough milk and never enough honey for us; all we had were Daddy's arms.

I sang my sermon that morning in the old way, long meters, dragging the melody until the words bled into one another and rested in the hollow caverns of our throats.

> I'm going to sit at the Welcome Table,
> I'm going to sit at the Welcome Table one of these days.

Far beyond the inherited and distorted Anglo creeds and evangelical formulas of a salvation American style, that melody shook up calcified memories. The Spirit walked the aisles and touched two other displaced southerners sitting in the congregation. They met me at the door at the close of the service and related to me their story of Frogbottom. They reported that only a week earlier, thirty years later, Daddy's boss-man's son had burned his wife in the fields that my family once worked. Daddy wanted me to *remember*; even the rising eerie smoke from the parched, bloody land that bore witness to his travail and the suffering of many broken black bodies cried out to me to *remember*.

How do you remember black fathers, their strong arms and old songs, without romanticization and nostalgic wanderings into places filled with the horror of *going nameless up and down the streets of other minds where no salutation greets and where there is no place to call one's own*?[12] I choose to remember my father as the one who never left but resides in secret places hidden from the master's rage. Arna Bontemps in *Black Thunder* says of Bundy, the field hand killed by old Marse, that you can't hurt a smoke man 'cause "Dying ain't nothing. The smoke goes free. Can't nobody hurt smoke. A smoke man—that's you now, brother.

A *real* smoke man. Smoke what gets in yo' eyes and makes you blink. Smoke what gets in yo' throat and chokes you. Don't let them cover you up in that hole, Bundy. Mm-mm-mm-mm."[13] Daddy is a *real* smoke man, now! And he is ghostly, free and dangerous because where there is smoke, there is *fire*!

When I am most myself, that is, mySelf, which has nothing to do with the illusory patterns of bondage that play out in the minds of lost boys who have never known their fathers—those mortgaged by society and sent to Never Never Land from the urban centers of America without charming Peter Pans and sexy nymphs to defend them—when I am most mySelf, I can hear distant murmurings of the "black and angry dead"[14] who visit in dreams and songs and testify to a day of reckoning in America and the world. They say (and I pause here, to affirm that it is true) that one day, *The bottom rail will be on the top rail.*

To remember black fathers is to reenter lost time, time-swept-under-the-rug, and to play in broad open spaces far from the fear of predators who lurk behind the curtains of social fictions. It is to soar in flight above the madness in ever-widening concentric patterns of freedom heralding a new day when Million Man Marches and apocalyptic gangsta paradises are moving pictures set to the rhythm of old songs with fresh meanings for struggle and redemption in a land where our fathers' and mothers' bones await a new Breath of Pentecost. It is to remember that our names, our destinies, our soul journeys are in the valley of these bones and that only with the invocation of the Holy Ghost can we see a mighty army clothed in flesh.

I await this day—better, I run screaming through the valley of dry bones and challenge them to live again, to see again, to know again, to be again, to begin again. Dare we see this, we who believe in ghosts?

* * *

During a 1977 family reunion in Winona, my father, mother, older brother, and sisters took me back to Frogbottom. Twenty-one years had passed since my family had traded the croaking of frogs for the

Promised Land. I was anxious to see the place, the little house where I was born. I had warm and cheerful memories of the house and of my family living there. It was *home*. I remembered the animals, the smells, the sounds, and what Du Bois called "the sensuous spirituality of the southern environment." Although I was raised in Chicago, my family remained essentially southern. The experiences, feelings, associations, jokes, stories, etiquette, behavior, laughter, language— indeed, the culture of the South—were so deeply embedded in my way of being in the world that someone in New England remarked once that I was "more Mississippian than Chicagoan," a compliment I graciously acknowledged.[15]

I was eager to see the place, this "site of memory,"[16] and to relive those time-swept days that my father rehearsed in stories about High John the Conqueror, Brer Rabbit, and h'ants in country churchyards. Ah, the magic of those ecstatic rituals that translated us from the madness of urban existence to sacred spheres of redemption as we sat at his feet for hours. I discovered, however, that these memories were perhaps more an amalgam of my father's stories about the South that he loved and missed so much than factual recollections from my early childhood. "Memory (the deliberate act of remembering) is a form of willed creation," writes Toni Morrison. "It is not an effort to find out the way it really was—that is research. The point is to dwell on the way it appeared and why it appeared in that particular way."[17]

After experiencing considerable difficulty in locating the place, we finally came upon the remains of what was once "our house," the place we called *home*. In fact, it had been a little four-room, wooden structure nestled in the woods off a dirt road. But now, not even the simple elegance of a weatherworn shanty remained to give testimony to my family's intimate and sacred history in this forsaken place. *Even the ground where the house once stood had shifted. The earth had moved, the foundations had fallen. Only ruins remained. The little house in which we lived and "made do" was no longer there. Nothing remained except the memories—like wandering ghosts without habitation.*

2

Haunted Houses

Black Churches and the Ghost of Post-Racialism

All houses wherein men have lived and died
are haunted houses.
—Henry Wadsworth Longfellow, "Haunted Houses"

This past, the Negro's past, of rope, fire, torture, castration, infanticide, rape, death, and humiliation; fear by day and night, fear as deep as the marrow of the bone; doubt that he was worthy of life, since everyone around him denied it; sorrow for his women, for his kinsfolk, for his children, who needed his protection, and whom he could not protect; rage, hatred for white men so deep that it often turned against him and his own, and made all love, all trust, all joy impossible—*this past, this endless struggle to achieve and reveal and confirm a human identity.*
—James Baldwin, *The Fire Next Time*[1] (italics added)

There is an uncanny correspondence between the experience of returning home to Frogbottom and the task of reimagining black religious practices for this new time of fragmented discourses about the meaning and role of black churches in the United States.[2] The memories of the past are no longer adequate to sustain the mission of black churches in these turbulent times. The little house in which we lived and made do cannot contain the new moments to which black churches are called. The ground has shifted, and memories and metaphors like ghosts speak to us and drive us on. But memory and metaphor without critical engagement and historical suspicion are dangerous and destructive.[3] How then shall we think about the inherited burdens of race and culture in what is being called a *post-racial* America, in which African American religious scholars and church leaders must engage this new time and rhythm of *lifeworlds* and *systems* and their many deep-textured transitions and transformations?

This book analyzes the meanings and ramifications of "post-racialism" for black churches in the United States, highlighting the ways scholars and religious leaders can usefully engage and reframe critical questions relating to the historical problems of racialized, sexualized, and gendered politics of the church and the larger culture. The term "post-racial America" is presented here as a postulate that is subject to argument and investigation: that the United States is or will be at some time in the future free from preferences, bigotry, discrimination, and prejudices that are based on race. It is put forth in this way because even though it is not a statement of fact, it still functions as if it were or could be true and therefore informs our cultural reasoning and national conversations surrounding race.[4] This book interrogates the functions and assumptions of post-racial reasoning in black theological and ethical discourse and practice by identifying its damaging effects on the questions of institutional memory, vision, and mission. It looks particularly at the influence of the idea of post-racialism on the *religious* discourse of black churches and its implications for self-identity. If we are in a post-racial era, then what is the future of the black church?

This volume invites readers to consider how black churches' historical identity and agency have been stymied by the shifting grounds of a post-racial era, thus forfeiting their prophetic role in the world. It argues that black churches need to determine whether they can effectively use race as an emancipatory instrument, and it offers ideas for the *conjuring* of new liberating practices for churches. As we will see, black churches must employ the Holy Ghost—that Spirit who helps us to see our *somebodyness* and our *possibilities*—against the ghost of post-racialism, the "unholy ghost." In this way, black church leaders will be empowered to use *tools of the spirit* to embrace *hope* in the strangeness of its possibility and combat the tragic dilemma of failing to believe in the ultimate justice of the human drama.

Pushing beyond older race-based language and metaphors that have outlived their utility, this book is concerned with offering a global vision for black churches, involving new ways to model citizenship in diasporas and exiles. It also focuses in particular on African American young men, given their often-desperate situation in U.S. society. The focus on young black males is in no way a trivialization of the atrocities of injustice meted out against other black female, queer, lesbian, gay, transgender, and crip bodies.[5] Rather, it is a statement first and foremost about the field of work with which the author is engaged and a daring proposal to look at the intersectionality of our complex and multidimensional oppression. These youth are in particular need of tools to foster a sense of identity and human flourishing, and black churches must provide them.

Post-Black Churches and Post-Racial Ruminations on the Black and Living Dead

One grand example of what is at stake for black churches in this new moment is the controversial proclamation by Professor Eddie Glaude that rocked the proverbial boat of black theologians and church leaders in a provocative essay entitled "The Black Church Is Dead." Glaude wrote, "The Black Church, as we've known it or imagined it, is dead. Of course, many African Americans still go to church. . . . But the idea of this venerable institution as central to black life and as a repository for the social and moral conscience of the nation have all but disappeared."[6] By Glaude's own admission, the title of his essay was hyperbolic and meant to stimulate debate about the state of the black church. Glaude outlined three reasons for making the statement. First, black churches and narratives about them are very complicated. While the metanarrative of prophetic, engaged churches tends to be embraced by contemporary scholars and nonscholars as the main way to think about black churches and their leaders, the truth is that it is not accurate. There is a mixed bag, so to speak. It's not all prophetic, concerned with exhortations to social justice and confronting the question of race in America; there is a long, complex history of conservatism in black churches, "but our stories about black churches too often bury this conservative dimension of black Christian life."[7]

Glaude's second point was that African American communities are highly differentiated. Hence the continuing belief that the black church is at the center of all that happens in these communities needs to be re-examined and addressed; we need to understand the place of the church as one social institution alongside other religious and nonreligious institutions and organizations.

The third and perhaps hardest-hitting critique made by Glaude was that the prophetic voice of the church has become *routinized*, echoing Weber's notion of *disenchantment* (as one astute respondent to Glaude suggested). This, by far, seemed to be the profound challenge, according to Glaude, for the future of the black church. "But such a church loses it power. *Memory becomes its currency*. Its soul withers from neglect. The result is all too often church services and liturgies that entertain, but lack a spirit that transforms, and preachers who deign for followers instead of fellow travelers in God" (italics added). Ironically, Glaude closes on a prophetic note miming the absence of the prophetic:

> The death of the black church as we have known it occasions an oppor-
> tunity to breathe new life into what it means to be black and Christian.
> Black churches and preachers must find their prophetic voices in this
> momentous present. And in doing so, black churches will rise again and
> insist that we all assert ourselves on the national stage not as sycophants
> to a glorious past, but as witnesses to the ongoing revelation of God's love
> in the here and now as we work on behalf of those who suffer most.[8]

Glaude's dissenters and supporters alike were moved to provide their rebuttals and affirmations to his 790-word essay, which was likened to "the Digital-Age equivalent of nailing a set of theses to a church door."[9] Rumors about the death of the black church, of course, are always premature and greatly exaggerated, as some scholars suggested. Nonetheless, the spurring of debate that arose as a result of Glaude's annunciation was helpful in drawing attention from church leaders and academics. One in particular was Professor Josef Sorett of Columbia University, who made the following perceptive assertion about black churches:

> At their best, [black churches] . . . are often "progressive yet co-opted." This simply means to recognize that black Christians are a part and parcel of . . . the Protestant establishment. Yet even this view of black churches says little about what is religious in the discussion. We might ask, what distinguishes "post-black church" rhetoric from claims of a post-racial America?[10]

Sorett asks a difficult question about the relationship of the *religiousness* of black churches and its various forms and functions to the shifting metaphors and practices of black churches in the United States.[11] Are we now in a post-black church and post-racial America? And if so, how do we understand the relationship between these two signifiers? And what ought to be the response of black church scholars and leaders? This book provides answers to these questions.

I agree with the raison d'être for Glaude's rhetorical exaggeration of the state of black churches, and I also understand that sweeping generalizations are always problematic—a fact to which Glaude himself eloquently confesses. His own prophetic utterance that "The death of the black church as we have known it occasions an opportunity to breathe new life into what it means to be black and Christian"[12] is reminiscent of "raising the dead," as in Ezekiel's vision of the dry bones. If his intention was to wake up the dead, then he at least performed the preparatory removal of the grave clothes with grand form and effect. Indeed, at a deeper level, if the critical task of black scholars and leaders is to *wake up the dead*, then it should be to wake up (black) subjectivity and to examine its relation to an *imaginary national identity*. In respect to (black) subjectivity, this book is concerned with notions of identity, agency, otherness, and human flourishing, all of which we will attend to in the following chapters. National identity as imaginary refers to black churches' fidelity to the unfulfilled promise of equality that Benedict Anderson calls "ghostly national imaginings."[13] These are imaginings enshrouded in death and anonymity, like the quasi-religious response that we offer at the tombs of unknown soldiers—a universal transcendental that everyone can believe in without attending to the complex historical and social realities of death and suffering. Black churches operate in a national imaginary of "dead space"—that is, what the literary scholar Sharon Patricia Holland identifies as "an unaccomplished imaginative shift from enslaved to freed subjectivity and the marked gap between genealogical isolation and the ancestral past."[14] Along with Holland, we must ask why black churches and their leaders continue to reside in the nation's imaginary "space of death" and offer their loyalty at the tombs of the unknown. Or, more biblically referenced, why do black churches continue to seek the living amongst the dead?[15] I think it is because an old ghost inhabits the living and the dead, dwells in the in-between, living-dead linguistic spaces, and haunts black churches. We must therefore learn to speak from those spaces inhabited by *the living dead* as part of our ongoing theological and churchly missions in order to disrupt the categorization and binary symbols of blackness/whiteness and provide a middle way of speaking from this spectral space to the possibilities of our future.

I would thus state the problem in different terms from those used by Glaude. The black church, as we have known, loved, and imagined it, is haunted by an old ghost that has shape-shifted into the language of post-racialism; by extension, perhaps the God whom African Americans have come to know, love, imagine, and worship in wonderfully creative and ecstatic styles is in conspiracy with the ghost; and thus this idea of God reinforces the ghost's racial haunting and possession of many of the church leaders and scholars who are its loyal defenders. The ghost of post-racialism is embedded in the dominant ideological discourses of American culture, which are manifested in possessive individualism and religious narcissism. By possessive individualism, I am referring specifically to the moral language of *utilitarian individualism*, which is a by-product of an acquisitive, bourgeoisie-oriented culture that is centered on individual interests within a market-driven system that exists, for the most part, as a national and cultural imaginary for black and other poor people in this nation.[16] Possessive individualism is concentrated on *capital* and its promised, but elusive, rewards of recognition and prestige that perform a séance with race, religion, and culture, conjuring the ghostly entrancement of many of our church leaders who embody and speak for an "unholy ghost."[17] Consequently, a large majority of black churches are in a state of possession, suffering from social-political narcolepsy, a condition of uncontrollable sleeping.

The religious narcissism that afflicts many of our churches is also a form of this ghostly inhabitation. The term *narcissism* comes from the tragic Greek myth of Narcissus, the beautiful lad who rejected the love of Echo, the nymph, and dismissed her. Echo consequently died of a broken heart. Echo, as the name implies, could not speak her thoughts, she could only "echo" what others said. The gods punished Narcissus by making him fall in love with his own reflection in the lake, and in his self-admiration, he fell into the waters and drowned. Religious narcissism is the deadly conjurer of many of the manifestations of the ghost that haunts black churches; among these are heterosexual normativity, insularity, and apathetic dismissal of the subaltern voices in its midst who cannot speak for themselves. Put another way, these churches are so infatuated with their own images and religiosity that they refuse to attend to the echoing cries of the dismissed in the shadowy wastelands of post-racial political and cultural configurations. Narcissism is not only a cultural-political malady that afflicts many of our churches, it is also in alliance with the aesthetic wanderings and practices of churches that have become so obsessed with style, ecstatic worship, ritualistic practices, dogma, doctrines, religious paraphernalia, and excessive scrupulosity that they cannot hear the voice of God calling them to service in the world, a world that includes the dismissed who sit in their pews.

These apparitions of the ghost have lulled many of our churches to sleep. Hence, prophetic activism, as we have chosen to remember it, has been anesthetized by the controlling dramas of possessive individualism and religious narcissism. This is a very difficult statement. In some quarters, such a statement will be heard as heresy; in others, it will be interpreted as the expected ramblings of an out-of-touch academic who is guilty of a misreading of the black religious experience, but few can argue that we have not fallen asleep in the midst of one of the most dangerous periods in our history, where *memory*, as Glaude argues, has become its currency.

The Shape-Shifting Ghost of *Post-Racialism*

From their beginnings, black churches were conceived in *race* and birthed into a struggle for an institutional identity and social space that was not controlled by the dominant gaze of white authority and legitimacy. Yet ironically, black churches, with few exceptions, still rely upon inherited theological symbols, metaphors, and signs that have been syncretized, recycled, and made usable for their worship and service to God and black communities without critical engagement and interrogation of their contemporary utility. In the United States, our loyalty and allegiance to the nation serves as an eschatological hope in the unrealized dream toward which African Americans continue to aspire: a nonracist society that upholds the fundamental principles of equality and freedom. I agree with Peter Paris's claim that "the normative tradition for blacks is the tradition governed by the principle of nonracism which we call the black Christian tradition." This critical principle of *nonracism*, according to Paris, is fundamental for "justifying and motivating all endeavors by blacks for survival and social transformation."[18] But I argue that this principle of nonracism in black churches and black communities is a radical egalitarian hypothesis that has been tested with uneven results from the earliest movements of independent black churches to the present, in every major war fought by the United States, and in every struggle for civil and human rights, including contemporary movements like Black Lives Matter. The "radical egalitarian hypothesis" refers to the Enlightenment ideals of the equality of humanity associated most definitively with Locke, Hume, Montesquieu, and Kant, all of whom were avowed racists. The ideal of equality being grounded in the capacity to reason or in divine creation was not intended to apply to Africans and others whom these thinkers associated with savagery and animality. African American life and history abound with examples of this problematic concept, variously referred to as "double consciousness," the "normative gaze," and the crippling labels of intellectual and social inferiority based on race, class, sexual orientation, and gender. African Americans' belief in the radical egalitarian hypothesis is like the belief in what William James calls the *religious hypothesis*: a *living, forced*, and *momentous option* that has been interpreted as meaning that we must continue our steadfast loyalty to the "American Idea," for to choose otherwise is a *dead, unforced*, and *trivial* path to nonbeing. In other words, the hypothesis is forced—there is no option but to believe. Much of the stirring protests of Black Lives Matter, for instance, rejects this hypothesis as elusive and consequently, as no choice at all and a denial of agency.[19] Ironically, as a result of black churches' attachment to the principle of nonracism, even in their most radical forms of resistance and transformation, black church leaders have sought not so much to leave or separate from America, but to take the American national imaginary with them.[20] A curious matter of concern is that the majority of black churches not only extol American values and virtues of patriotism alongside their various forms of resistance and protests, but they continue to adhere to an uncontested loyalty to the nation and to self-monitor and correct their own practices that conspire against American interests. In this respect, *nonracism* bears a strange symbiotic relationship with what is now being called *post-racialism*.

To be clear, *post-racialism* is a problematic moniker that ascribes legitimacy to a host of destructive cultural and political conversations and public policy decisions that retard serious progressive deliberations on the continuing significance of race in the United States and elsewhere.[21] Moreover, its insinuation into the theological discourse of black churches has had far-reaching implications for the questions of institutional self-identity, praxis, and transcendence.[22] This is because *post-racialism*, as I am using the term, is *ghostly* and *shape-shifting*. It is *ghostly* in the sense of Jacques Derrida's treatment of *hauntology* as ideology born of the materialization of a nonmaterial phenomenon that is simultaneously a specter and a thing that evades, elides, and coerces a certain mode of allegiance to itself as a transcendent good and as a sign of divine creation.[23] A key question that will be revisited throughout is, How then do we negotiate (*touch* and *not touch*) and find balance between *transcendence* (the *movement of super-, the step beyond* that *is made sensuous in its very excess*) and *death* as in *falling*? We need not touch it to know it is there; rather, we must learn to live in this space, *fluid center(s)* where we experience transcendence and immanence simultaneously. I will argue that this is the space of freedom or nonfreedom (bondage, subjugation) where the agent chooses his or her freedom even at the risk of *falling* (death). Transcendence exists as a ghost, as a sensuous nonsensuous phantom; therefore, we experience it only in its absence, in its untouchability, yet it is necessary for us to go on, to *hope*. "Negotiated transcendence," then, is the consciousness of something that is there and not-there at the same time—it exists in this infinitesimal space between life and death, between the nonsensuousness and the sensuousness of body as potential, not yet but there to be believed. It is something that is lost, like the woman sweeping for the coin, or the shepherd looking for the lost sheep, or my father, sometimes *limping* through the world, "making a way out of no way." Freedom, like hope, is coiled up in the arms of death. And *we are saved by hope*.

The ghost of race shape-shifts and conceals itself in post-racial language of transcendence and in performances that point to the radical egalitarian hypothesis while it simultaneously conjures and transforms itself into the deadly and destructive antithesis of the aspirational ideal of American fairness and desert.[24] This ghostly apparition of race that masquerades as post-racialism demands that we swear allegiance to it, yet it is difficult, if not impossible, to locate in time[25] because it is a "bodiless body," a thing that is invisible, intangible, inaudible, and odorless, yet it affects every dimension of our sensuous existences in language, signs, symbols,[26] and—most importantly—public policy decisions that negatively impact the lives of black people and poor people of every color and national origin. Its cultural hauntings correspond to a "paradoxical incorporation" of a *spectrogenic* process that appears and disappears, leaves and returns, which makes it extremely difficult to define and talk about publicly.[27] In relation to the *spectralization* of history and time, this means that the ghost is neither time-bound nor limited to one epoch or construction—it shape-shifts, appears, and reappears in different forms of language and speech with different connotations. Race as *post-racialism* is not bound by a specific history, but rather reinvents itself; it appears as an angel of light, a normative ideal that has been realized (a future that is already present), even as it surreptitiously undermines the onto-eschatological conception of history and the future of *race*.

One example of this phenomenon is the controversy surrounding the Confederate flag that resurfaced in 2015, as a result of the racially motivated vicious murder of the pastor and parishioners of Mother Emanuel African Methodist Episcopal Church in South Carolina by a white gunman who had earlier posted photos of himself with the Confederate flag on the Internet. In many respects, the congregation's willingness to forgive the virulent young racist responsible for the murder of nine people during Bible study was reflective of most churches' dispositions toward Christian virtues of love, generosity, and hospitality to the stranger. But in the case of Mother Emanuel, there was more than Christian forgiveness and love of the enemy going on. Given its strategic geographical and historical location, it reminded the nation and the world that we not only have a long ways to go, but in respect to deeply entrenched customs and practices associated with the synonymy of southern heritage and white supremacy, we have not moved much beyond the legislative victories symbolized in the Civil Rights and Voting Rights Acts of 1964 and 1965 (whose respective fifty-year anniversaries were, ironically, celebrated in 2014 and 2015 amidst public outcry against a number of high-profile acts of violence directed at African Americans by the police). The murders at Mother Emanuel occurred in the midst of Black Lives Matter campaigns that were inspired by a long-standing unresolved historical antipathy toward black progressive politics since Reconstruction; and a growing national disrespect for the legacy of President Barack Hussein Obama, a disrespect that was serendipitously undermined by Supreme Court decisions on the Affordable Care Act and the Defense of Marriage Act. Remarkably, few of these historic victories or the protests against the Confederate flag and the Black Lives Matter campaign were initiated or led by black church leaders, but mainly by young activists with moderate, if any, relationship with the church. In fact, Black Lives Matter was initiated by three black women, two of whom self-identify as queer.[28]

Shape-shifting is a form of postmodern self-reflexive critique of all signs that claim to be absolute, including race, blackness, and theological discourse. In this respect, it has formal affinity with *post-blackness* as a quest for identity, authenticity, and agency in black cultural and religious life and practices. My understanding of the shape-shifting character of race and blackness, however, is not as fluid as it is for some writers;[29] it is, rather, a form of critical signification on how we understand the remembered past of the life and practices of black churches and our often uncritical allegiances to those traditions. This book examines how post-racial ideology as a shape-shifting, ghostly specter resituates the discussion of race in African American religious discourse and practice, and considers its implications for black church leadership; it asserts that remembering, retelling, and reliving the stories of black churches highlight the need for us to revise the language of race in African American ideological, cultural, and religious practices.

At stake in this discussion of black churches' often uncritical allegiance to the principle of *nonracism* is a revelation of how deeply *race* is embedded in American culture and of how race as a cultural and social ghost shape-shifts and reinvents itself in myriad figurations. In some respects, the method employed in this analysis draws on the image of the trickster, as in Ananse, Esu-Elegba the Signifying Monkey, or Brer Rabbit, as race *shape-shifts* by taking advantage of the indeterminacy of language, which signals how it can be used as a tool that allows for the revisability and reappropriation of meaning in new situations.[30] Historically black churches have taken their metaphors, parodies, and transformations of Western stories and ideas too literally. They have mistaken these rhetorical devices for preordained things, essences. Sallie McFague, for instance, claims that all theological metaphors are human constructions of the divine and may never fully reveal the divine presence. As such, McFague argues that the metaphors theologians draw upon to construct theologies should remain relevant to the current situation, rather than relying upon the authority of the past as if language about God were somehow static or fixed. For her, theological metaphors that remain fixed upon the past lead church communities to misrepresent their present condition in the world in relation to divine presence. In this sense, all guiding theological metaphors reveal and conceal aspects of human relation to the divine.[31] For example, the idea of Exodus is not a fixed reality but a metaphor that must be revisable if the black church is to survive and interpret its mission in this new century. Relatedly, I contend that the symbol of God, rather than an unchangeable, fixed reality, is better understood as a dynamic, relational process in which and to whom we are called to participate in our quest for citizenship and human identity. Therefore, black churches must be open to the revisability of theological language by remembering, retelling, and reliving their own tradition of *shape-shifting* and signifying as part of their hermeneutical, kerygmatic, pedagogical tasks and social engagement. In this sense, I am calling for a return to a theological-process orientation that is already present in the traditions of the Black Atlantic, yet at the same time, this process begs for new approaches and ways of thinking, speaking, and acting in a new world.[32]

Remembering, Retelling, and Reliving Our Stories

A critical tool in this analysis of black church life and practices is a methodological strategy of remembering, retelling, and reliving our stories that parallels a correlated conceptual movement of *memory* (past), *vision* (future), and *mission* (present). These three movements should not be conceived as a linear process but rather as a spiraling, liberated circle that corresponds to a counterclockwise *turning* of memory, vision, and mission, ensuring a dynamic flow that captures the notion of *fluid center(s)*. The language of *fluid center(s)* is related to what the theologian Howard Thurman believed is the pulsating, rhythmic movement of life, which, like a river, is moving and still, old and new, being and becoming simultaneously.[33] Therefore, the narrative method employed here invites readers first of all to *remember*, to return to the complex, sometimes contradictory discourses embedded in the African American psycho-social, political-cultural metaphors of Dilemma and Diaspora; the theological-ethical metaphors of Exodus and Exile; and the existential-aesthetic metaphors of the Frying Pan (hell) and the Fire (the Holy Ghost). Second, vision includes the critical step of *retelling* or revising these metaphors by identifying the in-between spaces of language and agency, imagining possibilities beyond entrapment in national imaginaries and ghostly narratives of the radical egalitarian hypothesis. The third critical methodological task is defining mission, *reliving* the story by developing new *enfleshed* approaches and practices that speak to our contemporary situations marked by the slippery language of post-racialism. In order to *remember, retell*, and *relive* the story of prophetic black church life and practices, black church scholars and leaders are asked to *congregate, conjure*, and *conspire* in *common(s)* in a type of *fifth moment* called for by the scholar and pastor Raphael Warnock.[34] The book is organized respectively around these three tropes of memory (chapters 1–3), vision (chapters 4–7), and mission (chapters 8–10). Throughout the discussions that follow, the yearning for *home* serves as a metaphor for the existential and elusive quest for identity, intersubjectivity, and human flourishing.

Remembering refers to the way we must utilize *memories* of our past as points of departure and sites of excavation as first steps in reviving prophetic black religious discourse and practices in our existing struggles with the ghost of post-racialism. These practices did not arise from a historical vacuum; rather, they were deeply rooted in what Cornel West calls the "utterly and undeniably tragic character of life and history."[35] Prophetic African American religious and moral practices must be understood in this context of American history, culture, and ideology. African Americans in the United States have gone through tumultuous, horrific experiences that are often hidden from memory and hence have become *learned ignorance*.[36] The first moment of remembering, therefore, marks the critical sociopolitical location for investigating substantive discourse as *sites of memory*.[37] James Baldwin offers a strategic clue into remembering *this past, this endless struggle to achieve and reveal and confirm a human identity*[38] that in my humble estimation is the core of the African American struggle (and the human struggle).[39] More generally, an underlining and operative assumption of this discussion is that black churches, in their origins and institutionalization, were concerned as much with the question of their humanity as (or more than) with their religious liberty. Hence my understanding of the meta-mission of black churches continues to be the "endless struggle to achieve and reveal and confirm a human identity."

Toni Morrison's literary idea of *rememory* addresses the analytic relation of *habitus*, memory, and history in the quest for human identity.[40] *Rememory* acts to re-collect, reassemble, and reconfigure individual and collective consciousness into a meaningful and sequential whole through the process of narrativization. The significance of *remembering* is the narrativization of the past, the reclaiming of bodies of disparate and disconnected meaning lodged in the unconscious matrices of the psyche and in the body. It is not only a return to intellectual excavation of historical data, but is also associated with deep emotional energy, which is spiritual and empathic. Remembering personal stories in the context of larger historical narratives offers entrée into forgotten worlds of meaning, and allows recovery of dismembered bodies of experience otherwise invisible to consciousness.[41]

Remembering is also related to ancestral knowledge, knowledge that triggers imaginative yearnings for a connection with the past as Great Time, typified in the distinction between Sasha and Zamani, two conditions of being related respectively to everyday time and infinity, and the notion of *being-in-between* (potential time, spectral time, trickster time), where time bends like a river to meet the road, creating a *crossing*, represented by the symbol of infinity or a yoke that binds temporality and infinity: ∞. Great Time, I argue, is a fluid space of negotiated transcendence and can serve as a basis for hope. It finds affinity with Sheila Smith McKoy's notion of "diaspora temporality" as discussed in LeRhonda Manigault-Bryant's excellent ethnohistorical investigation of Gullah/Geeche cultures in *Talking to the Dead*. At stake for scholars like McKoy and Manigault-Bryant is that "lived memory" is not something that happened only in "the long ago," but is present in rituals, music, "suspended time, which also coincides with the entrance of the Holy Spirit," dance, and practices that have persisted in African American women's religious and cultural institutions, yet are largely unnoticed and unobserved by Western religious scholars and practitioners.[42] For Howard Thurman, the relationship between time and infinity is analogous to the flow of the river that empties itself into the sea. The analogy yields key insights from enslaved Africans and their cosmological perspectives: the river leads to a deeper appreciation of the tragic African American past, which Thurman calls "flood time" in his reflection on death and freedom in the Negro spirituals, which I will refer to as "old songs."[43]

What, then, is the fundamental significance of all these interpretations of life and death? What are these songs trying to say? They express the profound conviction that God was not done with them, that God was not done with life. The consciousness that God had not exhausted His resources or better still that the vicissitudes of life could not exhaust God's resources, did not ever leave them. This is the secret of their ascendancy over circumstances and the basis of their assurances concerning life and death. The awareness of the presence of a God who was personal, intimate, and active was the central fact of life and around it all the details of life and destiny were integrated.[44]

Thurman also thought that the river analogy allowed for an empirical investigation into the tragic circumstances of enslaved existence that provided greater knowledge of the source of life and death, which leads to greater awareness of our relationship with the "aliveness of Life" and therefore the power of hope. So in returning to early sources of African American culture, especially old songs, we have the opportunity to trace the impact of long memory on African American spiritual and cultural practices in both their tragedy and hope. In ancient and early Christian traditions, this *in-between* space is where heaven and earth intersect and time and space *bend*, so to speak. Hence it is a place of power—power to rename, to refashion, and to manipulate material conceptions of reality. This concept will become clearer as we examine notions of revisability and conjuring that involve language and bodies that *turn* in ecstatic, ritualistic, rhythmic sequences and cadences to sound.

In addition, as we discuss *memory* in African American life and culture and attend to historical and religious perspectives, we must constantly bear in mind that the early prophetic African American religious leaders were shaped by the complex interaction of history, ideology, and culture, and the third, *in-between space of potential time*—the presence and experience of the *living dead*. The German Egyptologist Jan Assmann calls this process "mnemohistory," which investigates the history of cultural and communicative memory. To return to *memory* is not merely to dwell in the past, but to examine how we still participate in the accumulated debris of that past. Assmann reasons that since we are what we remember, then "the truth of memory lies in the identity that it shapes." In other words, memory has faces, names, and stories; and the truth of memory "is subject to time so that it changes with every new identity and every new present." Therefore, identity and consciousness lie in the story, "not as it happened but as it lives on and unfolds in collective memory." At the collective level, these stories are called "myths." They are the stories by which a group, a society, or a culture lives. Myths are narrative constructions with their own inherent logic and history that "organize action, experience and representation" for groups and individuals. Zamani is the world of myth and sayings and knowing that defies linearity and *dead spaces* that trap and ensnare us into fixated ways of being that inhibit agency. Zamani is not disassociated, however, from historical discourse; rather, it is "a kind of textual conversation or debate which might extend over generations and centuries, even millennia, depending on institutionalizations of permanence such as writing, canonization, educational and clerical institutions, and so forth."[45]

Toni Morrison's literary work is helpful in pointing out the significance of memory, counter-memory, and, most importantly, the constructive agency involved in remembering for healing and creating liberative practices. For Morrison, the body—*enfleshed life*—is a "site of memory."[46] The ethicist Emilie Townes takes up Morrison's examination of *enfleshed* memory, which she says is "the truth of proceedings that may have been too terrible to relate but must be told nonetheless."[47] For Townes, cultural symbols such as Aunt Jemima and the Tragic Mulatta evoke tragic memory and history, but also counter-memory and paths of discovery of truth that point to freedom. Memory and history are both subjective concepts for Townes. She rejects the traditional view that memory is subjective and history is objective or scientific; rather, she argues, both can lead to a diverse and expansive amount of resources from which to draw to dismantle cultural forms of evil, and both are open to being reinterpreted.

Our stories can be told in multiple ways. Since we recognize that both history and memory are ideologically constructed, we can also use them as tools of healing and freedom. We tend to remember that which confers an identity upon us. Thus to remember, retell, and relive is to participate in a continuous cycle of identity, purpose, and meaning that is dynamic and unfinished, like a spiral that infinitely ingresses and egresses (and, perhaps, progresses). As such, memory wedded to imagination is a powerful tool of the spirit that revisits the horrors and joys of the past, but is never ultimately defined by them because of the infinite possibilities unleashed in remembering, retelling, and reliving the story.

As we remember, retell, and relive stories of African American pasts, we must also check for *madness* and its relationship to *bestiality*, the evil of American slavery and Eurowestern supremacy, because cultural perceptions of madness and bestiality conspire against any sanitized abstraction of the social practices and moral expectations of those located on the "underside of history" of American slavery and its continuing traumatic dramas that play out in contemporary captivating narratives, which impact black youth in particular. Integrally related, bestiality and madness are conjoined notions. In Western history, the cultural production of the bestiality and savagery of African Americans was linked to madness (as in being uncivilized) and to public spectacle. The "discovery of the savage" from the Renaissance through the Enlightenment provided philosophical, legal, and moral justification for definitions of the "nonhumanness" of Africans, who were associated with darkness and "out of which the light of Europe's reason would be delineated."[48] Hence, it was a remarkable feat of human dexterity and resilience that some early African American prophetic leaders not only survived but also resisted in the throes of this madness. Isabella Baumfree, called Sojourner Truth, lamented at the news of the death of her sister Nancy, who had been sold into slavery seventeen years earlier and whom she had met and prayed with, but did not know to be her sister, "Oh Lord, what is this slavery, that it can do such dreadful things? What evil can it not do?"[49] Sojourner Truth and other early African American prophetic leaders addressed "a situation characterized by *anomie*, a loss of 'world,' or erosion of structure, psychic and cultural, with the consequent nakedness of Being or immediacy to the dynamics of existence."[50] In apocalyptic, prophetic utterance, David Walker asked,

> Can anything be a greater mockery of religion than the way in which it is conducted by the Americans? It appears as though they are bent only on daring God Almighty to do his best—they chain and handcuff us and our children and drive us around the country like brutes, and go into the house of the God of justice to return him thanks for having aided them in their infernal cruelties inflicted upon us. Will the Lord suffer this people to go on much longer, taking his holy name in vain? Will he not stop them, PREACHERS and all? O Americans! Americans!! I call God—I call angels—I call men, to witness, that your DESTRUCTION is at hand, and will be speedily consummated unless you REPENT.[51]

In this respect, *madness* is deeply entrenched in what Cornel West describes as the "prophetic tradition in Afro-America," in which he delineates the moral practices of a deep-seated moralism, an inescapable opportunism, and an aggressive pessimism.[52] Here the concern is with the ways memories of the religious and moral practices of black elites, many of whom were church leaders, conspired with this "deep-seated moralism" to the detriment of the masses of African Americans who were not able to incorporate the etiquette and manners associated with the "politics of respectability."[53] Hence our understanding of theological discourse and moral practices is best considered in respect to the tragic character of black life and existence, and to the "madness and melancholia, doom and death, terror and horror"[54] of the black condition, especially the poor and despised. Consequently, the "deep-seated moralism" arises from a particular sociocultural context best expressed by the Du Boisian metaphor of "double consciousness," or what Raphael Warnock calls "the divided mind of black churches."[55] In this root metaphor of moral agency, the tragic and often fatal dilemma of daring to believe yet disbelieving in the ultimate justice of the human drama, contextualized in the American radical egalitarian hypothesis, creates a schizoid mode of discourse and practice that West identifies as "inescapable opportunism" and "an aggressive pessimism," and which I will refer to as *Dilemma*. The core around which these distinct yet related modalities revolve is the continual, insufferable confrontation of African Americans, especially the poor and black subaltern masses, with unjust, recalcitrant power relations that reveal the contradiction in what Alasdair MacIntyre calls "internal" and "external goods."[56]

African American elites' complicity with sex, gender, and class biases has had a deleterious impact on the ways the "illiterate, uncultured and uncivilized" black masses were viewed. The intellectual and cultural historian Kevin Gaines has argued that at the turn of the twentieth century, black elites who called for "self-help and Negro improvement tacitly confirmed the commonplace view that the impoverished status of blacks was a matter of moral and cultural deficiency, not coercion and economic exploitation"—a remarkable description of how the quest for citizenship and the embrace of bourgeois morality conspired against liberative claims and agency.[57] Outstanding male and female leaders participated in the quest for full citizenship while embracing a "politics of respectability" that had both aspirational and destructive outcomes for the poor and disinherited masses of blacks. Key to the quest for citizenship was the role of literacy as liberation, which was a theological trope of salvation that simultaneously designated a curious cultural and structural divide between the saved and unsaved. To be a citizen suggested a belonging to, and fellowship in, a quasi-sacred narrative of nationhood. Hence, education was viewed and used as *symbolic capital*, as a means of racial uplift, but it had the paradoxical disadvantage of inculcating certain habits and practices that encouraged bourgeois manners and morals, ensuring the perpetuation of difference and religious and theological interpretations of human subjectivity. At stake for certain black female and male leaders was not only the promotion of "manners and morals" of the masses, but also a campaign against pejorative images of black womanhood that depicted black women as shameless, bestial, sexually licentious, and sinful.[58] Hence, African American women and men alike sought in education the morals and manners of bourgeois civilization not only as a goal of respectability but as the public ideal for leadership and deliverance from sin. The civilizing influences of education, despite great ideological divides as to which type was most effective for uplift, had a paradoxical impact on black leadership in respect to the public practices of recognition, respect, prestige, and loyalty to democratic values that created a dilemma. I will return to this argument and the problematic role of the "politics of respectability" in the mission of black churches in chapter 8.

Historically, African American religious and cultural practices have been marked by an unresolved contest of dualities, binary oppositions, and dialectics that are expressions of the difficult psychosocial and political frames of relating captured in tropes of "double consciousness," "accommodation/protest," and "Dilemma."[59] The inimitable and ever-hard-hitting Harold Cruse wrote, "American Negro history is basically a history of the conflict between integrationist and nationalist forces in politics, economics, and culture, no matter what leaders are involved and what slogans are used."[60] As we will see, this dilemma played out in a variety of ways in the psychosocial world of the first African American president of the United States, Barack Obama.

Black intellectuals and race leaders, such as Ida B. Wells, Anna Julia Cooper, W. E. B. Du Bois, Booker T. Washington, Thomas T. Fortune, and Mary Church Terrell, all embraced the polite and gentle pursuits of bourgeois morals embodied in *thrift, industry, self-control, piety, temperance, and the work ethic*—all necessary, they believed, for successful citizenship and economic independence. Over time, these practices became more and more related to personal and individualistic betterment related to the accumulation of various forms of capital: social, economic, and symbolic.[61] This observation is important because it demonstrates how discursive formations provide the means for the articulation of moral languages that over time become distinct from the *reasons* for which they were originally related, or assumed to be related—the historical project of their discursive features or, to use Bourdieu, their *field*, the struggle *qua* ideology of racial uplift. In other words, the *habitus* of racial uplift became the dominant ideology and, as such, the moral practice of generations of black leaders who followed. The black elite ideology of racial uplift was accompanied by a specific moral vocabulary, born of the rigors of slavery and Jim Crow. In its most basic formulation, it was a language that sought *recognition, respectability*, and *loyalty* to an ideal embodied in democratic life and practices.[62] Furthermore, the moral vocabulary of black elites evolved over time to embrace a bourgeois worldview that promoted self-reliance and social egalitarianism—and now, without the benefit of historical memory (memory that has been reframed by mass media and buried in social-political narcolepsy), a *possessive individualism* that accentuates the language of prosperity and success. This worldview has proved to have complex and aggravating features that have impacted the way black leaders, especially some contemporary black church leaders, understand themselves and their respective missions.

West's identification of these practices arises from a hermeneutical perspective that takes possessive individualism seriously as an integral dimension of racist practices. Here the concern is with property and the means of controlling and protecting relations surrounding it by cultural elites who tend to be white and male, but are by no means limited to white male bodies. Black elite complicity with the reigning values and mores of the culture continues to displace masses and to perpetuate sexual, gender, and class differences through theological, moral, scriptural, and metaphysical justifications. Consequently, "morality" dons the garment of the thief—that is, the moral demand perpetuated by class structure and cultural configurations unwittingly leads the leader into a design of its own. Ideology, like an unseen ghost, in this sense traps, conjures, commands, and conspires with its victim to do its bidding. The end product is as remarkable in its creation as its impact on the poor and marginalized. The birth of the *black cultural asylum*, its conspiracy in the subjugation of black leadership, and its damning effect on poor black youth result in the patient controlling himself or herself, as discussed in chapter 9. That is, the *madman's* behavior is no longer the distinct responsibility of the keeper, but is performed by the patient himself or herself. Consequently, "inescapable opportunism" and "aggressive pessimism" are often disguised as *hope* in African American life and culture. At their best, they serve as means of maintaining some measure of personal sanity in an increasingly unjust, compassionless society that perpetuates madness, but neither can provide the basis for the politicization of the deep-seated moralism to which West refers above. In fact, this kind of perverted hope perpetuates the vicious circle of madness—it relies on progress, the ignominious and idolatrous worship of the machine culture of postindustrial bourgeois sentimentality. The hope to which I am referring lies elsewhere. Unlike the Pollyannaish optimism of Western consumer culture, this hope is born of the acknowledgment of the tragic character of human existence, yet it refuses to give up. *There is hope for this world, there is hope for this world, it's all going to be all right, there's hope for this world.* (An old song I first heard sung by a children's choir. The innocence and purity of their voices struck a dissonant chord that awakens memories from another time—perhaps mythological time—long memory, forgotten and shipwrecked, but still singing.)

Dangerous Memories and Hope

The anatomy of this hope is rooted in *dangerous memories* and redemptive possibilities that hurl us into the trysting places of faith and courage.[63] But before this hope can be expressed as liberative speech and action, it must be translated through memory: a return to *the day before yesterday*, where voices long lost and forgotten are given permission— better, opportunity—to join the conversation about the meaning of black faith in America and the world. Dangerous memories offer entrée into forgotten worlds of meaning. They allow recovery of dismembered bodies of experience otherwise invisible to consciousness. Black church traditions are repositories of these lost and dismembered bodies of experience that return from the dead to haunt and guide us as we negotiate safe places in the dark.

Dangerous memories also involve the simultaneous acts of *weeping, confession*, and *resistance*. Black preaching is an example of this methodology, as has been suggested by the homiletician and cultural critic Christine Smith.[64] The narrative history of black preaching, from the Great Awakenings and frontier revivals of the late eighteenth and early nineteenth centuries, is punctuated with diachronic and synchronic weeping, confession, and resistance in response to Eurowestern hegemonic practices. Today, however, there is more at stake than identifying systemic patterns of injustice that breed suffering and perpetuate violent acts of racial hostility. The *lifeworlds* of twenty-first-century, postindustrial black lives reflect behaviors deep and ominous enough to qualify as demoniacal possession. The critical task of *rememory* includes these three infra-centers of weeping, confession, and resistance, but distances itself from any critique that has the effect of undermining the liberative yearnings of black life and struggle. Black churches and black lives are sites of dangerous memories.

One of the *lost* virtues of African American leadership is precisely this deep-seated, politicized *hope*. But this *hope*, as West mentions above, is a belief in the ultimate justice of the universe, that somehow ancient wrongs will be righted (*the bottom rail will be on the top rail*) and that the daring of faith in the dream of human community will be justified. Hope, as I am using the term, also refers to *commitment to the strangeness of the future*—a future that is uncertain, fragile, carefully negotiated, and often wrenched, strained, and disfigured through suffering, yet it is situated in the narrow space of transcendence, like the element of surprise in the narrative, the imagined possibility that brings resolution and redemption to the tragic and ironic, only to be upended and returned again to the struggle. It mimes the movement of the "inch worm"—"keep a inchin' along like a po' inch worm, Massa Jesus comin by and by."[65] It emerges from *fluid center(s)*, the aperture of agency that declares, "If you just hold out until tomorrow; / if you just keep the faith through the night / . . . everything will be all right."[66] Or as the mother says to her son, in Langston Hughes's celebrated verse, "I'se still climbin', / And life for me ain't been no crystal stair."[67]

The source of this hope for African American church traditions has and continues to be in theological constructions of the Cross. I will refer to *crossing(s)* as a quest for appropriate ways of speaking to movements, pluralities, and temporalities associated with *marginalized* bodies and the birthings of consciousness at different *turns* in individuals or collectivities.[68] *Crossing(s)* point to the yoke of infinity and time ∞, as that *in-between space*, a place where *congregating, conjuring,* and *conspiring* in *common(s)* take place; it is also where the living and dead speak and God is *enfleshed* in black life and struggle.[69] *Crossing(s)* are spaces where we become aware of the intersections between transcendence and immanence; eternality and time—spaces where liminality intrudes, breaks in, and leaves a crack—an aperture of light, a tiny opening through which we peer at the world and ourselves. See over there! The path to the River—no, the path that crosses the River—or is it the River crossing the path, who knows? One must be careful at *crossing(s)*, for while they bring information, knowledge, and possibility, they are also fraught with danger and peril, for we do not quite know who or what goes there and where to set our feet on shifting grounds![70]

Baby Suggs's sermon in *the Clearing* is an example of *crossing(s)*, this powerful space of *congregating, conjuring,* and *conspiring* where weeping, confession, and resistance meet:

Baby Suggs called the women to her. "Cry," she told them. "For the living and the dead. Just cry." And without covering their eyes the women let loose. It started that way: laughing children, dancing men, crying women and then it got mixed up. Women stopped crying and danced; men sat down and cried; children danced, women laughed, children cried until, exhausted and riven, all and each lay about the Clearing damp and gasping for breath. . . . This is flesh I'm talking about here.

This is flesh that we are talking about here, where (black) subjectivity conspires with language and the body as a conjurer of hope.[71]

Hope joined to dangerous memories is a signifier on impossibility. As political praxis, this hope is incarnate in defiant speech, first-order, embodied language: the speech of the black *living dead,* which proceeds from *conjured in-between* spaces of death and possibility. From the early slave rebellions to modern black protest movements, African American social history is replete with examples of this defiant speech that is inspired by hope.[72] Nowhere is this posture of hope more clearly dramatized than in the deep, surging river of African American religion and culture. Hope is rooted in long memory that returns in dreams, songs, sermonic cadences, and dancing in the Fire of the Holy Ghost that brings life. But this long, lingering memory must be retrieved and embodied in practices that *congregate, conjure,* and *conspire* in the contemporary *lifeworlds* of those who have been dismissed and left behind in a world of globalized capital, which is discussed in chapter 8. Until scholars and church leaders remember, retell, and relive our stories, the old ghost that masquerades as post-racialism and promises the fulfillment of an egalitarian hypothesis will continue to haunt our churches and communities. How shall we begin this delicate, arduous, and complex task until we *turn* from language (symbols, signs, and metaphors) that have become calcified in dogma and doctrines that are contrary to liberative quests and yearnings for *home*? Behold, the bones in our post-racialized valley of the twenty-first-century nation language are very dry, and nothing less than the Holy Ghost can breathe life that revives, renews, and resurrects black churches for this moment to which history has called us. What tools of the spirit are in our hands to help us remember, retell, and relive this beautifully tragic and tragically beautiful journey of Dilemma and Diaspora, Exodus and Exile, and *turning* from the Frying Pan to the Fire? To this task, we *turn.*

3

Cultural Hauntings

Black Church Leadership and Barack Obama

What the cynics fail to understand is that the ground has
shifted beneath them, that the stale political arguments that
have consumed us for so long, no longer apply.
—Barack Obama, inaugural address, January 20, 2009

He died, but we who live must do a harder thing than dying is.
For we must think, and ghosts shall drive us on.
—Howard Thurman[1]

The troubling dilemma of believing in the radical egalitarian hypothesis and yet confronting deeply enshrined hegemonic practices of race
and the politics of respectability is an aspect of the cultural haunting
of America. The dilemma reveals how the ghost of post-racialism borrows from the romanticized past of African Americans and feeds on
the failure to retrieve dangerous memories that nonetheless seep into
the present in dissonant performances of mixed aspirations and mocking despair. In this forgetfulness, black churches and African American
leaders fall into a sense of estrangement—an alienation from that past,
the impossibility of knowing and realizing a livable future as citizens and
reclaiming a prophetic agenda for those most affected by the politics of
Dilemma. This chapter addresses this in-between space of anonymity
and immobility wrought by masked performances in the face of radical evil. The election of Barack Obama and his presidency is a case in
point; indeed, it points to the performance of a masterfully gifted African American intellectual and pragmatic politician who had to negotiate

the binary of whiteness/blackness without, on the one hand, *falling* into the vicious caricatures of the uncivilized beast—a madman in disguise performing in whiteface—and, on the other hand, failing to signal to African Americans that he was "black enough." I think of this dilemma often in respect to the story of Icarus's waxen wings. In the Greek myth, Icarus flies too close to the sun and crashes to the earth because of his sin of pride (*hubris*). In black public life, the sin is the opposite; it is sensuality that signs madness and bestiality—a type of inverted Icarian narrative—where leaders fly too close to the ground by claiming their black enfleshment. The lesson for black churches and their leadership is that there is no safe way to "be black" in America without falling into the most dreadful of sins (embodying and embracing your truth); nor is there a safe way to "become white" without falling from the sky. This chapter is less about the legacy of President Barack Obama, and more about the dilemma of black leadership and the concomitant performances of mirroring America and masking identity for the sake of salvation.

The inauguration of our first African American president was hailed as a proud moment for the United States, a jubilant moment for the world, and a surreal, fantastical, disembodied experience for many who live and breathe, work in, and think about the black church. And yet there was a troubling dimension to this incredible passage: something said to me—maybe to many of us—that *the ground had shifted*, and that maybe African Americans had lost something precious even as we gained what so many had fought for, prayed for, hoped for, and died for. For some, the moment was, and still is, strange and mixed with anxiety (*angst*), a distrust of feelings that were too joyful, too hopeful, and perhaps deceptive. Did this moment bring with it *erasure of memory*, a type of *anomie* as in loss of world? Did not some silently wish and ask, "Are we now becoming a *post-racial America*?"

On November 5, 2008, the day after the historic election of Obama as the forty-fourth president of the United States, I was invited to write an article for *U.S. News and World Report*, in which I raised the question of the cultural haunting of race in America.[2] I wrote that for many, Obama's presidency marked a new beginning, and for others it provoked suspicion, fear, and distrust because our nation is haunted by an old ghost. This ghost is not quite like the ones with which we have become comfortable: Banquo visiting his cunning and power-hungry murderers; Hamlet's father's specter demanding that the young prince swear to avenge his heinous murder; Washington Irving's headless horseman spooking the quiet village of Sleepy Hollow in Ichabod Crane's early America; Edgar Allan Poe's tell-tale heart pounding from beneath the floorboards; or ghosts gazing from the framed portraits on the walls of the staircase in Hogwarts in the Harry Potter chronicles.

No, I argued, this was a different kind of eerie visitation that represented a twenty-first-century *cultural haunting* of America. This ghost is more like the ha'nts in the country churchyard that my folks talked about, or like Toni Morrison's Beloved, who is a full-bodied, central character in the American narrative. To use the language of Kathleen Brogran, the ghost "serves to illuminate the shadowy or more repressed aspects of our [national] character"[3] that played out ignominiously in both of Obama's campaigns and elections and haunted his presidency.

During Senator Obama's presidential candidacy, this old ghost showed up everywhere: in an elderly woman in Milwaukee expressing her suspicion and distrust of the "Arab"; in an old man screaming, "I am fed up and mad as hell!"; in the unidentified shouts at Republican political rallies: "Kill Obama!"; on the cover of the *New Yorker* depicting Barack Obama wearing a turban and his wife, Michelle, toting an AK-47; in the sign of a backwards "B" on the face of the young McCain campaign worker in Pennsylvania; and in a foiled assassination plot that, thank God, was hatched by simpletons.

After his first election, Obama was verbally assaulted by an irate GOP congressman in the U.S. House during his health care address; demands were made upon him to submit his birth certificate as authentication of his U.S. citizenship; and he was caricatured and minstrelized in thousands of backwater creeks and in the romanticized hegemonic imaginings of a nostalgic America that never really existed. These were all signs of the ghost that stalks in the shadows of the American collective consciousness. We know all too well now that it is alive, very dangerous, and will not go away.

Ironically, while our nation celebrated the fiftieth anniversary of the 1965 Voting Rights Act and the Selma March in 2015, we were also struggling to make some sense of the shootings of black seventeen-year-olds Trayvon Martin and Jordan Davis and eighteen-year-old Michael Brown, the strangulation of forty-three-year-old Eric Garner by the police, and the controversy surrounding "stop and frisk" practices in neighborhoods of color—all grim reminders of the legal and moral implications of what is at stake in this era of *post-racialism*, not just for black and brown people, but for the future of our democracy.[4] President Obama's remarks that "Trayvon could have been me thirty-five years ago" came, on the one hand, as a source of encouragement for many mass protests of righteous indignation and cries for justice from citizens around the nation. On the other hand, many felt that he had inserted the proverbial race card into an already volatile situation of fractured race relations in this country. Some conservative pundits blamed him for acting as the "Racist-in-Chief," while some critics in the black community felt that he said too little, too late, that his statement was like "pre-sweetened Kool-Aid," suggesting that it was palliative at best and failed to address the deep structural issues at stake for the poor and black hopeless masses who needed his engaged and embodied leadership.[5] One has to ask why this continued cultural haunting of Obama appeared to be intensifying as Supreme Court rulings carefully and effectively dismantled some of the hard-fought gains of the civil rights movement (the Civil Rights Act, the Voting Rights Act, and affirmative action) a half century after Martin Luther King Jr.'s historic "I Have a Dream" speech. If it is clear that the subject of race is alive and well in the United States and around the globe, then what does the label *post-racial* mean? Does it signify something else that continues to elude, elide, and resist critical analysis, public debate, and policy-based solutions? How does it authorize and demand allegiance to an egalitarian society with equal justice for all and at the same time eviscerate and denude hard-fought-for and well-earned gains of generations who made simulacra of justice possible in the election of an African American to the highest office in the land?

As we have seen, on the one hand, the concept of post-racialism serves as a symbolic, eschatological hope in the unrealized dream toward which African Americans continue to aspire; and it functions alongside *nonracism* as a normative principle of *black churches* and *black communities.*[6] On the other hand, *post-racialism* is a problematic moniker (*problema, shield, mask*) that ascribes legitimacy to a host of contagious cultural and political conversations and public policy decisions that inspire violent actions and retard serious progressive deliberations on the continuing significance of race in the United States and elsewhere. Since the election of Barack Obama in 2008, *post-racialism* has increasingly become part of the language of our culture and informs many of the political and economic, religious and social, conservative and liberal judgments that determine our corporate destiny.[7]

Jeremiah and Barack: A Tale of Two Perspectives on Race

When my father died in 1984, my family and I returned to Centennial Missionary Baptist Church for his funeral service. As the only ordained minister in the family at the time, I took on the task of planning the service and eulogizing my father. It was a very difficult time for all of the family because my father represented the strength and core of our identity as children and, of course, we wondered how his passing would impact my mother. As I was delivering the eulogy on that gray October day, I was surprised to see the Reverend Jeremiah Wright seated in the back of the small congregation with his winter coat on and a heavy scarf around his neck. Accompanying him was the head deacon of Trinity United Church of Christ, where Reverend Wright pastored and which has become a site of national discussions about race within the American cultural and political landscape in recent years. Jeremiah, or "Jerry" as I fondly call him, came uninvited to the funeral and under doctor's orders not to speak because of a severe case of bronchitis. He had literally gotten out of his sickbed to be with me and to share in the homegoing of my father. I shall never forget this moment or his demonstration of compassion to my family on that day and his continuing friendship. I should not have been surprised that he came to be with us on this unhappy day. My family and I were not exceptions, we were simply part of the way he shared his deep empathy and pastoral care with everyone.

I met Jeremiah Wright when I was a seminary student at Garrett-Evangelical Theological Seminary in 1978 as the nascent black theology movement began to gain momentum in the academy alongside womanist, feminist, and LGBT movements. He was a guest in one of my classes, and I was among students who later visited with him at his then small but growing congregation on the Southside of Chicago. After matriculation from Garrett, I served St. John's Congregational Church, United Church of Christ, in Springfield, Massachusetts, a historical landmark in New England, whose history included activist pastors like William N. DeBerry, Albert Cleage, and Charles Cobb, spiritual leaders who were deeply committed to black liberation struggles. As a young pastor, working on a Ph.D. at Boston University, I diligently sought to create an ecclesial model that embraced St. John's tradition of prophetic leadership around race, gender, class, and sexuality. Among the many guest preachers were the theologian Delores Williams, the activist and later executive director of the NAACP Benjamin Chavis, the writer and cultural critic James Baldwin, and the Reverend Jeremiah Wright. Later, I would preach at Trinity, and I continued to invite Jeremiah as a featured speaker at convocations and conferences that I led at Colgate-Rochester Divinity School and Morehouse College. I share this personal history because I cannot distance my personal experience and appreciation of Pastor Wright from the ways he was depicted and demonized in the media as an irate, irresponsible, and irrational black madman.

Barack Obama joined the Trinity United Church of Christ in 1998, having built a relationship with Pastor Wright during his days as a community organizer on the Southside of Chicago in the mid-1980s. Obama admired the charismatic, intellectually engaged, and socially conscious preacher and used one of his popular sermons, "The Audacity of Hope," as the title of his bestselling book.[8] At the time of Senator Obama's official presidential candidacy announcement on February 10, 2007, at the old State Capitol in Springfield, Illinois, Reverend Wright had been invited to offer an invocation, but at the last minute was mysteriously disinvited. David Axelrod, Obama's chief strategist, later summed it up: "There was no doubt that there was controversy surrounding him. And we didn't want to expose him . . . [or] to make him the target and a distraction on a day when Senator Obama was going to announce his candidacy."[9] A number of Wright's speeches had been discovered by the media and were depicted as "anti-American" in their critique of injustices in American society and around the globe, particularly a sermon that he had delivered on April 13, 2003, titled "Confusing God and Government."[10] Later, in his presidential campaign, Senator Obama ultimately denounced the statements, and Reverend Wright was vilified in the media for raising issue with the campaign of Senator Obama at the Washington Press Club.[11] In the tragic fallout of these events, it is important to note that Wright's entrée into the partisan battles surrounding Obama's ascendancy was not initiated by him. He responded out of his own enfleshed narrative of black prophetic preaching and consequently was drawn into a media quagmire and suffered the fate of black leaders who, in the inverted Icarian narrative, fly too close to the ground. With few exceptions during the debacle, prominent black church leaders avoided Jeremiah Wright like the plague. The question of post-racialism that emerged in the media-driven tension between Senator Obama and Jeremiah Wright extended beyond the personal assaults on Obama's character, motives, and place of birth, and critiques of Pastor Wright's public remarks and "black nationalist" rhetoric. Rather, the controversy illustrated the very political and social character of the nation. Obama's leadership can be read as an example of the ways race disguises itself in the predatory attacks of right-wing conservative factions and the sometimes veiled, but equally vicious, assaults of the liberal left and progressive black leadership. It is also a statement of an old dilemma between cultural and political strategies of black liberation: moral and political reform versus black nationalism, to which we will attend in the following chapter.

The Dangers of Post-Racial Reasoning

Several writers have examined the debate surrounding the efficacy of Obama's political leadership and black prophetic leadership,[12] but what is needed is a broader critique that asks questions about what his leadership means for the nature and destiny of the American democratic experiment and the ways the question of race appears and reappears in ghostly apparitions that haunt the radical egalitarian hypothesis. Gary Dorrien's book *The Obama Question: A Progressive Perspective* is helpful in examining the diatribes concerning Obama's leadership.[13] Dorrien provides a balanced critical assessment of President Obama's leadership and his vision for our country, and offers insightful commentary on the progressive movement and a retelling of the troublesome, contentious debate about the meaning of America in a post-racial quagmire of political theater and social anxiety. Dorrien warns us of what is at stake when the endgame of political contests is primarily about winning and what happens to those whom the late Samuel DeWitt Proctor called "the lost, the left-out and left behind." *Post-racialism*, as a *ghostly* language and as a *shape-shifting* performance, poses very real and present dangers for the future of this nation and the world that are rooted in the competitive nature of *realpolitik*, in which we are most concerned about winning, *saving face*, and, when possible, stretching for ideals. In a post-racial and post-American world (which are not one and the same but curiously attached to the era of Obama's presidency),[14] the *Obama question* has been more than an interrogation into the assumptions of fair play and just orderings of racial and ethnic configurations and a host of other valid agenda items that include gender, sexuality, and religious discourse; it is also a question about governance that rests on the wise use of power in a high-stakes game of winning and losing.

President Obama also inherited the burdens of long-range economic, political, and social costs of war, a failed market economy, a permanent underclass at home, a dangerous and often clumsy American empire supported by a wobbly supercapitalism and the rapid crusades in technology and science, the global yearnings and eruptions of democracy expressed in the Occupy and Black Lives Matter movements, the "closed, alternative knowledge systems" of the conservative right, and the makings of a social anarchy that threatens the very foundations of our social purpose.[15] Ironically, the United States' increasingly fragile role as empire in a *post-American world* and the continued global eruptions of democratic freedom created peculiar difficulties for the first African American president in his first term. I am speaking to the intrinsic contradiction of the U.S. exportation of capitalism and democracy, which for some is akin to riding two horses going in different directions: a strain on the anatomy.[16] This problem presented even greater challenges for President Obama in his second term, as evidenced in how he dealt with an asymmetrical new world order where the law of unintended consequences is at work—for example, contending with ISIL, Iran, Syria, Libya, Egypt, and so on. With a bankrupt European economy, the rise of China and India as economic powers, the challenges of a new Russia, alliances of unaligned, developing economies, the continued conflict between Israel and Hamas, and the encroaching confrontation with Iran, it had become increasingly clear that the United States is no longer the Goliath of the world.[17] This would have been a major challenge for any president, but for Obama, exercising strong global leadership was even more difficult because the old ghost haunted him. Consider the Republican congressional leadership's and Prime Minister Benjamin Netanyahu's snub of the leader of the free world in his acceptance of an invitation to address Congress in March 2015 that bypassed the White House. Such a breach of diplomatic protocol could be interpreted as a *detour* around *blackness*. It would be hard to imagine this completely arrogant and dismissive public dishonoring if the president had been other than Obama. "I am invisible, understand, simply because people refuse to see me," writes Ralph Ellison.[18]

The Coach Bell Question

When my son played Little League baseball, concerned parents approached Coach Bell because some of the kids were not getting enough playing time. A tense moment ensued, filled with deep feelings about equality and fair play and self-interest (low on the enlightened and rightly understood part—more Hobbesian state of nature, in fact). Several parents felt that their children deserved the right to equal time on the diamond; after all, they had paid their fees, purchased uniforms, and exerted as much effort as other parents whose children played in nearly all the games. It did not matter to them which kids were the best hitters, outfielders, or pitchers. The game was about learning the discipline of democracy and good citizenship, they explained. Coach Bell, in his accentuated black southern drawl, with a combination of Georgian civility and black Baptist deacon's charm, reasoned with the parents and decided to play several games in which he rotated players so they could have equal time. After several losses were racked up, he called another meeting of the parents and asked a hard question: "Now, do you want everybody to play, or do you want to win?" While the analogy does not account for the troublesome particularities of contending with issues of justice and fairness in national and global policy, the larger point is that any fair assessment of President Obama's leadership and his legacy must take this question into account.

How do black church leaders respond to the *Coach Bell question* in the competitive arena of *realpolitik*? A major question that critics of Obama and his legacy must ask is along these lines: the bank bailout, the public option, and two wars are examples of what is at stake when leaders in the public domain want to win. Did this analogy apply to Obama any less than to his white Republican presidential and congressional rivals, who were willing to hold the future of the nation hostage rather than yield to Obama's proposals for the Affordable Care Act? It seems to me that there was a *personal* struggle within Obama, an internal crisis of values coupled with the perennial political task of *saving face*. Leaders in the public domain use inestimable personal energy, time, and intelligence *saving face*, but for Obama, who was lauded as the embodiment of post-racial ideology and was under constant intense surveillance and scrutiny, this task was more severe, perhaps impossible. It is true that Obama leaned toward the middle, that he manifested an inner need to find common ground and to be accepted, and that this was a strength (especially during his ascendancy to national politics), but largely it was a liability during his two terms in the White House.[19] The risks and the losses entailed in this strategy have been colossal, and progressives have proffered innumerable critiques and apologies for Obama's style of negotiation and compromise. But there is something else that characterizes Obama's leadership. Obama's leadership style is an example of a tendency toward Dilemma.

The *Coach Bell question* is raised by the political scientist Frederick Harris in his book *The Price of the Ticket: Barack Obama and the Rise and Decline of Black Politics*.[20] Harris traces the rise of black politics in the United States, especially the coalition strategies used by black politicians in pursuit of the white vote. Harris suggests that there is an unspoken, time-honored, and well-understood covenant between black politicians and black voters called the "wink and nod" strategy. Most blacks, Harris argues, understand that in order for black politicians to secure the majority vote and get elected, they must make universal promises and minimize race-specific issues during the campaign; they must "deracialize" their public image and "cover" (that is, "when stigmatized minorities engage in conscious acts that 'tone down a disfavored identity to fit the mainstream'").[21] Barack Obama, according to Harris, represents a long line of black political leaders (Edward Brooke, Douglas Wilder, and Deval Patrick, to name a few) whose success depended on building diverse coalitions that responded to universal appeals and claims ("I am a candidate for all the people" or "Rising tides raise all boats") rather than race-specific agendas. Obama ran not as a black presidential candidate, but as a presidential candidate who happened to be black. According to Harris, for loyal black voters, the symbolism of having a black president far outweighed substantive issues regarding black empowerment. Over time in the Obama administration, this strategy of symbol versus substance (i.e., the political strategy that addresses only universal, race-neutral policies and neglects questions of black unemployment, incarceration, and education) created a special dilemma for black voters and for President Obama: Do black voters continue to "wink and nod" or do they call out the Obama administration for its failure to address the overwhelming needs of black citizens once he had been twice elected? Clearly, Harris thinks, symbolism prevailed over substance in the fact that the race-transcendent leader represented the larger goal of black citizens—a post-racial society. Harris writes, "Instead of fading away in an era celebrated as 'postracial,' race as ideology demonstrates convincing staying power, endowed with the ability to readapt and readjust as new political situations arise."[22] *Everybody plays . . .*

Several related questions arise pertaining to Obama's deracialized leadership style and the kind of country we want to be. Is this "middling predisposition" related to his biracial story,[23] which is not just an American story but also a story that spans three continents? Does this reading of Obama conform to the characterizations of Shelby Steele (the "bargainer/challenger duality"[24]) and hence Obama's seeming invisibility (read: the absence of voice or more dramatically, Clint Eastwood's failed parody of the *empty chair*[25]); or Cornel West's charges of betrayal (Obama is "a black mascot for Wall Street," "the Johnny Mathis of American politics," "a Rockefeller Republican in blackface");[26] or Dinesh D'Souza's outlandish African postcolonial conspiratorial diatribe?[27]

Obama's Inner Theater

A closer look at these characterizations and the questions that arise from them teaches valuable lessons about the *post-racial* leadership of Obama and, by implication, black leadership in general.[28] In fact, they tell us more about America and progressives than we may really want to know. Taking a sort of dramaturgical gaze,[29] I suggest that race plays a major role, if not the most significant role, in what went on backstage in Obama's leadership decisions, and this is as much a statement about Obama *the man* as it is about Obama the *president of the United States*. It is also a disclosure of the staple ideological dogma of the white American psyche, often masked and unspeakable, which Obama mirrored and of which he is the mirror. No wonder he appeared Janus-faced and tongue-tied in matters of racial doublespeak and presidential leadership. He was America! Americans are afraid of race—not just to talk about it, which is to acknowledge it, but to see it embodied in *black face*, as this is to see who *we* really are. Behind the frightened, raced imagination of most white Americans, conservatives and progressives alike, is the lurking threat of being devoured.[30] Wisely or unwisely, until pushed by the Reverend Jeremiah Wright, Professor Skip Gates, the deaths of unarmed black youth, or the atrocities visited upon innocent parishioners in South Carolina, Obama handled the race question as if it were nitroglycerin.

Black church leaders can learn much from our first African American president about mirroring and masking. "We, too, are America," to channel the poetic spectral voice from the past,[31] but the time and the new moments to which we have been called will no longer allow the doublespeak and duplicity that come from mirroring and masking. We must set a new course for activism that discards the false faces and ventriloquized voices of the ghost. Frantz Fanon reminds us that "to speak means to be in a position to use a certain syntax, to grasp the morphology of this or that language, but it means above all to assume a culture, to support the weight of a civilization."[32] A critical question going forward is how do we appear to ourselves as civilized actors who perform on the stage of Western empire, and how shall these performances appear and reconstitute themselves in the eyes of others who have had to deal with the civilizing effects of the modern world? Can we think about a sophisticated and usable diasporic vision that allows black church leaders to find "home" in a world as global citizens?

Obama and the Question of Civility

The *doubleness*, the two-faced cautiousness, of Obama leads to the question of civility in a contested post-racial America that has notable historical precedents among African American elites, especially religious leaders. But the question of civility has implications for how we understand democracy and the future of this society. I have suggested elsewhere that there is a huge difference between dysfunctional civility and transformative (subversive) civility as it relates to the etiquette of democratic life and principles.[33] The early stages of Obama's presidency are excellent examples of what can happen when an anemic and uninformed civility substitutes for healthy suspicion and consistent interrogation of power—in other words, civility in public discourse demands a requisite cultural knowledge base so that one's response, while civil and appropriate to the demands of the situation, is able to differentiate between truth and falsity, hospitality and entrapment, like the wolf in the tale of Little Red Riding Hood. Some argue that Obama's willingness to trust Timothy Geithner, Ben Bernanke, Lawrence Summers, and Henry Paulson with the "crashing and bailing" of Wall Street was akin to leaving the foxes in charge of the henhouse.[34] Civility can also become a transformative and subversive practice that exposes unjust practices and calls upon the highest within a leader's character.

By subversive civility, what I have in mind is akin to the observation of Jeffrey Goldfarb, professor of sociology at the New School for Social Research and the founding editor of Public Seminar, that intellectuals "contribute to a democratic life when they civilize political contestation and when they subvert complacent consensus; when they provide enemies with the discursive possibility to become opponents and when they facilitate public deliberations about problems buried by the norms of civility."[35] Obama did this in his dealings with his Republican and Democratic opponents alike. The outcomes have been uneven mainly because his political opponents were determined from the beginning of his presidency to ensure his failure. In order to facilitate civic decorum in public debate, minimally there should be a commitment to procedural knowledge and norms and values of public discourse. In President Obama's case, the game was rigged so that his best hand had to be played with a consummate poker face, masking serious deliberations and strategies that often surprised his adversaries as much as his supporters.

Hence, for Obama the critical question, "Do we all want to play or do we want to win?" was an ethical one that was utilitarian, pragmatic, and creative. Sometimes it worked well; in other instances, he appeared indecisive, weak, and naïve. It is a challenge to handle—in the context of a *post-racial* America—and to hold in tension the dynamics of the right's unyielding commitment to the primacy of liberty, race, and capital over and against the larger egalitarian vision of the left. Who will win, and how that will be determined, are huge questions for the future of democracy and for the future of black religious leadership. However, the question remains for America whether a leader with a *black face* can pull it off. Whether or not America's obsession with its original sin, or what Condoleezza Rice calls its "birth defect,"[36] will prevent future black leaders and others representing historically marginalized communities from moving forward is *the Obama Question*.

"I Didn't Die Right": A Ghost in the House

One of my favorite childhood stories was the one my father told about the ha'nt who lived in a house and who had a nasty habit of visiting its tenants after they moved in and began to feel comfortable. At midnight without fail, the ghost would come into the room of the unsuspecting new occupant and exclaim, "I didn't die right! I didn't die right!" This haunting chant would go on and on, until the terrified tenants rushed out of the house to escape the eerie intimidation. At last came High John the Conqueror, who, when confronted by the ghost, declared, "If you stay in this house, you're going to die right tonight!"

My father told the story with great flair and humor, though the lesson of the story was that the ghost could not haunt John because he was not afraid to directly confront it. An old ghost that didn't die right haunted the Obama White House, and many claim that President Obama did not demonstrate the necessary fortitude and commitment to racial justice during one of the most devastating periods for black life since the 1960s. What some critics fail to understand is that the ghost in Obama's White House was no ordinary h'ant—and this was and remains a postracial haunting of America. As I argued earlier, this ghost evades, elides, and eludes capture and confrontation; its *spectrality* is an abstract space that is not a space, a thing that is not a thing. Its haunting is accompanied by the disjuncture of time and the pluralization of temporalities and meanings—even justice is pluralized in languages of diversity and differences that conceal black materiality and specificity.[37] Therefore, as a *spectrogenic* process the ghost appears and disappears, leaves and returns, which makes it extremely difficult to catch and hold on to long enough to fight it head-on. Yet we see evidence of the ghost's haunting everywhere. Its appearances, though episodic, are part of the very architecture of American society portrayed in the shape-shifting demographics of black migrants' travel from inner-city ghettoes to suburbs and exurbs and finding that they have not left the ghetto behind. It is manifest in the continuing challenges of income inequality, food deserts, incarcerated populations of black and poor youth, inequitable educational policies, public health disparities, and other signs that portray the ghost's resilience and indirectness.[38] Therefore, future leaders of the church and society will need to learn different ways of dealing with this old ghost that refuses to die in America and that continues to avoid apprehension. Some lessons can be learned here that require more than political confrontation and mass protests.

President Obama was not John the Conqueror, nor a pugilist or a puppet, but a pragmatist through and through. One could argue that as a pragmatist, he took seriously the ambiguity and contingency of the post-racial era that gave birth to his candidacy and two elections—and waited patiently for opportunities to point to the ghost and its nefarious masquerade. He knew the danger and the sometimes futile enterprise of speaking about race in *post-racial* America, yet in two of his most publicized speeches on race in America, "A More Perfect Union" and the "Eulogy for the Honorable Reverend Clementa Pinckney," both responses to race-provoked incidents, he delivered stirring addresses in which we caught a glimpse of the old ghost in the house and its chilling effects not only on President Obama, but on black leadership in general and on black church leadership in particular. Most striking, and perhaps telling, was the eulogy for the Honorable Reverend and Democratic member of the South Carolina Senate Clementa Pinckney, in which President Obama boldly spoke to the nation and the church in an unmistakably black voice, accentuated by his theme of "American Grace" and closing with the hymn written by a converted slave trader, "Amazing Grace."[39] President Obama, unlike Senator Obama of the "More Perfect Union" speech, was less reserved and more on point. In the syncopated rhythm and pause of black preaching, he briefly rehearsed the history of the invisible institution's revolutionary past of "hush arbors," "praise houses," and "rest stops on the Underground Railroad"; its service as "bunkers for foot soldiers of the Civil Rights Movement," "community centers," "places of scholarship and networks," and spaces "where children are loved and fed" and "told that they are beautiful" and that "they matter"— all of this, he suggested, was hidden from the view of "the killer of Reverend Pinckney and eight others" in South Carolina and, perhaps, from America. He added,

That's what the black church means. Our beating heart. The place where our dignity as a people is inviolate. When there's no better example of this tradition than Mother Emanuel, . . . a church built by blacks seeking liberty, burned to the ground because its founder sought to end slavery, only to rise up again, a Phoenix from these ashes.[40]

From where did this unambiguous black voice and vibe come? Was it deliberate—an intentional, calculated jab at the old ghost—or was it a totally unconscious expression of his weariness with the racist sins of the nation? Or was it both? Whether conscious or unconscious, President Obama spoke from this in-between space in a voice and enfleshed language that were undeniably his own. We saw Barack Hussein Obama both dance with his brothers and sisters in Kenya and sing "Amazing Grace" at Mother Emanuel African Methodist Episcopal Church in Charleston, South Carolina, accompanied by black church leaders and congregants—a black American civil religion moment of transfiguration. At a July 28, 2015, address to the African Union in Addis Ababa, Ethiopia, a month later, we heard another edge in that voice when he announced his lineage—not as a genealogical isolate but as a son of Africa and America: "I stand before you as a proud American. I also stand before you as the son of an African. Africa and its people have helped shape who I am and how I see the world. In the villages in Kenya where my father was born, I learned of my ancestors, the life of my grandfather, the dreams of my father and the bonds of family that connect us as Africans and Americans."[41] One could be accused of making much ado about nothing, but I think he was *turning*.

In that black voice and in that black body and in those resplendent, fleeting moments in which he reclaimed authorial intent, was Obama signifying on white America (and maybe on the "black church" as well)? Can we arise again "from these ashes"? Is it possible to awaken from our social-political narcolepsy and reclaim this tradition of which President Obama spoke, and if so, how? For the most part, we have not; rather, we have been caught in the in-between spaces of the living dead where the old ghost sidesteps, rope-a-dopes, and hides in the Christian language of forgiveness and reconciliation and comes back to assault us with greater tyranny. How shall we learn to *turn* from those spaces inhabited by the *living dead* as part of our ongoing theological and churchly mission?

Caught in the Middle: Black Church Leadership in the Age of Obama

Most significantly for our purposes, the apparition of *post-racialism* in the age of Obama and beyond has haunted texts, practices, and performances of black church leaders and scholars by insinuating and incorporating the radical egalitarian hypothesis into cultural and sociopolitical, theological, and ethical constructs that undermine prophetic praxis. One example is how the ongoing debate between structural and behaviorist perspectives of black American culture is translated in black churches as a contestation between mainline religious practices and the rise of the prosperity gospel. It can be no coincidence that the theological and ethical perspectives of these two polarities fall alongside social and political positions that are deeply embedded in the contentious debate of progressive black church leaders and leading prosperity gospel figures. Progressive black church leaders, following in the prophetic tradition of Martin Delany, Martin Luther King Jr., the Reverend Pauli Murray, the Reverend Adam Clayton Powell Jr., and the Reverend Prathia Hall Wynn, hold that the causes of poverty, sexism, homophobia, health disparities, incarceration, and deteriorating educational systems are related to larger issues of systemic injustice. These and other extra-church black prophetic leaders like Frederick Douglass, Ella Baker, Ida B. Wells, and Malcolm X have been brilliantly analyzed and discussed by contemporary scholars such as Vincent Wimbush, Cornel West, and Christa Buschendorf.[42] For the most part, religious scholars in the academy tend to embrace this tradition as normative for the black church, but this stance is mistaken because alongside this tradition, and perhaps overriding it, has been another long-standing tradition that has come to be known as the "prosperity gospel," which commands the attention and loyalty of millions of black Christians in the United States and around the globe.

Jonathan Walton, Plummer Professor of Christian Morals and Pusey Minister of Harvard's Memorial Church, is among a group of scholars who have helped us to better understand the historical religious and cultural roots of the prosperity gospel in the United States through the lens of televangelism. Through historiographies offered by the media and religious scholars in the development of African American televangelism, Walton identifies the paucity of serious analytic reflection on and investigation of the phenomenon. For instance, his discussion of the cultural and religious sources that informed the theology and praxis of the Reverend Frederick Eikerenkoetter (Reverend Ike), a critical figure in the history of African American televangelism, illustrates how religious practices and cultural myths are portrayed in African American lifeworlds, denoting the "naturalization" of select religious/cultural ideas that resonate with succeeding generations of African American communities. In doing so, Walton provides a perceptive ethical and aesthetic analysis of popular culture versus the radical embrace of religiosity that perpetuates rituals and practices of three traditions that he designates as neo-Pentecostal, Charismatic Mainline, and Word of Faith, whose complex cultural and historical roots, and multifarious configurations, have been rendered relatively invisible until now. Walton's work has been praised and criticized. Most critiques are related to the gender imbalance of the representatives he studies and a lack of serious historical attention to, and treatment of, questions of racial reconciliation.[43]

Contemporary prosperity church leaders in these traditions, represented by pastoral leaders such as T. D. Jakes (neo-Pentecostal), Eddie Long (Charismatic Mainline), and Creflo Dollar (Word of Faith), maintain that the problems of black success and wellness are primarily behavioral, not structural. Blacks are poor, they tend to argue, not because of what government has done or not done, but because African Americans have not lived by *the word of faith* and practiced prescribed scriptural forms of holiness. Consequently, these two traditions—historically activist black churches and new prosperity gospel churches—are at loggerheads over the theological, social, and political mission of black churches. The danger of post-racial metaphors and fixation with *ghostly* narratives that compete for prominence in black churchly discourse and practices is also manifest in the tendentious debates between the academy and "prosperity gospels" in the United States and Africa. Prosperity gospels will continue to play a significant role in the shaping of black church leadership and its embrace of post-racial ideology.[44]

In summary, in chapter 2, we identified the place and role of memory as a critical tool in accessing a past that informs much of our present struggles with race and post-racialism. This chapter has continued the theme of memory by remembering the cultural haunting of President Barack Obama. This remembering provides for black church leaders and scholars an analytic frame through which we can begin to see the devastating and destructive practices associated with Dilemma-oriented leadership, and perhaps a glimpse of its possibility in Barack Obama's *turning*. Therefore, it is important to further understand the nature and function of Dilemma as an anchoring metaphor of black church life and practices. This will be treated in the next chapter. This understanding will enable us to proceed further in speaking specifically to psychosocial and cultural-political strategies for transformation. It would be equally instructive to explore some ecclesiological models for black church leadership (although this cannot be adequately done here) that speak to prevailing shifts toward an embodied and engaged notion of global citizenship and critical multiculturalism for transatlantic black church activism. A necessary step that helps us to proceed is to first better understand how scholars have understood post-racial discourse as both a theoretical and practical construct and how that language might be utilized as a tool in the reconstruction of black churches. This discussion begins in part 2, "Vision."

PART II

Vision

Retelling Our Story

Lord, I fashion dark gods, too.
—Countee Cullen, "Heritage (For Harold Jackman)"[1]

4

Turning from Dilemma to Diaspora

The overweening, defining event of the modern world is the mass movement of raced populations, beginning with the largest forced transfer of people in the history of the world: slavery. The consequences of which transfer have determined all the wars following it as well as the current ones being waged on every continent. The contemporary world's work has become policing, halting, forming policy regarding, and trying to administer the movement of people. Nationhood— the very definition of citizenship—is constantly being demarcated and redemarcated in response to exiles, refugees, *Gastarbeiter*, immigrants, migrations, the displaced, the fleeing and the besieged. The anxiety of belonging is entombed within the central metaphors in the discourse on globalism, transnationalism, nationalism, the break-up of federations, the rescheduling of alliances, and the fictions of sovereignty. Yet these figurations of nationhood and identity are frequently as raced themselves as the originating racial house that defined them. When they are not raced, they are . . . imaginary landscape, never inscape; Utopia, never home.
—Toni Morrison, "Home"[1]

The Revisability of Race-Based Language and Consciousness

How do contemporary black religious scholars and church leaders begin to think, speak, and act in *hope* in an era of *post-racialism* and negotiate the effects of its *ghostly, shape-shifting* character? The metaphor of race as a ghost-like social entity that shape-shifts into different guises in order to adapt to changing cultural and sociopolitical situations continues to be a hotly contested one in contemporary academic discourse.[2] On the one hand, *eliminativist* philosophers such as Kwame Anthony Appiah argue that since the concept of race is a biological fiction, it is a meaningless term that should be discarded in academic, cultural, and sociopolitical life. To continue to employ the concept of race as though it were a scientific fact simply reinforces and encourages historical oppression and divisiveness on the basis of skin color. This perspective shares deep affinity with the problematic radical egalitarian hypothesis, which is incapable of achieving substantive accounts of justice for those damned by the modernist project. As the rapper Common chants, "Justice is juxtapositionin' us / Justice for all just ain't specific enough."[3] Moreover, *conservationist* thinkers such as Richard Jones, Lucious Outlaw, and Charles Mills argue that eliminating the concept of race will not lead to an egalitarian society. The opposite is actually true. If we eliminate the concept of race from our academic and sociopolitical discourse, we render racism and its consequences beyond rational critique.[4] The danger of post-racial/eliminativist thinking in the conservationist viewpoint is that it easily degenerates into an outright denial of racism, a theoretically sophisticated, mutated, shifting form of racism in the name of antiracism. This perspective is reminiscent of the proverbial ostrich that hides its head in the sand in the presence of imminent danger in order not to see what is happening. The danger of this position, of course, is that when we bury our heads in the sand, more is exposed than is hidden. It has become increasingly clear with mass incarceration and police-sponsored deaths of young black men and women, and the rise of new movements like Black Lives Matter, that this is not a rational option. Those who adopt this perspective must also attend to a type of double jeopardy to all nonwhite oppressed classes. The philosopher Naomi Zack writes,

> It's one thing to understand within a safe forum that race is a biological fiction. [But] in American culture at large, the fiction of race continues to operate as fact, and in situations of backlash against emancipatory prog-

ress, the victims of racial oppression, non-whites, are insulted and injured further for their progress against oppression. If those who practice such second-order oppression begin to employ the truth that race is a fiction, gains already secured against first-order oppression (or in redress of it) could be jeopardized.[5]

So how do we employ the concept of race in academic, theological, and sociopolitical contexts without reinforcing it as a biological fact or treating it as social fiction? Michael Eric Dyson suggests that "fiction may not be the problem; the trouble may be our storytellers and the stories about race that they are telling," which suggests that the concept of race has utility in a purported post-racial era.[6] Dyson's perspective finds resonance with Richard Jones's thinking about race as a resilient, shifting, and revisable historical reality that is constantly adapting to new social situations.[7] Drawing from American pragmatism and W. E. B. Du Bois, Jones redefines race as a linguistic tool, infinitely revisable, that we use in myriad ways to ascribe meaning to ourselves and others. As it assigns difference and value to varying configurations of class, gender, sexuality, and tribalism, race also ascribes and inscribes notions of identity, otherness, and definitions of human flourishing. In this sense, race is

> a tool in a language game, or a tool for achieving viable forms of life—that is infinitely revisable as the dynamic relationships (processes) between frameworks (or environments) and agents (or organisms) evolve over time as they work out internal inconsistencies. In this instrumentalist view, race as a linguistic concept can be seen diachronically as having been a tool for domination and subordination in "master/slave scripts"; [and can be viewed] synchronically as a developing linguistic instrument for human liberation.[8]

A critical question that the revisionist perspective raises is related to the intersectionality of race, class, gender, sexuality, and a host of other markers. In other words, we cannot analytically engage race without taking into consideration these other important social and cultural determinants.

Another problem is that of structure and agency. A bifurcated diagnosis of what ails black communities and their leaders yields to deep cultural and political assumptions and either/or polemics (structural justice versus personal behavior and responsibility), which is problematic and insoluble. Here the work of the late sociologist and philosopher Pierre Bourdieu, which advocates a form of scientific humanism that respects the capacity of human agency even while acknowledging the structural determinants of human behavior, is invaluable.[9] One key to developing a method that balances religious and humanistic perspectives to studying persons and groups is what M. Brewster Smith calls a "cross-cultural approach."[10] Most important for our purposes is the idea that "self-awareness and self-evaluation are social emergents"—that is, human beings become aware of themselves partly by assuming shared meanings within society that provide persons with points of reference to understand the nature and meaning of their own selfhood and to shape group behavior through *mirroring* and *masking*.[11]

The theorists A. Paul Hare and Herbert Blumberg summarize some of these more contemporary contributions to the symbolic interactionism theory developed by George Herbert Mead by drawing from Erving Goffman's dramaturgical theory of self-presentation, which likens all social interactions to theatrical performances: "An instance of social interaction is a *performance*. Any performance, including a theatrical one, starts out from an *idea* about a situation and the action that will unfold within the situation. The idea may be a single *image* that has the program for action packed into it, much as a symbol in a dream may be a merger of waking events."[12] But very often, much like racial stereotypes, symbols and images that inform social roles are imposed without our conscious consent. We breathe them like air, and participate in a socially constructed *habitus* extended intergenerationally in "learned ignorance."[13] We simply know and do not question what is expected of us; rather, we seek to *save face* in front of others and to adapt to ways that garner acceptance by appearing to conform to certain social standards.[14] Cultural situations, scenes, symbols, and metaphors hypnotize and bewitch us like unseen ghosts, providing us with scripts to perform that diminish our agency and our ability to genuinely appreciate our and others' worth, and to work toward human flourishing. This means that human persons and groups self-reflect and understand their experiences on the basis of narratives, metaphors, and symbols they derive from within cultures. Ideas, images, symbols, or metaphors that shape human behavior are informed by a social audience, and performed with a social audience in mind. Actors, so to speak, are given specific roles, ideas, or metaphors to enact by the larger society and in specific local situations in their everyday lives that perpetuate schematizations of cultural domination. But when agents consciously engage these roles, override them, or seek to create new ones, they are simultaneously constructing what I shall call *tools of the spirit*, which are dispositions of agency and hence imaginative practices that assist in the work to liberate self and others from forms of psychosocial and political-cultural domination. Here I have in mind spiritual practices that conspire with liberative praxis in the transformation of thoughts, feelings, and behaviors that perpetuate the vicious and punitive cycle of racialized otherness.

My academic performance in high school was very poor. In fact, I am sure I was in the last quadrant of the 1969 graduating class of Dunbar Vocational High School in Chicago. Yet I enjoyed writing, and during the end of my senior year, my homeroom teacher found an internship for me in a downtown advertising agency. Everyone in the agency, except me, of course, was white and suburban. It was my introduction to the professional and socially constructed white world, and my first experience of what the theologian and public intellectual Thandeka describes as "learning to be white."[15] It took a major adjustment (and some more adjustment), but after several months, I learned "to be white." What an incredible power it conferred upon me as I learned what to say to the secretaries to make them and me feel comfortable as I entered the office;

or how to speak to the white men about baseball at the coffee station and so on. I wore the mask; better, over time the mask wore me. But as I learned the power and danger of the mask, I studied ways to adjust it to various situations. So much was involved in my performance—affects, inflections in speech, mannerisms, and dress—that I learned to consciously change my habits and practices to accommodate this new environment where everyone was watching. I mention this yearlong episode to suggest that there was never a moment when I forgot that I was black (nor did they), but as long as I was acting and talking "white" there was little or no tension. Indeed, there was a lot of paternalism and unmistakable racism, but in my shape-shifting Rodney King fantasia, we all got along. I identified as "white" in my shamed-racialized-underclass-black-male-body, but I was never "white" and neither were they. We were playing parts imputed to us from a larger sociopolitical, historical dramatic repository.

I would like to engage the reader in another way of thinking, acting, and speaking that assumes consciously experimenting with racialized roles as social and political performances in the work of social and political transformation. What might be the implications of this experimentation for questions of identity, otherness, and human flourishing among black churches and its leaders? Might we begin to think not of *fixed identities*, but of *identifications*—where subjects choose where they locate themselves in the political and cultural struggles surrounding race, in their quests for a *sense* of identity that is not delimiting but fluid and empowering?[16] Thus, positing race as a tool in the creation of religious and political meaning recognizes that race is not a biologically or historically fixed reality; rather, it encourages us to be aware that race exists nevertheless in mutable social forms that constantly adapt and blend into new sociopolitical situations. It also suggests the notion of racial identifications as conjured narratives that we perform in a shared sense of utilizing race as a tool, as a type of *pharmacopoeia*, a dangerous but potent possibility of an admixture of poison that heals. On the one hand, might we consider race in its most literal sense to be a social toxin that harms and kills, in the ancient sense of *pharmakos*, and make of it an instrument for healing and transformation? In other words, we need to further investigate the ghostly meanings and obscured absences (and traces) of *race* as an unmentionable in public discourse and acknowledge its diseased presence in the Christian theological imagination.[17] In my understanding of *pharmacopoeia*, I am referring to the assorted connections of the scapegoated black body to systemic patterns of injustice evidenced in violent acts of unspeakable cruelty: enslavement, lynching, rape, incarceration, poverty, and so on. The scapegoated black body bears affinity with the *homo sacer* or *sacred human* who may be killed but not sacrificed as an indistinct sphere of sovereignty in a biopolitical context. The black body as *homo sacer* exists at the threshold of the living and the dead and bears the ban of sovereignty (a "bandit"), a "hieroglyphics of the flesh,"[18] a monstrosity "who is precisely *neither man nor beast*, and who dwells paradoxically within both while belonging to neither."[19]

On the other hand, in order to use these evidentiary markers of *pharmacopoeia*, we need to identify and demonstrate their ghostly nature as phenomena that are not always spoken though they are there in every reading, linguistic formulation, and action as signs that signify on and point to our difficult yet possible redemption.[20] As *conjuring agents*, therefore, we have the responsibility to discern, deliberate, and decide to use race effectively as an emancipatory instrument in the *alchemic transformation* of social evil or for demonic oppressive ends. Hence, the double jeopardy of *racing* as fact or fiction becomes simultaneously instrumental and revisable, and, therefore, potentially a *tool of the spirit*. It is an invitation to play with the trickster who is constantly inviting us into dangerous territory—*crossing(s)*—that incite possibilities through shape-shifting transfigurations of language, symbols, and signs.

In *Slave Culture*, the cultural historian Sterling Stuckey relates the powerful folktale of "Bur (Brer) Rabbit in the Red Hill Churchyard," which illustrates the African trickster role in burial ceremonies and the raising of the dead through the instrumentality of the fiddle. The tale in its simplest telling is that Brer Rabbit uses his fiddle like a "magic wand" for all sorts of things—to "realize his will against predators or in competition for the hand of a maid."[21] In similar ways, Babacar M'Baye underscores how trickster tales in Antigua reveal strategies of diversion, playfulness, and musicality that helped enslaved Africans to survive in hostile, alien environments.[22] In the Red Hill Churchyard, Brer Rabbit is a conjurer and Obeah man, who uses his fiddle to create community among the various small critters, including the songster Brer Mockingbird, who joins him to "whistle a chune dat would er made de angels weep."[23] The graveyard represents "dead space," but in that space of powerlessness and desolation, Brer Rabbit's performance shifts and transfigures the alienation of the slave culture through a counterclockwise dance circle (ring shout) where enslaved Africans and the ancestors—living and the living dead—create *common(s)*: common consciousnesses, *common grounds* on uncommon grounds, and common rhythms through the agency of the fiddle. Stuckey connects the origin of this trickster tale to the funerary ceremonies of Central and West African peoples, varied in ethnicity and language but able to find *common(s)* in the power of the music and the embodied performance of the counter-circle dance—a spiraling configuration of embodied meaning[24]:

> If they had been preserved, the lyrics of what was sung would tell us much about the impact of slavery on the consciousness of first-generation Africans and much about African religious ceremonies generally. But given the context of the songs, the overall meaning is clear enough: they were songs concerning the ancestors, songs some notes of which, like those of Brer Mockingbird in the Red Hill Churchyard, conveyed the pain of being on the ground of the dead in an alien land far from the ancestral home.[25]

As we have seen, a significant part of retelling our story(ies) involves memory, the remembering of our story(ies) that reaches back beyond national imaginary time to yet another time, distant and near, in the embodied language of "home." The fiddle is a metaphorical *tool of the spirit* that points us to a space that Morrison identifies above as *home*. As we return to the shape-shifting characterizations of the ghost of post-racialism and the attendant questions of eliminativism, conservationism, and revisability of race, it will be important to remember that those to whom this work matters most are those who are in search of home—*never inscape, not Utopia*, but home as a spiritual quest for a sense of wholeness, of belonging, of meaning that is always elusive, always far from *home* as *negotiated transcendence*.

It is helpful to keep the notion of *turning* in mind as I apply this pragmatist, conservationist perspective of the revisability of race (against post-racialism) to U.S. black church contexts to consider how the major metaphors that have shaped the psychosocial/politico-cultural, theological/ethical, and aesthetic/existential dimensions of this phenomenon in the previous centuries have become inadequate guiding paradigms for this ecclesiological community in the twenty-first century. *Turning* connotes the playfulness, the gesturing, and the musicality of enfleshed life, not unlike Stuckey's presentation of the counterclockwise ring shout or the community's dance in *crossing(s)* at the Clearing, where weeping, confession, and resistance emerge from a *conjured fluid center*. *Turning* is important because we are always re*turning*, re*membering*, retell*ing*, and re*living* our stories in the context of larger social-historical events—a spiraling, counterclockwise dance of embodied mind and imagination. Here this movement in time and space bears affinity with what Michelle M. Wright, associate professor of African American studies at Northwestern University, calls *Epiphenomenal time, spacetime* that bends backwards, so to speak, to incorporate the past in the present ("now") and forward to capture the future ("not yet" but can be). At stake in this argument, for Wright, are the ways "blackness" has been epistemologically defined as solely a linear, sociohistorical narrative construction that creates a host of problems associated with ontological and intersectional readings. Her approach is to define "blackness" through the lens of *Epiphenomenal time*, which also sees it as phenomenological or imagined and performed "through individual perceptions in various ways depending on context." I am suggesting in my reading of Wright that *Epiphenomenal time* as phenomenological and historical points to a certain *negotiated transcendence* that includes the burdens of the tragic and political while allowing for agency and subjectivity.[26]

This chapter begins to reconstruct the notion of *home* in respect to vision or envisioning the future based upon the first moment of retrieval of memory or remembering. Any authentic or substantive sense of vision is impossible without memory. "Surely my soul remembers and is bowed down within me. This I recall to my mind, therefore I have hope. God's lovingkindnesses indeed never cease, for God's compassions never fail."[27] Memory precedes vision, but vision relies also on *enfleshing* mission, as we shall see going forward, in a spiraling dance with temporalities that proceed from *fluid center(s)* that are *turning*. Vision beckons us to *turn* to the future but its home is in the past; as memory signals a short and long past that *hopes* in the future for home like the symbolic Sankofa *turning* to preen its feathers.[28] That hope, however, is always turning and negotiating the difficult terrain of tragedy and transcendence—home here and home beyond this time. Home, I argue, is near us in the present reliving of the story that informs mission . . . always *turning*.

The meta-metaphor guiding this reevaluation of black churches is "the ground has shifted but the ghost still haunts us." It is also a symbolic marker that pushes us to think and speak about—and act on—the need for African American religious scholars and church leaders to engage a new time and rhythm, a shift of *lifeworlds* and *systems* in what is being called a *post-racial* American society. I structure each moment respectively as a *turning*, first *from* Dilemma *to* Diaspora, then *from* Exodus *to* Exile, and finally *from* the Frying Pan *to* the Fire.

Psychosocial/Politico-Cultural Contexts of Black Church Practices

I have noted in several places thus far that the metaphor of Dilemma characterizes the trope of double consciousness in black church leadership and practices. In an earlier work, I suggested that since Gunnar Myrdal's classic study *An American Dilemma*,[29] the metaphor of Dilemma has come to represent broad and conflicting ideologies in respect to African American life and culture and our understandings of identity, otherness, and human flourishing.[30] The subtitle of Myrdal's work, however, underscored the fundamental character of the issues at stake. He characterized the dilemma as "The Negro Problem and Modern Democracy." *The Negro Problem* (sometimes called *the Negro Question*) has been the staple ideological proclamation, rivaling the Emancipation Proclamation, defining and representing the life and place of the African in American society since slavery. The Negro Problem, formulated by all sides of the male-dominated white power elite, was "What shall we do with the Negro?"[31] "Betwixt and between"[32] is the ongoing ritualized dilemma of African Americans in respect to both national and religious identities, constituting a spasmodic reaction to religious time and democratic time that exclaims in utter exasperation, "O wretched creature that I am! Who will deliver me from this body of death?"[33] The dilemma is related to the "dead space," or the "unaccomplished imaginative shift from enslaved to freed subjectivity and the marked gap between genealogical isolation and the ancestral past" referenced earlier. In fact, for the most part, the religious and nationalistic imaginaries are so integrally related that they appear as one hegemonic shadow that haunts black churches and their leaders, mainly because they are cultural productions of the architecture of race, or what Wahneema Lubiano calls "the house that race built."

Recently, I worked as part of a team with a large group of corporate executives on issues of leadership, diversity, and change in Atlanta, Georgia. One of the exercises was to revisit the civil rights monuments and sites in the city. The most significant moment was the tour of the old Ebenezer Baptist Church building, which has been registered as a historic landmark. This haunted site of memory retold the story of Martin Luther King Jr.'s life and work in the modern civil rights movement. But it retold other stories as well, beginning with the stories of those early pioneers who founded the church in 1886 during Reconstruction and their troubles with ghosts, and continuing through the late twentieth century, with the recollection of the tragic shooting of King's mother at the church organ six years after his assassination. It told of the contributions of the many souls who built this structure and contributed to the most powerful religiously inspired and led movement of the twentieth-century United States. But more emphatically, it chronicled the journey of raced religious and national yearnings and tragedies embedded in the American story. To understand black churches as part of the national imaginary of a *raced* house helps us to better identify the power of the ghost, not simply as a political and economic asset to powerful elites who benefit from its operation, but in its constitutive role in the production of the idea of American democracy itself and the problem of Dilemma. What is the United States of America without the idea and operation of race as a binarism that promotes other forms of opposition in the public and religious imagination?[34]

In his classic meditation on "doubleness," W. E. B. Du Bois posed Dilemma as a question of identity: "What does it *feel* like to be a problem?" On one hand, the question implies a psychosocial/cultural-political inquiry: "What does this mean for the social life and personal sanity of African American citizens?" Du Bois's question, however, is not simply personal, sociological, or cultural-political, but a religious and theological one that demands historical, sociological, and cultural analysis. Du Bois's famous question is both an existential query denoting the angst of *doubleness* in African American life and practices, and an interrogation of the socially constructed *habitus* that framed the practice of Dilemma in social policy and the quest for citizenship at the dawn of twentieth-century America. It is also a critical signification on the *bitter cry* of dereliction and abandonment (remember, Du Bois also asked, *"Why did God make me an outcast and a stranger in mine own house?"*). The *bitter cry* of lament is a plea of theodicy that arises from the deep processes of social alienation and estrangement in a world constructed in the image of whiteness, where black subjectivity is subjugated and incarcerated by its own agency—a consciousness that monitors and participates in its own confinement. The discursive features of the problem, of course, precede and succeed Du Bois's eloquent, poetic analytic of black agency and the concomitant structural injustices of race that have received wide scholarly attention.[35]

The Dilemma is hardly resolved; it still exists at the heart of African American life and practices and has far-reaching implications for the ways African Americans understand themselves and others, participate in civic life, and interrogate the ghost of post-racialism. In recent years, a number of scholars working in critical race theory and historical, literary, cultural, multicultural, and philosophical studies have addressed the problematic in other terms.[36] More progressive critiques look at the question of Dilemma in respect to macroeconomic and political variables and their relationship to cultural and aesthetic meanings, and in respect to the place of the *body*.[37]

In *The Social Teaching of the Black Churches*, in the chapter "Autonomy in Dilemma," Peter Paris discusses this long-standing struggle within African American communities between loyalty to faith and loyalty to the nation. The dilemma, Paris informs us, is how we reconcile these contending demands for loyalty: the inclusive moral demand of faith versus the more particularized and often self-annihilative demand of the nation. These loyalties, he suggests, "represent, respectively, theories of politics and ecclesiology that imply moral conflicts in theory and practice."[38] Historically, we have tended not to reconcile them at all, but rather to acquiesce to the demands of the nation, as illustrated in our participation in the two world wars and the wars in Korea, Vietnam, Iraq, and Afghanistan. This posture has not only stymied our autonomy within the political landscape of the United States, but has prevented U.S.

black churches from authentically participating in the global community. The controversy stemming from the jeremiad of the Reverend Jeremiah Wright and then Senator Barack Obama is but one example of the ways this binaried sense of loyalty to nation versus faith manifests itself.

In this sense, for U.S. black churches, Dilemma is a boundary metaphor, or what Robert Neville calls a broken religious symbol. According to Neville, religious symbols are complex phenomena that arise out of the imaginative engagement of persons and communities with "finite/infinite boundary conditions" in the world through the use of signs. As potential vehicles of revelation, these signs or symbols point beyond themselves to an infinite source, even as they remain partial, finite, and "broken" by the particular cultural, social, and political concerns of the subjects they embody.[39] As we will see, a theological interrogation of Dilemma as a boundary metaphor in black churches would lead to new ways of understanding and utilizing theological doctrines such as creation and the fall, sin and salvation, and agency and eschatology.[40] Suffice to say here, analysis of the boundary metaphor of Dilemma is the first moment in the passage toward reconstructing a new political and ecclesiological ground for black churches in global perspective. While Dilemma might have been unavoidable in the past in claiming an African heritage and yearning for U.S. citizenship rights, it cannot at this point in our history and in the contemporary global context help us to deal with the massive concerns of human and nonhuman flourishing. Nor can it direct us toward envisioning a future for our churches in the United States in which they fully participate as global citizens. Black churches, for instance, must not only acknowledge the complicity of race within national borders, but also identify its presence in the searing *glocal* issues of immigration, poverty, health inequity, poor education, the destruction of the earth through the relentless and avaricious search for fossil fuel, the depletion of natural resources, and the destabilization of entire nations through war, massive surveillance, and the spread of super-corporatism.

I would suggest that scholars and church leaders pay close attention to an emergent second coming of Diaspora (or Diasporas) that arises from within the notion of Dilemma. The metaphor of Diaspora has always been present in African American religious, political, and cultural discourse, in the illustrious examples of the call for Pan-Africanism in the work of Robert Alexander Young, David Walker, Edward Wilmot Blyden, Henry Highland Garnet, Henry McNeal Turner, Martin Robison Delany, Marcus Garvey, W. E. B. Du Bois, and Malcolm X.[41] In another tradition in the African American Christian community, the notion of Diaspora was ably articulated by the later King in his excoriation of the Vietnam War and the call for a "world house" signifying on "the house that race built." His dream of a "world house" has striking implications for the plight of black church leaders and scholars as we prepare to meet the challenges of a new era.[42]

Dr. King's prophetic insight of a global community is not the same as the "I Have a Dream" speech of 1963, of which many are so fond. That was a speech directed to the issues of jobs, freedom, and civil rights that African Americans had been denied. But the notion of a "world house" places our struggle in the context of liberation movements throughout the world. It implies that the freedom of African Americans, our human rights and religious predilections, are inextricably bound with the yearnings and hopes of oppressed people everywhere. King often reminded the nation that "injustice anywhere is a threat to justice everywhere." Diaspora, in King's perspective of a "world house," is a shape-shifting metaphor that emerges from Dilemma as a way of addressing issues of identity that are not confined to religious and nationalistic ideologies that bind one to potentially narrow visions of peoplehood. Rather, Diaspora, in this sense, places African Americans in the world context as global citizens.[43] What Diaspora ultimately does is to give U.S. black churches a more appropriate paradigm and symbol from which to talk about ministry in global perspective; and it affords a prophetic position relative to the loyalty to nation motif that has in many respects prevented African Americans from more fully approximating the ideal of their faith convictions and global solidarity.

A nagging question, however, that accompanies this kind of thinking is, Can a complex notion of Diaspora, as we have understood it in *nation language* and in *migratory patterns* of black religious and cultural practices, serve as a foundation for a more radical proposal for national and global citizenship?[44] The question is difficult to answer, partly because of the antagonistic tendencies among scholars working in black religious and black church traditions surrounding essentialist and postmodernist critiques of black religious nationalism. On the one hand, there is the tendency to view Africa as an ontological assemblage of the displaced, disparate, disembodied, dismembered Africans dispersed throughout the globe, but still united in a common sense of racialized and ethnic identity and hope. "Thus," according to Tracey Hucks, "in understanding diasporicity both as a historical event and a subsequent set of conditions and ongoing processes, the Africa most sought after in the New World was the Africa of symbol that could assuage the alienation of exilic ontology."[45] On the other hand, there are critiques of tendencies to maintain an onto-eschatological vision of Africa as home for all people of African descent. For this reason, some religious scholars, following the work of Paul Gilroy, prefer the metaphor "Black Atlantic" over "diaspora" to refer to the ways passing ships carried various human cargos in multiple directions to create a multidirectional black culture.[46]

The cultural anthropologist J. Lorand Matory argues that, starting with the transatlantic slave trade, the Black Atlantic was the first self-conscious transnational modern community that was and is simultaneously "a geographical focus, an identity option, and a context of meaning-making, rather than a uniquely bounded, impenetrable, or overdetermining thing."[47] In other words, the existence of the Black Atlantic has always represented an argument against modernity, nationalism, and master narratives about the homogeneity of human cultures, even if this fact has been ignored in the literature on modernity, postmodernity, and transnationalism. For Matory, the metaphor of "African Diaspora" shares some of the misleading implications of *arborescent* metaphors, insofar as the "diaspora" concept suggests that homelands are to their diasporas as the past is to the present. Candomblé, Yoruba, and many other African-diasporic religious phenomena are not simply outgrowths of their homelands but also, and just as important, outcomes of an ongoing dialogue with a coeval homeland. African homelands and diasporas— much like Europe and its American, African, Middle Eastern, and Australian settler colonies—have engaged in a long and influential dialogue of mutual transformation.[48]

Instead, borrowing from Deleuze and Guattari to describe Black Atlantic communities as co-directional entities, Matory encourages the use of "rhizome metaphors that mimic the network-like roots of grasses, which unite multiple roots with multiple shoots."[49] Thus, he suggests that we reject "monocausal narratives, single source constructions of group history, and inattention to the multidirectional ramifications of any genealogy of events."[50] Similarly, Awad Ibrahim prefers the rhizomatic metaphor as a way of countering facile notions of "roots," "origins" that give rise to doubleness and Dilemma. He suggests, rather, that a rhizome is always in the middle (*milieu*) from which it grows and which it overspills. Therefore, the rhizome resists verticality and chronological *lines of flight*, where its growth is contained and conceived in a linear, arborescent, and systematic line.[51]

My revisionist approach to the process of becoming black and the general politics of diasporic identities is closer to a third way between essentialism and postmodern critiques. Scholars such as Diane Stewart-Diakete suggest that "we must be willing to surrender, or at least, suspend postmodern critiques that render diasporic ethnocultural and racial identifications with Africa essentialist, romantic, and, therefore inauthentic and contrived."[52] This does not mean that we ignore the analytical problems associated with modernist protocols of identity and agency; rather, the suggestion of suspension by Stewart-Diakete offers an opportunity for scholars to freeze the moment, so to speak, in order to search for *common(s)* or temporary, experimental strategies that allow spaces for consideration of the questions of tool-making and the revisability of racial discourse in an ongoing, unfinished communicative project. This perspective has its merits with respect to producing what Lucious Outlaw calls a "practical universality," that is, a quest for "unity in diversity" that is appreciative of the materiality of race and ethnicity but does not inscribe ontological status to them; rather, it is in part a project fueled by communicative reason that points to, but is always under the scrutiny of, democratic eyes.[53] The emphasis in such a democratic, communicative process is on continuing the conversation, not necessarily on finding the "right" answer(s), but engaging in pragmatic approaches that seek common understandings and solutions to questions of identity, otherness, and human and nonhuman flourishing that are not fixed, monocausal, and monolithic. In this respect, honoring, testing, listening to, arguing for, and producing multiple identifications created in a rhizomatic third space are the result of a long, arduous struggle to be and become (*devenir*).[54] This is both possible and necessary because we share *complex semiological languages* (signs that are open for signification and different readings because they cannot produce verbal utterances, yet are ready to speak) that we produce and perform as actors in public spaces. Therefore, as Awad Ibrahim reasons, "if this is so, then *one is not born Black either, one becomes one*, where Blackness is a set of norms, narratives, and everyday performative roles and acts."[55]

In many respects, being and becoming black or becoming aware of blackness as a fluid, unfixed reality is to encounter the deeper search for meaning and possibility that Toni Morrison calls *home*. *Home*, for Morrison, refers neither to the national imaginary that is the site of binary fixations of gendered, raced, and sexualized identities nor to the onto-eschatology of a new world order; rather, it is more like an unfixed *line of flight*, a spiraling, liberated circle, the embodied yearnings or the yearning embodiments for a sense of wholeness that is a journey toward a destination that is always beyond us, elusive and eliding. In this sense, it deterritorializes and seeks "social space that is psychically and physically safe," where one is no longer "prey."[56] Yet the yearning for home is not just a *line of flight* in the imaginative sense, but a tool that allows for analysis of the very question of territorial dominance or sovereignty as a symbolic marker. *Home* is the place over Jordan, not here yet, but always coming to itself in myriad configurations of meaning and sounding—*speaking* as the spirit gives utterance.

In my understanding, diasporas, like all signs and language, are shape-shifters, indeterminate and yet necessary for navigating the world. Therefore, shape-shifting diasporas find affinity with the "assemblage" approach of Gilles Deleuze and Felix Guattari and their interpreters,[57] and with Morrison's yearning for *home* that is immediately and emphatically spiritual; *home* also refers to spaces where U.S. black churches can recognize their multidirectional affiliations and interconnections with *roots* and *shoots* around the globe, but are not ultimately determined by them. The metaphor of Diaspora also resonates with the black churches' ultimate affiliation with that which the process philosopher Theodore Walker called the *God of all Creation*, who has guided us beyond our attachments to Exodus from enslavement into a new global exilic reality of struggle and transnational possibility.[58] I will refer to the *God of all Creation* as the Holy Ghost who bears witness to our exilic condition and yearnings for new language(s) to speak about and point to *home*. How might we begin to think of black churches in diasporic transformations, in new times that displace dysfunctional linearities of identity, otherness, and human flourishing? Where might we find models that speak beyond the limitations of imposed blackness without falling captive to eliminativist docetism that supports post-racial boundedness and Dilemma?

In the meditation "I Will Not Give Up," Howard Thurman captures what is at stake in this personal and collective struggle of *becoming* and the search for *home*.[59] He tells the story of his encounter with what appeared to be deformed evergreen bushes that somehow had grown above the timber line. "The steady march of the forest had stopped as if some invisible barrier had been erected beyond which no trees dared move even in single file." These bushes were really branches of trees that somehow had survived despite their restricted movement. They did not appear "lush"; in fact, Thurman writes, "they lacked the kind of grace of the vegetation below the timber line, but they were alive and hardy." His further investigation revealed a rather stunning phenomenon: these branches were gathered together as vines hugging the ground, developing trees that were different from anything he had ever witnessed. For him it was a statement of the force of life daring to live, not merely survive, but in order to live the branches had to reconstitute themselves, which also reshaped their anatomical structure—hardly recognizable as evergreens (or whatever they were *becoming*)—a *rising from the dead*.[60] Thurman exclaims,

> What must have been the tortuous frustration and the stubborn battle that had finally resulted in this strange phenomenon! It is as if the tree had said, "I am destined to reach for the skies and embrace in my arms the wind, the rain, the snow and the sun, singing my song of joy to all the heavens. But this I cannot do. I have taken root beyond the timber line, and yet I do not want to die; I must not die. *I shall make a careful survey of my situation and work out a method, a way of life, that will yield growth and development for me despite the contradictions under which I must eke out my days.* In the end I may not look like the other trees, I may not be what all that is within me cries out to be. But I will not give up. I will use to the full every resource in me and about me to answer life with life. In so doing, I shall affirm that this is the kind of universe that sustains, upon demand, the life that is in it." I wonder if I dare to act even as the tree acts. I wonder! I wonder! Do you? (italics added)

A major concern going forward in our discussion is the question of religious identity. For the most part, African American church traditions have held tenaciously to their Christian identity while maintaining practical affiliations with other religious practices (Santería, Vodun

Spiritualism, and Yoruba, among others). The critical question that confronts many black churches in this century is how to maintain what appear as conflicting faith claims and obligations without compromising, or worse, *despoiling* their Christian identities. At this point in our history—a history that stretches beyond the raced house of modernity to a world house where differences are honored and religious loyalties are at least ecumenical—we must accept the fact that purity of doctrines and statutes of holiness must be reexamined. As Stuart Hall suggests, "The future belongs to the impure. The future belongs to those who are ready to take in a bit of the other, as well as being what they themselves are. After all, it is because their history and ours is so deeply and profoundly and inextricably intertwined that racism exists. For otherwise how could they keep us apart?"[61]

Black religious practices might be advised in this new and dangerous reconfiguration of symbols and signs to follow the way of the *shrub-tree-becoming-other* that adjusted and revised its trajectory and appearance for the sake of survival and the possibility of flourishing. Thurman's intriguing analogy posits a certain resilience in human strivings that follows the path of all nature in its seemingly rugged determination to live and grow. While Thurman's tree image harkens to an arborescent metaphor, it is more like the rhizome in its complex, unfinished, and incomplete particularity—in its indeterminate *lines of flight*. Identity as such is always an unfinished project,[62] just as the flow of life, like the river, is in constant motion—fluid, dynamic, and alive.[63] How might contemporary black churches begin to remember, retell, and relive their stories within the framework of rhizomatic particularity and the reimagining of possibilities as unfixed lines of flight?

If we look again at Thurman's analogy of the branches-become-trees phenomenon, we might find some clues to what is at stake in revisiting narratives and histories that have been lost to memory. To rethink the history and (de)formation of black churches in the United States along these *lines of flight* without *falling* into the traps of essentialism might be helpful.[64] The historical *fatedness* of the raced house of American slavery, segregation, and now, post-racial legacies of bondage and separation are socially constructed and deeply affected by religious protocol and doctrine. These religious beliefs and assumptions of cultural domination do indeed proceed from binary, oppositional forces, yet there are *fluid center(s)* out of which opposition *appears*. The language of *fluid center(s)*, as I am using the term, is related to the pulsating, rhythmic movements of life, which, like a river, is moving and still, old and new, being and becoming; and from these centers we must launch a search for a sense of wholeness—or what Thurman called "common ground" and what Morrison calls *home*—which is manifest in varied and myriad forms of creative vitality and intelligence that are never fixed, but always becoming. The larger project, therefore, has to do with the question, How shall we make a careful survey of our situation and work out a method, a way of life, that will yield growth and development for black churches despite the contradictions under which we must eke out our days? Shall we do away with the historical identity of U.S. black churches altogether in the new and emerging diasporas of this century, or can we find a third way to live as black churches in what has been lauded as a post-racial world? I note here three possibilities that we will discuss later on: (1) congregating, (2) conjuring, and (3) conspiring in *common(s)*. But before we do so, let us *turn* to the theological and ethical shape-shifting of Exodus and Exile.

5

Turning from Exodus to Exile

No single story captures more clearly the distinctiveness
of African American Christianity that that of the Exodus.
From the earliest days of colonization, white Christians had
represented their journey across the Atlantic to America
as the Exodus of a New Israel; slaves identified themselves
as the Old Israel, suffering bondage under a new Pharaoh.
White American preachers, politicians, and other orators
found in the story of the Exodus a rich source of metaphors
to explicate the unfolding history of the nation. Each section
of the narrative—bondage in Egypt, rescue at the Red Sea,
wandering in the wilderness, and entrance into The Promised Land—provided a typological map with which to re-
connoiter the moral terrain of American society.
—Albert J. Raboteau, *A Fire in the Bones*[1]

Deep river, my home is over Jordan
Deep river,
Lord, I want to cross over into campground . . .
Oh, chillun
Oh, don't you want to go, to that gospel feast
That promised land, that land where all is peace?
—"Deep River"[2]

Sometimes I feel like a motherless child
A long ways from home
—"Sometimes I Feel Like a Motherless Child"[3]

Exodus

From its earliest beginnings, Exodus has been the central paradigmatic theological and ethical statement of black church life and practices. The idea of Exodus has served multiple functions in an ongoing cultural narrative of African Americans that is "deeply anchored in themes of captivity, Exile, enslavement and deliverance."[4] Exodus has referred to the language of *nation* espoused by early nineteenth- and twentieth-century church leaders and activists; it marked the transition from slavery to freedom in the historical events of Emancipation and Reconstruction; it evolved into the "second Exodus" during the Great Migration that began around World War I, when large numbers of African Americans left the Southeast, mid-South, and Southwest for the urban Northeast, the northern Midwest, and Canada for "the warmth of other suns";[5] and in the modern civil rights movement, Exodus language was a powerful symbol of the journey to the Promised Land of full citizenship and equal opportunity.[6] According to Robin D. G. Kelley, the long and aggravating history of the Exodus metaphor essentially encapsulates a "freedom dream" of a new land, composed of imaginative yearnings for return to a glorious past in Africa or an Afro-futurist intergalactic space travel exposition to "anyplace but where we are now."[7]

Nowhere is this metaphor more powerfully demonstrated in the organization of the religio-political consciousness of African American peoples than in the early nineteenth-century productions of independent black churches, the black press, and the National Colored Convention Movement. According to Eddie Glaude, the Exodus served as a metaphor for the development of nation language and formed the basis of the politics of respectability and nascent articulations of black nationalism. This language of nation, for African Americans, found its source in the ritual enactments of the Exodus story in ways similar to those performed by other early Americans, especially the New England Puritans. But unlike the Europeans, who utilized the story for "an errand into the wilderness,"[8] African Americans decentered and inverted the narrative, so to speak, and constructed their own sociohistorical narrative of Middle Passage, slavery, and freedom. The reversal of the narrative appropriated the biblical themes of bondage, wilderness, and Promised Land of early America and provided African Americans with pragmatic tools to remember, retell, and relive their story as a means of maintaining personal sanity and a sense of collective identity in a sociopolitical environment that was antithetical to their existence. Their feat of revisability produced a national imaginary that honored their own *chosenness* and *messianic* claims to be a "peculiar people" set apart for a special purpose in the ordinances of God. For these pioneering religious, political, and social leaders, Egypt was not Europe and Pharaoh was not King George III of England; rather, America was Egypt and "Pharaoh was on both sides of the bloody-red waters."[9]

Glaude complicates the Exodus narrative by returning to the historical context of early nineteenth-century America, which witnessed the rise in the utilization of race science, geography, and complexion in the construction of racial identities, and which justified the horrid lot of African Americans. He identifies the National Colored Convention Movement (later known as the American Moral Reform Society) as a site of excavation and the context for the development of a specific racialized vocabulary and grammar that emerged as nation language during this period. For Glaude, there tended to be two prevailing modalities of this language: on the one hand, an intra-discursive politics of respectability expressed by William Whipper and Frederick Douglass, and on the other hand, an immanent use of the language of nationalism by African American notables such as David Walker and Henry Highland Garnet. These two contending streams, he argues, issued forth to serve as "grammars of sort"[10] for moral reform and black nationalism and set the terms of the debate on the means of racial progress and liberation through most of twentieth-century African American history and culture. The early debate reached its apotheosis in the confrontation between Douglass's Garrisonian abolitionist ideology of protest and moral reform and the call for the violent overthrow of the system of slavery heralded by nationalists like Garnet at the 1843 National Colored Convention in Buffalo.[11] Critical for our purposes are the ways the language of Exodus, which included strategic moments of migration, pilgrimage, and progress, were reversed in African American resistance, both as embryonic forms of the politics of respectability and as black nationalist claims to autonomy and separation (both of which bear striking parallels to the struggles of Dilemma and Diaspora discussed earlier). At stake in the following discussion are these historical precedents for the revisability of language, symbols, and metaphors embedded in black church leadership practices, which allow us also to reclaim and resituate traditions of struggle for contemporary black religious leaders. Central metaphors like Exodus should not be viewed as static metanarratives that confine and restrict the possibility of emancipatory movements. New global sociopolitical contexts beg for the articulation of theological and ethical language that honors and critiques the past in order to envision new forms of liberative practice.

A helpful guide in this respect is the Hebrew Bible scholar Herbert Marbury's most interesting and creative project, *Pillars of Cloud and Fire: The Politics of Exodus in African American Biblical Interpretation*.[12] Marbury analyzes African American readings of the Exodus from antebellum to mid-twentieth-century intellectuals and activists (Absalom Jones, David Walker, Francis Ellen Watkins Harper, John Jasper, Zora Neale Hurston, Adam Clayton Powell, Martin Luther King Jr., et al.), each in dialectical tension underscoring not only the accommodationist-resistance motif in African American political struggles but diasporic and global connections as well. In short, Marbury's uncovering of the ambiguity and contingencies of black existence is brilliant, owing as much to his readings in philosophical, literary, and cultural studies, perhaps, as to his astute biblical scholarship that forms the foreground of this work. For example, his treatment of Frances Ellen Watkins Harper and the Reverend John Jasper highlights the dualities of accommodationist-resistance while exposing in both the art of *subversive civility* to which we referred in the previous chapter. The high language and etiquette of Victorian morality (Harper) are contrasted with the common (vulgar) speech of the subaltern preacher *qua* philosopher (Jasper), but both subvert the dominant discourse and ideology of the master narrative and create new space for unfettered conversation. Here Marbury's fine eye sees clearly the issues at stake in an interdisciplinary effort to interrogate the *silences* of the biblical, cultural, and political meanings of Exodus that demand a more collaborative approach between church leaders and biblical scholars. This is an area in which his work finds fertile ground, especially surrounding the questions of ambiguity, contingency, and complex subjectivities in moral speech and agency in African American religious and cultural life as it pertains to the Exodus metaphor. For Marbury, the story of the Hebrew Exodus played a prominent role in grounding the religious imagination that made the human project tenable for these representatives of African American church leaders and cultural critics. Marbury's use of the Exodus is also helpful as we look more closely at the historical, discursive features of its development in African American religious and cultural discourse and our scholarly and churchly tasks "to reclaim black bodies from vitiating discourses and their epistemologies."[13]

In addition, his treatment of Exodus in African American readings of the biblical text underscores the obvious but inconvenient truth that all theological metaphors are human constructions and can never fully reveal the divine presence. The African American attachment to Exodus has been both helpful and harmful in black churches' quest to discern and respond to the activity of the divine in history. No one can read the great orations of the African American past or listen to the spirituals without knowing that the Exodus has played a prominent role in our thinking about liberation, God, and history. Lyrics from early songs of enslaved Africans, like "Go down Moses, way down in Egypt's land, / Tell old Pharaoh: Let my people go," are representations of the genius of African American improvisational artistry and prophetic utterance. An assemblage of African American religious, political, and cultural figures from Phillis Wheatley to Frances Ellen Watkins Harper to W. E. B.

Du Bois to Barack Obama have continued this tradition of Exodus with varying degrees of success and failure, but most importantly it has served as a lens through which the march toward the Promised Land in ideological linearity predisposes it to repeated backstops, unfinished performances, and dashed hopes. For example, Rhondda Robinson Thomas argues that Phillis Wheatley's appropriation of Exodus in her "Letter to Reverend Samson Occum" (1774) inaugurates the tradition in African American cultural narratives; and that W. E. B. Du Bois's earlier identification of Booker T. Washington as the potential Joseph of African Americans in *The Souls of Black Folks* (1903) marks the end of the initial phase of its utilization to explain and justify liberative functions of the symbol. Moreover, Thomas claims that the Joseph and Joshua narratives of the Hebrew Bible "provide the essential bookends of Exodus" for African American appropriation.[14] The Exodus narration included mixed interpretations of late nineteenth-century and early twentieth-century black emigrationist strategies, questions of redemptive suffering, and the eschatological ends of black church and religious existence, represented most powerfully among leaders like Bishop Henry McNeal Turner, Bishop Daniel Payne, and Marcus Garvey.[15] Martin Luther King's sermon "The Death of Evil on the Seashore" or his last public address, "I've Been to the Mountaintop," are excellent examples of the kind of sermonizing that utilizes the Exodus as a symbol of the historical plight of African Americans. During the rise of Black Power, Professor James Cone's theology took as its point of departure the Exodus of God's oppressed peoples from the bondage of Pharaoh.[16]

The late William R. Jones, in what was probably the most controversial book written during the nascent days of black theology, *Is God a White Racist?*, challenged the appropriateness of the Exodus metaphor for the experiences of African American people. However historically situated, Jones argued, Exodus suggests that there has been or will be an actual, historically verifiable liberative act for black people by the Hand of God. Jones contended that we could not point to such an act in history.[17] He maintained that the historical plight of African Americans cannot be equated with the biblical Exodus of the Hebrews or early American evangels, nor can we point to an eschatological event with historical certainty. The eschatological event of the future is based on the claims of a liberative Exodus event from the past. Since we cannot refer to an actual historically verifiable Exodus of the past for African Americans, we risk serious error in anticipating an eschaton in which God will deliver the oppressed.

One has only to walk the streets of any major urban center or witness the increasing incidences of incarcerated black bodies in correctional facilities around the country, the murder of young black men and women by the police, the continued sexual violence meted out against black female, LGBT, queer, and transgender bodies, and the sheer carnage of black humanity to know that there has not been a definitive, historically verifiable Exodus from Egypt or Mississippi or Chicago or Cleveland or Sanford or Staten Island or Ferguson or North Charleston or Baltimore or Waller County, Texas, for African Americans. Similarly, the affinity for the Exodus also has striking parallels for African American theological discourse in a post-American world.[18] The spiritualization of the Exodus story by the growing surge of Afro-Pentecostal, charismatic, prosperity gospellers and some mainline churches has all but erased social/political quests for justice, reparations, and peace.[19] In a way similar to the Dilemma motif, African Americans have tended to respond to the ghost of post-racialism out of an antiquated notion of Exodus that is, at this point in our history, more challenging than supportive when it comes to articulating a global vision of ministry for black churches and their leadership. In the twenty-first century, the Exodus motif prevents the masses of black church folk from thinking deliberatively and historically about their present political and social predicament in the context of global struggles for justice.

Most of the challenges related to this attachment to Exodus are rooted in the long-standing sociopolitical/sociocultural connection to Dilemma. The deep-seated ideological tension of Dilemma revolves around citizenship and belonging to a *territory* as part of a national imaginary that breeds "dead space," anonymity, and shame, which has deep-seated implications for the ways African Americans understand themselves, individually and collectively; the ways we relate to others and to *difference* within and outside our racial and ethnic categories; and our (onto-eschatological) religious and social definitions of human flourishing. The long struggle between the contending forces of moral respectability and belonging to a nation and the search for *home* elsewhere are products of our anxiety and struggle with modernity. Some critical questions attend to this deep cultural angst that haunts black churches in the United States: Might Black Atlantic or diasporic investigations as countercultural critiques of modernity provide different points of departure for an adequate theological and ethical reconfiguration of meaning-making in a post-racial era that is haunted by the ghost of race? What is at stake for black churches and their leaders in this way of thinking about identity, others, and human and nonhuman flourishing? I cannot adequately address these complex questions in the present text, but I will suggest a road less travelled as a way to begin this journey.

Exile

Some experimentation with the biblical and cultural notion of Exile as a more appropriate mode of discourse for the present sociopolitical and theological-ethical situation of African Americans seems called for. In fact, Michael Battle writes, "in many ways, the Black Church was forced into existence—perhaps, even exile."[20] Only a handful of Christian social ethicists have explored this trope in African American religious discourse. For instance, the ethicist Cheryl Sanders's excellent monograph *Saints in Exile* argues for the dialectics of exilic existence as the most appropriate paradigm and hermeneutical strategy for understanding black Pentecostal and holiness traditions in the United States.[21] These dialectics, she argues, include "in the world but not of the world," "egalitarianism and exclusivism," and "refuge and reconciliation." Though not all aspects of the "Sanctified Church's" exilic

methodology and identity are beneficial for effective community formation, it does form a bulwark around the oft-assaulted identity of black
people. Additionally, the exilic methodology espoused by the "Sanctified Church" decentralizes the oppressor/oppression conundrum that
threatens the oppressed by creating an understanding of existence that
does not reduce black identity to a mere response to white racism. As
a result, black identity is not defined by ideas of Du Boisian "twoness"
or "double consciousness" (which Sanders asserts maintains white racism at its center), but by the cultural values, aesthetics, experiences, and
traditions of black people. Sanders argues that the "in the world, but not
of the world" approach of the "Sanctified Church" provides oppressed
communities with a strategy for effectively responding to oppression
that does not make the oppressed's response to oppression the center
of their identity: "The exilic concept allows for honest appraisal of and
response to white racism without, at the same time, having one's own
identity totally shaped by it; the dialectical understanding of existence
need not become totally collapsed under the weight of oppression."[22]
In essence, the "Sanctified Church" is a response to the "problem of
race, sex, and class in American Protestantism." It is a dialectical construction that reveals parallel egalitarian and exclusivist notions that
are characteristic of exilic existence. Sanders identifies three features
as distinctive of Sanctified Church ecclesiology: ethics, spirituality, and
evangelism. In her view, these three areas can be enhanced to make the
"Sanctified Churches" more "viable centers of Christian formation and
totalistic transformation," inclusive of all people regardless of sex, race,
and economic status.[23]

Key considerations for Sanders's work are the notions of reconciliation and refuge as dialectical pointers toward "home" for the alienated and the stranger. Black churches have served as exilic, "substitute
communities" for African Americans, who historically have had limited choices between acceptance of a national imaginary that is buried
in "dead space" or identifying "home" as elsewhere as the birthing of
new understandings of self, world, and relation to ultimate meaning.

Peter J. Paris makes a similar point in his discussion of "moral agency in conflict":

> Whenever persons are rejected by society, the result is a loss of place; the result is Exile. Whenever a pattern of oppression persists from one generation to another and is firmly rooted in an ideology, the rejected ones become destined to a *veritable permanent state of Exile* wherein they have no sense of belonging, neither to the community nor to the territory. Since it is necessary for persons to be nourished by a communal *eros* in order to become fully human, an imposed Exile necessitates the formation of substitute community, and . . . that has been one of the major functions of the black churches. Born and reared in an alien sociopolitical context, blacks have had little hope for any sense of genuine national belonging.[24]

Such a Long Ways from Home

Paris's reference to *a veritable permanent state of Exile* speaks to the existential condition of African Americans being "a long ways from home." Listening to lyrics from the old Negro spirituals, like "Sometimes I feel like a motherless child, such a long ways from home,"[25] "Deep River, my home is o'er Jordan," or "Swing low, sweet chariot coming forth to carry me home," one gets the sense of homelessness, desolation, alienation, annihilation, and death. Such a rendering of embodied feeling and tone is emphatically spiritual and offers entrée into a national imaginary *space of death* that must be recognized in order to gain some appreciation of African American interpretations of Exile as "an unaccomplished imaginative shift from enslaved to freed subjectivity and the marked gap between genealogical isolation and the ancestral past."[26]

In this space of death, as alluded to in our earlier discussions of Sterling Stuckey and Howard Thurman, is the underlying theme of life and hope—tragic soul life and aggravated and troubled hope, to be sure.[27] A repetitive theme of the spirituals is suffering and hope. On the one hand, they speak to the deep sorrow of a dispossessed and disinherited people. Indeed, W. E. B. Du Bois called the spirituals *sorrow songs*, "the music of an unhappy people, of the children of disappointment; they tell of death and suffering and unvoiced longing toward a truer world, of misty wanderings and hidden ways."[28] On the other hand, they speak of the spiritual strivings of a disenfranchised people, who in spite of their hopeless situation, dared to believe that they would "see the goodness of the Lord in the land of the living." Howard Thurman writes, "The load is so heavy that nothing is of any avail. Hope is destroyed by its feeding on itself, and yet their destiny is placed in God's hands."[29] Thus, in the spirituals, suffering and hope sit side by side and inside each other—but somehow, because the singers believed that suffering and death did not have the final word in the universe, they were able to live through their suffering even when hope was exhausted and find *a place to stand*. Where could they stand? Being denied personal mobility and social values of citizenship, having no say over the disposition of their bodies or in shaping their existence, they took imaginative flights to a world where the builder and maker was God. "These songs represent the voices of those for whom active participation in the shaping of the world is denied. They [enslaved Africans] claim a share in the world, if only by condemning it and contrasting it with the vision of the world made whole, a world in which they will be full and active citizens."[30] They sang, "Soon I will be done with the troubles of the world, / troubles of the world / . . . I'm going home to live with God." For these early American singers, trouble constituted a *falling* into nothingness, an apocalyptic shattering of the world and an encounter with the nakedness of existence; a disjointed sense of time and no place to call their own.[31] Stripped bare, literally, without any hope except the faith in a God who restores worlds—their world and ours—they needed *a place to stand*, a sense of stability. Home was a place to stand in the midst of exilic existence. These black and unknown bards sang, "O, I got a home in dat Rock! / I've got a home in dat rock, don't you see? / I've got a home in dat rock, don't you see?"[32] These are songs of exile—songs born in a strange land "a long ways from home." Home was not escape or inscape, but a yearning for freedom, a sense of identity, and a place to stand in the *center of the world* (*le point le vierge*), "a still point, the 'center of our nothingness' where one meets God—and is found completely in His mercy."[33]

Related to the songs are the sermonic compositions like "Dry Bones in the Valley." Luke Powery rehearses the trope of the dry bones in the valley as a metaphor for black preachers, listing the commentaries of scholars like James Weldon Johnson, Allen Callahan, and Henry Louis Gates, who describe the sermonic tradition surrounding Ezekiel 37 as "one of the canonical narratives within African American experience." Noting the enslaved Africans' experience of exilic existence, Powery quotes Dexter Callender, who writes,

> The conditions of Jerusalem's deported were different given that they were largely people of means whose experience was not that of chattel slavery, and who retained some control of their economic destiny.... Still their tradition of exile as emblematic resonated with surviving victims of the African slave trade, who engaged it in a variety of ways.

Similarly, Allen Callahan writes, "Ezekiel's wind-swept valley continues to remind slavery's children of their blackness. They continue to be strangers in a strange land. And they continue to be haunted by the bones."[34]

Not in the least are these songs and sermons removed from the existential and intellectual constructions of meaning that, in large part, have determined the fiber and direction of the spiritual and cultural productions of black religious artistry. Yet the central themes that drive this improvisational life of playing on words and signifying on the persistent hopelessness and despair are the exilic condition of black life in the United States and the recurring haunting by the old ghost of race, which shape-shifts and disguises itself in language, signs, metaphor, and symbols. In this sense Exile shares striking affinities with Diaspora because it tells the truth about African American existence in the United States:

There is no *Promised Land* to hope for except our promises and commitments to form alliances and communities of discourse and practice with other diasporic communities in this nation and around the globe.

"Exile," like "Diaspora," speaks to a more world-oriented, historical picture of African American oppression in a contested post-racial world and allows black churches to take seriously their sociohistorical location as agents of world history rather than as passive nation-bound spectators. Exile as a shape-shifting metaphor, likewise, is a theological corrective to Dilemma, or what the political scientist Frederick C. Harris refers to as "the dualistic orientation of black oppositional civic culture."[35] Harris captures in this statement the paradoxical strivings of black leaders that combine the quest for social dignity with political activism within a parochialized theological/ethical context that colludes against a more globalized ethic of engagement. The exilic predicament of African Americans provides fertile ground for theologizing about our relationship with other brothers and sisters in the many diasporas that populate our postcolonial world; it also confronts us with the question of our existential and aesthetic *estrangement* and the question of the "stranger" (maybe our other sisters and brothers from whom we have been "estranged"). But there are some important biblical and theological investigations that pertain to the question of the revisability of Exodus language and to providing a rationale for the exilic metaphor, to which we now turn.

Exodus and Exile as Founding Myths

The revisability of Exodus and Exile language in black churches is complex and fraught with conceptual missteps. On the one hand, there is a temptation to view Exile and Exodus as dialectical twins, one feeding on the other, but neither "Exodus" nor "Exile" operated as a discrete "event" in the historical consciousness of ancient Israel or in African American religious, cultural, and political history. They are interdependent, one drawing its character and function from the other. The majority of Hebrew Bible scholars working in this area view the Exodus story as constructed in retrospect and in response to Exile as a way of giving meaning to post-exilic life among the dispersed Jewish nation. The biblical scholar Niels Lemche offers the clearest overarching narrative concerning the interlocking ways that Exodus and Exile function in creating an identity for ancient Israel. For Lemche, Exile is related to identity—ethnic, national identity. In its foremost ideological reach, Exile functions as a myth that "disconnects and unites the present and the past"; it is the basis for a yearning to return home to an ancient time that is simultaneously new, blessed in a covenant relationship with God.[36]

An important related function of Exile, according to Robert Carroll, is the ideological construction of the "myth of the empty land," referencing the Second Temple period and Israel's annihilation of the Canaanites.[37] Carroll argues that there were residents in the land ("the people of the land"), the poor and lower classes that were left behind in the first and second captures (597 and 586 BCE, respectively) and who were exterminated or deported upon the return from Exile. In fact, he prefers the language of "deportation" to the language of Exile and emphasizes the permanency of Exile as a condition or state of mind.[38] In other words, Exile should be interpreted as more than a historical event, but as a permanent condition or a state of mind or alienation from home, which is the way we will proceed with its usage in this context. *Where is home?* is an exilic question that cries out for an answer. *Home* is where I am fully human, respected as a citizen, and where I actively participate in the naming and shaping of my destiny—yet it is *more*. This question has not been resolved in the dilemmalistic political-cultural consciousness or in the theological/ethical discourse of African Americans because our condition is exilic, a permanent state of mind that engenders despair, sorrow, and death—and often a Pollyannaish but seldom politicized *hope*. Much of what we see in the second decade of this century in African American urban communities is the rioting of the souls of black people because of the unanswered question of *home*.

The Wilderness

Second, the use of Exodus as a paradigmatic theological construct is embedded within cultural and religious meanings that can be read in different ways. For instance, womanist theologians, like Delores Williams, have complicated the Exodus metaphor by interrogating and shifting the lens of the narrative, reinterpreting the idea of "wilderness," and placing more emphasis on Hagar's triple oppression (the intersectionality of gender, race, and class) than on the heteronormativity of Sarah and Abraham.[39] Williams was one of the early womanist theologians to challenge the intra-oppressive dynamics of the Exodus metaphor in respect to the language of "political empowerment and political oppression" undergirding African American appropriation of Exodus and its identification with Old Israel and the genocide of the Canaanites. According to the literary scholar Robert J. Patterson, "Williams's reading of the Exodus narrative not only complicates any rendering of the Exodus event as solely empowering but also reveals that the story's core values promote hierarchies of oppression that obstruct the development of equality within black communities and American society."[40] Moreover, other womanist thinkers like Kelly Brown Douglas and Irene Monroe have further complicated the usage of Exodus, calling for the incorporation of black queer critiques of the heteronormativity of the black male subject as the norm for black religious leadership.[41] According to Patterson, the Moses motif[42] has been read as an "urtext for black male privilege by asserting that it underwrites the modern notion of the endangered black male."[43] Moreover, this use of the symbol of Moses gives divine sanction to oppressive male-based hierarchies in black church leadership practices and the larger black community, issuing forth in a charismatic, Great Man Theory of leadership that is expressed in political messianism and cultural heroism.[44]

In addition, not only does the wilderness sub-trope have complex implications for how we interpret political messianic religious leadership, but emphasis on the heroic male warrior impacts social and political strategies of African Americans as well. In the wilderness motif, for instance, Moses's leadership is extended to Joshua in the conquest of Canaan. As Williams alludes to above, the appropriation of the slaughter of the Canaanites poses complicated issues for the religio-political rhetoric used by African American civil rights leaders. Put another way, How can those who embrace a progressive politics of justice and equality justify the genocide of an entire people as proclaimed in the text (Deut. 7.1–2; 20.16–18), including every man, woman, and child in the land of Canaan? Senator Barack Obama, for one, effectively utilized the Exodus metaphor as a political rhetorical strategy early in his first presidential campaign, comparing the civil rights movement to the "Moses generation" and the new post–civil rights activism to the "Joshua generation":

> I'm here because somebody marched. I'm here because you all sacrificed for me. I stand on the shoulders of giants. I thank the Moses generation; but we've got to remember, now, that Joshua still had a job to do. As great as Moses was, despite all that he did, leading a people out of bondage, he didn't cross over the river to see the Promised Land. God told him your job is done. . . . We're going to leave it to the Joshua generation to make sure it happens. There are still battles that need to be fought; some rivers that need to be crossed. Like Moses, the task was passed on to those who might not have been as deserving, might not have been as courageous, find themselves in front of the risks that their parents and grandparents and great grandparents had taken. That doesn't mean that they don't still have a burden to shoulder, that they don't have some responsibilities. The previous generation, the Moses generation, pointed the way. They took us 90% of the way there. We still got that 10% in order to cross over to the other side.[45]

Scholars like Homer Ashby also emphasize the language of wilderness as an appropriate site of investigation in order to understand the suffering and alienation of African Americans. Ashby's *Our Home Is over Jordan* offers a helpful critique of what is at stake in maintaining the Exodus narrative in the midst of the wilderness of African American peoples.[46] Ashby begins his text with an analysis of statistical data on violence, education, criminal justice, and economics in the African American community. His major argument is that the African American community is worse off in the twenty-first century than it was a century earlier. To put it plainly, he thinks that the survival of African Americans is in jeopardy. Ironically, he joins womanist theologians in his utilization of the "wilderness" language and motif. Consequently, for him, we are still wandering in the wilderness in search of the Promised Land, in search of *home*. Because of this wandering, displacement, and homelessness, Ashby argues, the future is much more confusing than it was even forty years ago, when almost all African Americans agreed upon desegregation, integration, and Black Power (which is a contestable assertion). Now, he argues, those unifying goals have been replaced with a diverse set of visions that do not have the power to rally the people. Unlike deconstructionist theologians, he regards this fragmentation as a major weakness, not a source of strength. He argues that we are disconnected and therefore less able to combat racism; and postmodernist interpretations and criticisms of black culture are idealistic and elitist. For him, efforts to move beyond ontological blackness threaten black connectedness. In some ways, Ashby's text suggests that Dilemma among African Americans is still alive and well. In other words, do postmodernist critiques really work in tough neighborhoods where people are just trying to survive facing racist institutions? Or is cultural criticism something successfully carried out only by black elites who already have a healthy sense of self and economic privilege? Ashby asks, for instance, Does Vanderbilt professor of Christian ethics Victor Anderson assume a baseline of privilege and community that is simply not present in the black underclass? Or, in some ways, is Anderson imposing a totalizing view of the black community as well? Ashby writes,

I, too, would like to pour all my energy into celebrating the variety of ways in which African Americans are achieving their fulfillment. If I did not have to concern myself with all the roadblocks, hurdles, fates, and ambushes along the way, that would be great. But the reality is that blacks are being murdered, lynched, infected, and failing to thrive in any number of different ways. . . . The cult of black cultural politics of difference fails to speak to these realities within the African American experience.[47]

Moreover, Ashby writes,

a healthy cultural identity is formed in community. Without a collective community there can be no transmission of a healthy sense of self-esteem or self-worth. Especially when a dominant culture is sending messages that constantly undervalue a person's self-worth and identity, there needs to be a counter balancing force to negate the false images and false definitions that the person is being forced to adopt.[48]

Unlike Anderson and others, Ashby thinks that cultural heroes are necessary in this situation.

For this writer, given the overt tension between these interlocutors, the critical question is, How might we find balance between the scholarly representations of Ashby's and Anderson's arguments—and are they not reflective of the Dilemma-Diaspora collective doubleness that plagues the psychosocial/political tension referenced above? Neither Exodus nor the wilderness offers a basis for the deep-seated politicized hope that African Americans so desperately need and desire at this critical passage in our history. Exodus and wilderness still pledge allegiance to the unseen ghostly narrative that perpetuates and licenses itself in a so-called post-racial society. I contend that there also exists a dynamic tautness between the theological and ethical characterizations of Exodus and Exile, and that the critical indices that inhere in these tensions call for a "new" sense of identity, understanding of otherness, and human fulfillment. I propose a new reading of the trope of Exile as a strategic counternarrative that makes it possible for us to reimagine *home* as part of a new global eruption of courage, justice, and compassion as we witnessed and participated in liberation struggles such as anti-apartheid in South Africa and most recently in specific contexts of the Occupy movement, the Palestinian liberation movement, and Black Lives Matter campaigns here in the United States.

The Exile motif strikes critical distance between the problematic triumphalist, heteronormative heroism in Exodus and the angst, wandering, homelessness, and despair experienced in the wilderness. I agree, in part, with Ashby's utilization of the wilderness as a metaphor for where we are, but contest the linearity of the term as it relates to the metanarrative of journey through the wilderness and into the Promised Land. Our existential condition will not allow for linearity and repetition of the same patterns of interpretation of our experiences that black churches and communities have traditionally appropriated. The wilderness itself can be refigured in support of the biblical, theological, and religious scholars who argue for deconstruction and reinterpretation of narratives from different locations. One could argue, for instance, that the wilderness is indeed a dangerous, complicated space where people compete to be heard. There are many voices crying in the wilderness, so to speak, extolling and sometimes even exaggerating differences in order to be heard. But most are not in or from the church. They talk, walk, and stalk black churches in our gardens of *learned ignorance* and *forgetfulness*, demanding our discursive locations, or better, where *we will choose* to locate ourselves in the human struggle for justice. These voices transgress boundaries, categories, and the order of things. They intrude, disrupt, and interrupt our quiet complacency—making the church and its interpreters anxious and uncomfortable. Sometimes they cry out in extremes, without respect to persons, places, or heritages, because they are unheard, unacknowledged. Unlike many of us who benefit from the privileges of academic and ecclesiastical authority, they do *not* seek to make *straight* that which is crooked and *right* that which is not in alignment with the order of things. These are the voices of those who dare speak for themselves, the voices of the muted, missed, and dismissed, the wretchedly fated who have no recourse but to cry out. Father David

Tracy writes, "The final indignity is to be forbidden one's own voice and robbed of one's own experience."[49] Tragically, the comfortable and secure seldom, if ever, *really* hear these voices until they scream. The terrible reality is that we have missed or dismissed these voices in places like Sanford, Florida; Ferguson, Missouri; Staten Island, New York; and Waller County, Texas—and we are shocked when they speak up and act out in tragic, tormented violence in places like Brooklyn, Baltimore, Boston, or Brussels.

For the most part, we know where to locate the wilderness that is outside ourselves, but the wilderness is not merely a geographical and political location—it is also within us as *embodied history*. Much of the violence in our communities and world is a result of long, complicated, and embodied histories that reach as far back as the birth of the modern, if we accept the arguments of scholars like Paul Gilroy and Charles Long. These embodied and coded histories collide at the intersections of our everyday worlds and remind us of our own vulnerability, detachment, estrangement, and complicity in our own bondage. On the other hand, the wilderness is a mirror of our own *wildness*, desertion, loneliness, and alienation. Should we be surprised, then, that there are so many voices crying in the wildernesses of twenty-first-century America and the world who appear as *wild* men and women, who haunt our sacred stories of religion and nation and call us to accountability where injustice reigns among the poorest of the poor; among black, brown, yellow, red, white, female, male, crip,[50] and queer broken bodies that are crucified daily by the relentless pursuit of global capital and power?[51]

So, while wilderness signifies wandering, confusion, and dread, it can also be interpreted as part of our exilic condition in a post-racial era, as a sign of difference and the space where cries for justice go unattended and unheard within the sovereign confines of a national imaginary. Privileging Exile provides a more excellent way, a more powerful space in which to locate the contemporary struggle of African American existence because it is a more accurate depiction of where we are: exiled from one another, from ourselves and even from the land of our birth—

exiled in a space of death, a national imaginary that is dysfunctional for the overwhelming majority of black people who exist not as citizens, but as resident aliens or worse. Exile also captures the yearning for home, which is where we must go and become in order to enter a different social and political purpose. *Home* is a signal, a lighthouse that stands alone amidst the crashing waves of postmodernist claims that gesture toward an aggravated and tragic future in which the possibility of hope is buried in new forms of territorialism. *But if we are saved by hope,* and if our *home* is indeed over Jordan, then Jordan must symbolize the transition from the psychic/political/cultural spaces that are beyond the restrictive boundaries of Exodus, which promises a land flowing with milk and honey—because there is never enough milk and there is too little honey for the least of these, like the African American poor in the raced, haunted house of American territoriality. As James Baldwin so eloquently and viscerally put it, "In my case, I think my exile saved my life, for it inexorably confirmed something which Americans appear to have great difficulty accepting. Which is, simply, this: a man is not a man until he is able and willing to accept his own vision of the world, no matter how radically this vision departs from others."[52] And yet we must not claim a superficial, nihilistic vision that fantasizes in this hegemonic atmosphere. *We,* leaders of black churches and others beyond our borders, must learn to breathe together, yes, conspire and conjure new narratives of this unfinished project where the internal and external modes of struggle are conjoined, perhaps melded in a symphonic, syncopated melody of songs (sounds) of freedom. Change becomes possible when we gather, reassemble, and congregate in *common(s)* on new campgrounds over Jordan. *Common(s)* is a rereading of common ground, ground that is shifting, and therefore must be reconfigured and translated into *common loyalties and commitments to justice and peace. Common(s)* is a narrative quest that is mutable and portable with a temporary-fixed character that is always in candidacy for argumentation, becoming other, differentiated, stretching, better, flowing like a river, searching for *home.* James Baldwin writes, "Nothing is fixed, forever and forever and forever, it is not fixed; the earth is always shifting, the light is always changing, the sea does not cease to grind the rock."[53]

An ancient Nordic myth speaks to this quest for *home* better than any other and informs our task of playing with the power in signs and language that tricks us into ourselves. The tale features Thor, Loki, and the lad Thailfi in a contest with their adversaries, the Giants, who challenge them to three tests: Loki is challenged to out-eat *Logi* (fire); Thailfi to outrun *Hugi* (thought); and Thor to out-wrestle *Ellie*, an old woman (old age) for whom he was no match, to drink from a horn (cistern) of water that never empties, and to lift a cat whose feet never leave the ground and whose arched back stretches forever into the sky (infinity). They are unable to carry out their adversaries' challenges. They leave the land of the Giants knowing their finitude and are forever chastened by this decentering experience. The moral to the story is that the real prizes they sought were not grasped by means of speed, strength, or material consumption; rather, the answer was just above their heads.[54] *Home* is the moment when we become aware of the long history that preceded us and (if only for an instant) grasp a sense of the infinite future that beckons us to envision what is possible if we dare to live freely and courageously in the present. We never arrive *home* because *our home is over Jordan*, not the fictive enterprise of conquest and annihilation of the other in death and dying for the sake of land; and for recognition and respect from ghostly puppeteers who hide behind the curtains of social fictions and manipulate the mindscape of black churches and their leadership. *Home* has to do with remembering, retelling, and reliving our stories in the quest for a sense of wholeness with ourselves (identity), others, and throughout creation that returns us to the struggle with humility, gratitude, and a scent of holiness upon us.

Whose Memory? Whose Culture?

A third problem that we must engage is the appropriation of themes from Hebrew memory and culture. The relationship between ancient

Israel's conceptions of Exodus and Exile and the ways they have become a part of the cultural narrative of Afro-Atlantic scholarship was noted in Paul Gilroy's *chronotope* of slave ships in *The Black Atlantic*.[55] Gilroy suggested that the appropriation of journey and exile in Afro-Atlantic discourse is related to the themes of Jewish cultural history and memory. Gilroy's closing conjectures in *The Black Atlantic* raise the question of social memory and the organization and collaboration of Jewish and black diasporas that are haunted by the common denominator of the ineffable terror of the modern world. African American appropriation of Jewish history and culture is problematic, as he acknowledges, but his suggestion raises more questions than it answers.[56] Laurence Mordekhai Thomas and Michael Lerner with Cornel West have made similar attempts to understand and compare African American religiosity in the larger orbit of Jewish cultural history and memory.[57] It appears that the relationship is inescapable, given the appropriation of narratives from the Hebrew Bible, except that there are serious questions to ponder in ways similar to those presented to the larger American religious and cultural inheritance.

Houston Baker's critique of Gilroy's use of the *chronotope* as an organizing symbol for ships transferring human cargo between Africa, the Caribbean, the United States, and Europe is helpful.[58] Baker brings the argument back to the "South" by bringing together *ships* and *plantations*. Baker argues that by "determinately fixing attention on this privileged locative site" of the plantation penal system and its protocols of subjugation and incarceration, we are able to identify the *telos* of the black body as a predetermined state of incarceration.[59] The criminalized and commoditized black body as a site for theological and ethical reflection reveals common and conflicting narratives of black and Jewish culture and memory, and by implication, the appropriation of Exodus. Exodus reveals shared themes of *sovereignty* and *bare life*, but also conceals "hidden imperialisms" that conspire with the notion of a "prophylactic state."[60] Matthew Lopez explores some of these questions in his play *The Whipping Man*. Amid the ruins of a Jewish slave owner's plantation in

Richmond, Virginia, at the close of the Civil War, a rebellious slave who was given his master's religion of Judaism says to the master's son, Caleb (who is later revealed to be his brother),

> Already before she [Caleb's mother] started to teach me, I was asking questions. Like when was God going to set us free like he did the slaves in Egypt. Or whether Nat Turner was our new Moses. That's when our lessons ended. But I kept reading. I pored over the books of the Torah. And I kept asking questions, if only to myself. You ever read Leviticus . . . "Both thy bondmen and bondmaids, which thou shalt have, shall be of the heathen that are round about you; of them ye shall buy bondmen and bondmaids. They shall be your possession and ye shall take them for your children to inherit for themselves. But over your brethren, the children of Israel: Ye. Shall. Not. Rule." You remember reading that? . . . It certainly got me to thinking. Were we Jews or were we slaves?[61]

The argument presented here takes seriously the notion of memory in rethinking and re-languaging both Exodus and Exile, but with important inflections. While I seek to excavate the symbolic meaning of Exile in association with the Middle Passage that speaks to the actual historical event of capture, enslavement, and commodification of human beings as chattel in the larger pattern of colonization, labor, and capital, I am also suspicious of overidentification with the ideological underpinnings of a linear return to a symbolic or actual homeland, whether it be Africa or Jerusalem. I also question the usage of Exile and the ways it reinforces African American churches' uncritical embrace of Exodus. Exile, in its functional equivalence with Exodus, conspires with the *telos* of the criminalized and commoditized black body and the *habitus* of a systemic practice, on the one hand; but, on the other hand, as a polyvalent metaphor, it speaks to the aesthetic and existential dimensions of *homelessness*. Such a perspective demonstrates the importance of African diasporic theologies, which subvert internalized forms of oppression within African-descended communities and open up avenues of collaboration between African-descended and other diasporic communities who live in particular contexts, and who similarly suffer from the continuing postcolonial permanence of exile that resulted from European conquest and the Atlantic slave trade. This is a complicated and uncomfortable challenge that will not be resolved here, but it bears noting. For instance, Michelle Gonzalez, writing from an Afro-Cuban theological perspective, argues that part of the challenge of moving into a new space that honors pluralities and particularities of diasporic theological contexts is being aware of the complexities that have emerged from different readings of race and ethnicity that are, at best, ambiguous, but hugely problematic if erased through the lens of ontological blackness:

> For black and womanist theologians, the heavy emphasis on the African-American community erases the existence of Puerto-Rican, Dominican, Cuban, Panamanian, and other black Latino/as whose culture and history are invisible within the discourse of black theology. . . . In a similar vein, Latino/a theology's refusal to address race and racism explicitly leads to the erasure of black Latino/as. Instead Latino/a theologians emphasize the border, the "both/and" reality of Latino/as as racially mixed and diverse peoples. This emphasis leads, however, to a disregard for black Latino/as, as well as to a refusal to confront the complex problem that while Latino/as are considered people of color, many Latino/a theologians benefit from white privilege.[62]

So how do African American scholars and churches avoid silencing those who do not fit into our neat ethnic and racial categories even as we construct theologies of liberation? Here is where the movement from Dilemma and Exodus to Diaspora and Exile becomes central, as a movement away from binary frameworks that *intend* to free oppressed people, but in actuality remain stuck in oppressive binaries, black and white, male and female, right and wrong, and so forth.[63] There is a surprising silence on Caribbean, African, and Latino/a negotiation of blackness in America and abroad.[64] The ambiguities and contingencies of Exile open new possibilities for forging new ways of relating to identity, otherness, and our understandings of what constitutes human and nonhuman flourishing without falling prey to binary functions of power that are illustrated in Exodus and its theological sub-trope of "wilderness." In my reading of the exilic motif, the emphasis is placed on the imaginary third way alluded to earlier, as an unfixed *line of flight* in which materially constructed, politicized hope is translated into language that yearns for *home—always incomplete, never quite there, but yearning for a home in self, others, and in the world house.* In this sense, *home* arises from our exilic conditions in our respective diasporas as a tool that allows for analysis of our attachments to modernist claims of territorial dominance and sovereignty as symbolic markers and reimagines space and time. Exile also takes us out of linear time, into a recurring long memory that transcends everydayness while it remains in the "now."[65]

The following chapter begins this process of reimagining possibilities of retelling our incomplete and complex stories by being bodily baptized in the Holy Ghost and Fire as a way to *that home o'er Jordan* that is always new, vibrant, and dangerous. The argument will also consider the body as a *somaesthetic* site where we *turn* from Dilemma and Exodus to Diasporas and Exiles as part of a global yearning for citizenship beyond the porous boundaries of territorialism and Christendom.

6

Turning from the Frying Pan to the Fire

And the devil, who deceived them, was thrown into the lake
of burning sulfur, where the beast and the false prophet had
been thrown. They will be tormented day and night for ever
and ever. . . . Then death and Hades were thrown into the
lake of fire. This is the second death, the lake of fire. And if
anyone's name was not found written in the book of life, he
was thrown into the lake of fire.
—Revelation 20:10; 14–15 NIV

The old meeting house caught on fire. The spirit was there.
Every heart was beating in unison as we turned our minds to
God to tell him our sorrows here below. God saw our need
and came to us. I used to wonder what made people shout,
but now I don't. There is joy on the inside, and it wells up so
strong that we can't keep still. It is fire in the bones. Any time
that fire touches a man, he will jump.
—Former slave, quoted in Clifton H. Johnson, *God Struck
Me Dead*[1]

The Frying Pan and the Fire

When I was growing up on the Southside of Chicago, we were frequently
visited by the Jehovah's Witnesses. My father, though not an active
church member, was curious about religion and would often invite the
eager evangelists into the living rooms of our various abodes and listen
to them expound on the scriptures. One of their favorite topics of discussion was the Book of Revelation. As a child, I was fascinated by these
conversations, especially the notion that there is no eternal damnation

of the lost; rather, where there is death of consciousness, one simply ceases to exist. The Jehovah's Witnesses believe that "our consciousness is not an independent system from our body that mysteriously survives the death of the body. God created the first man and woman to have a physical body formed from the 'dust.'"[2] To put it another way, we are "dust that breathes."[3]

The synonymy of death and loss of consciousness had great appeal for me because several of the references in the Book of Revelations mentioned a "lake of fire."[4] I feared the "lake of fire" where people like me who had been written out of the "book of life" would be tormented day and night forever and ever. *The second death*, the final throw-down between God and the devil and all the false prophets, and even death itself, offered little comfort because I could not figure out the secret formula for salvation. I thought that there must have been some secret to getting your name written in the book of life because the Jehovah's Witnesses who stopped by our apartment were so confident and always dressed like salespersons: nice suits and dresses, shined shoes, and smart-looking countenances. Obviously, they had information that the rest of us did not, just like the brothers from the Nation of Islam whom I would see on the streets and the Fuller Cosmetics man who would drop by occasionally to proffer his wares. They all looked the same to me—self-assured, bourgeois, and *saved*. I was very confused because I neither felt nor looked saved. In fact, I actually tried to join our church, Centennial Missionary Baptist Church, twice as a candidate for baptism by the time I was twelve years old because I was looking for the secret that would save me from the lake of fire, the second death.

It was not until I was drafted into the U.S. Army and became a born-again evangelical through the Navigators Ministries[5] that I was able to overcome this deep fear. Sadly, even this conversion did not wipe away my s(k)in and my inner torment; nor did it get my name written in the book of life. I always felt strange, disoriented, and not-at-home in my body. It was not until I returned to the old hood from the army and tried to "save" one of my buddies that I realized that I had not escaped the lake of fire. He resisted and stated, "Damn, man, you don' turned white!" Yes, that's right, I had turned into someone else and was looking self-assured and talking like the Fuller Cosmetics man—I had become a witness! I often remark that I was a "white evangelical" until I got saved—after I figured out that the second death, where the beast and the false prophets are, is the domain that James Baldwin called "being white and other lies."[6]

I was also visually attached to the aesthetics of the *Watchtower* magazines that the Jehovah's Witnesses would leave with my father. I recall that one of the magazine covers had pictures of paradise. The pictures were so beautiful—all the lovely white people walking around gardens with flourishing trees and abundant fruit hanging from their branches. I often imagined myself in paradise with these elect in a special place for those who were saved. I later discovered that hell often disguises itself as an Edenic paradise while hiding legions of devils, pitchforks, and knives. The nineteenth-century South African writer Olive Schreiner wrote that once she dreamt that God took her soul to hell. Upon arrival she was astounded by its beauty and exclaimed, "I like this place." And God said, "Really!" As she proceeded further she noticed beautiful women everywhere in long flowing robes draping their graceful bodies and tasting fruit from the trees. She noticed, however, that they never ate the fruit, but only touched it softly with their mouths and left it hanging on the tree. She asked God why they were only touching the fruit with their mouths but not eating it. God replied that they were really poisoning the fruit. She said to God, "Why are they doing that?" God said, "That another may not eat." She said, "But if they poison all of them, then none dare eat; what do they gain?"[7] God said, "Nothing." She said, "Are they not afraid they themselves may bite where another has bitten?" God said, "They are afraid. In hell, all [people] are afraid."

She went a little further and noticed a group of men busily at work. She said, "I should like to go and work with them. Hell must be a very fruitful place, the grass is so green." God said, "Nothing grows in the garden they are making." She examined the workers more carefully and noticed that they were working among the bushes digging holes, but set nothing in them; and when they were a way off they would hide in the bushes watching. She noticed that as each one walked, he set his foot down carefully, looking where he stepped. She said to God, "What are they doing?" God said, "Making pitfalls into which their fellows may sink." I said to God, "Why do they do it?" God said, "Because each thinks that when his brother falls he will rise." "Why, how will he rise?" God answered, "He will not rise." And she saw their eyes gleam from behind the bushes. "Are these men sane?" she asked. God answered, *"They are not sane; there is no sane person in hell."*[8]

Those early years of seeking salvation and being captivated by aesthetic attachments in the *Watchtower* magazine covers were *loci of apparitions* inspired by ghostly yearnings for identity and a sense of belonging somewhere beyond the troubles of my small black world. I did not yet understand the power of the ghost and its eternal return. Since then I have come to believe in the lake of fire as conscious torment day and night—as the exilic existential condition of millions of poor people around the world, many of whom are colored, who are casualties of progress, of *the terror of history*.[9] As it relates to black churches and their leadership, the lake of fire is the continuing drama of nurturing cultural imaginaries that tend to be antithetical to human flourishing. Given the incredible atrocities that are heaped upon entire peoples who are unaware of the massive sociohistorical casualties exacted by the rise and decline of modernity, the greatest challenge to leadership in the twenty-first century is to awaken from the dead. Increasingly, this will be the challenge for black church leaders who stand at the intersections of colliding *lifeworlds* and *systems* and continue to exhaust biblical metaphors that have outlived their utility.[10]

Implanted in most of our discourse about God, Jesus, and the angels is an old patriarchal formula that is based on inherited models and meanings that perpetuate cultural domination and the ongoing massacre of the black poor. Intricately related to these beliefs and assumptions are the sacralized aesthetics of the beautiful, true, and symmetrical

Greek body—a sort of black Adonis complex,[11] not unlike the Moses *urtext* that functions as a driver for privileged male hierarchies of leadership in Exodus. But far more is at stake. The very notion of salvation as it is interpreted through this lens is in complicity with the ghostly hauntings, apparitions that stoke the flames in the lake of fire. Jesus, for many black religious leaders and followers, is Adonis resurrected, the savior whose nectar-enriched blood spilled over into windflowers and a flowing river, a male god whom women love and worship and whose beautiful body and power males envy and lust after.[12] These cultural figurations of meaning have powerful implications for the ways we continue to perpetuate an existential and aesthetic trope of death, a necrophilic obsession with bodily images that contradict our own physicality and subjectivity. This existential desire to be judged by cultural standards of beauty and goodness that have been implanted within and that prevent us from loving our bodies is indeed a second death in the lake of fire that burns day and night, forever and ever. Paradise, *home,* for most black saints still is not far removed from the one I witnessed in my childhood on the covers of *Watchtower* magazine.

This theological displacement from *home,* according to Willie James Jennings, began as a "theological error" in the Christian imagination as early as the fifteenth century in the European colonization of "nonwhite peoples." Salvation, therefore, for black and other nonwhite people, was schematized on a grand scale of election in which whiteness represents "high salvific possibility, rooted in the signs of movement towards God (for example, cleanliness, intelligence, obedience, social hierarchy, and advancement in civilization)." But black bodies, along with Jews and Moors, were relegated to the lowest region of salvific possibility, because "Black indicates doubt, uncertainty and opacity of saving effects."[13] Before the sophisticated, analytic probing of contemporary black theologians like Jennings, Howard Thurman in his classic work, *Jesus and the Disinherited,* demonstrated how theological presuppositions were linked to ocular metaphors that served as cultural resources in the segregation of African Americans. At the heart of the following quote is Thurman's critical observation that relates cultural aesthetics to religion, morality, and law:

> Given segregation as a factor determining relations, the resources of the environment are made into instruments to enforce the artificial position. Most of the accepted social behavior-patterns assume segregation to be normal—if normal then, correct; if correct, then moral; if moral, then religious. Religion is thus made a defender and guarantor of the presumptions. God, for all practical purposes, is imaged as an elderly, benign white man, seated on a white throne, with bright, white light emanating from his countenance. Angels are blonds and brunets suspended in the air around his throne to be his messengers and execute his purposes. Satan is viewed as being red with the glow of fire. But the imps, the messengers of the devil, are black. The phrase "black as an imp" is a stereotype. . . . The implications of such a view are simply fantastic in the intensity of their tragedy. Doomed on earth to a fixed and unremitting status of inferiority, of which segregation is symbolic, and at the same time cut off from the hope that the Creator intended it otherwise, those who are thus victimized are stripped of all social protection. It is vicious and thoroughly despicable to rationalize this position, the product of a fear that is as sordid as it is unscrupulous, into acceptance. Under such circumstances there is but a step from being despised to despising oneself.[14]

A number of scholars have begun to look more deeply into the existential and aesthetic contexts of black church life and practices along the lines of the thinking presented here. They invite us to carefully straddle the diverse worlds of religious meaning and tradition, leaving space for a sustained conversation between black church scholars, religious humanists, and atheists, which, in my opinion, may be the most difficult yet most salient public conversation in a contested post-racial and post-American world. These writings are but prolegomena to a larger, more complicated set of questions that black churches will need to rethink in light of the nagging historical problems of racialized, sexualized, genderized politics of the church and the larger culture; but more importantly they challenge scholars working in these traditions to reframe these questions in respect to the shifting grounds of political and social realities that *shape-shift* toward complex subjectivity, diversity, openness, and inclusiveness.[15]

The Black Body as a Somaesthetic Site

A critical dimension of this *shape-shifting* will involve a new aesthetic sensibility and appreciation of *the body*, the many colored, crip, queered, and estranged bodies that are heirs to *somebodyness*.[16] The reevaluation of *somebodyness* places emphasis on the *body* as a critical source for somaesthetic investigations that challenge dominant cultural, political, legal, theological, and ethical perceptions of religious experience.[17] One can hardly imagine having a religious experience without a *body*. Moreover, the *body* constitutes a critical frame of reference for the aesthetic life, apart from which theological and ethical analysis is impossible. This is especially important for reflection in African American churches. Theology and ethics seek answers to questions not only about God and salvation, but also about beauty, truth, excellence, human and nonhuman flourishing, and the ways beauty and *eudemonia* are related to the truth of the body. In the context of the shifting grounds of black church practices and questions of leadership, the aesthetic/existential perspective beginning with the body becomes all the more significant. Anthony Pinn suggests that integrally related to the question of aesthetics is the leverage of control over black bodies, black beauty, and hence, black freedom. Referencing Michel Foucault's notion of economy of discipline,[18] he writes,

> The Black body had to be controlled and in this sense the manifestation of will by those with power in North America marks an economy of discipline reaching into every sphere of existence for the "Other"—those of African descent. The taming of Black flesh through violence and intimi-

dation in order to secure the "consent" of the victim to his/her own victimization was the function of this economy of discipline. This economy also connotes a wider framework by which Whites sought to maintain societal order with myths of creation and meaning that made sense of the world through a mythology of Whites' aesthetic superiority. The projection of Black Americans as lacking beauty made abuse of Black bodies easier to undertake. To understand this, one need only consider the numerous stories of whippings, mutilations, and disfigurements provided by slaves and White observers alike.[19]

The critical site of the body as a place for reflection on the psycho-cultural, bio-political dynamics of Dilemma and the theological-ethical models of Exodus invites questions about the ways embodied practices of black church leadership are possessed by the ghost and reveals challenges associated with their aesthetic predilections and existential situation. In 1989 Professor James Cone was invited to Vanderbilt Divinity School to deliver lectures on the twentieth anniversary of his celebrated book, *Black Theology and Black Power*, which launched the black theology movement in America. The Baptist World Center, on the campus of the historic American Baptist College in Nashville, had been recently constructed. I shall never forget the saddened and disappointed expression on Professor Cone's face when we entered the building to view the massive sanctuary and beheld a huge stained-glass image of a white, patriarchal Jesus Christ benevolently looking down over his family as a "caring father to his submissive child[ren]."[20] As we build new cathedrals and altars mortgaged on the blood money of those sacrificed to greedy, grinning gods of capital, are we not still in bondage to the ghost? Are we not still in the "house that race built" even when we build new gargantuan structures and adorn our bodies for worship in these haunted spaces? How do we free the body to speak, hear, feel, turn, and jump from the lake of fire to a place called *home*? To put it another way, Howard Thurman writes, "If thy soul is a stranger to thee, the whole world is unhomely."[21] At another place, in the same tone, he adds, "Every man lives under the necessity for being at home in his own house, as it were. He must not seem to himself to be alien to himself. This is the thing that happens when other human beings relate to him as if he were not a human being or less than a human being."[22]

As I reflect on that day at the World Baptist Center, I am reminded of Arrested Development's 1992 hit song "Tennessee," which tells the story of the ghostly search for home; I am also reminded of the aggravating features of analysis that constitute this search for *home*, the diasporic, exilic displacement of the black body even in the spaces that we have built and where we now worship and sing in order to "forget all that hurts" us as we try to make sense of and re-language our world.[23] Indeed, the long history of African American cultural and religious subjugation has been the subject of scholarship for some time now, and I will not attempt to repeat it here, but will explore the following questions: What about the *body* as an aesthetic site for pondering new and fresh approaches to Diaspora and Exile? What if we were to take the aesthetic/existential dimensions of *shape-shifting* seriously in respect to black church traditions that must be remembered and retold? What would be the content of our preaching, the form and shape of our liturgies, and our relation to the stranger, and who might that stranger be? Far from a more comfortable predicament, I am suggesting that we would be *turning*, to mix a metaphor I used to hear my mother say, from the Frying Pan to the Fire.

The Frying Pan, as an existential/aesthetic moment, incorporates the two analytically prior moments of Dilemma and Exodus. In respect to the actual sociopolitical condition of black lives, the Frying Pan finds its fullest expression, its apotheosis, in enfleshed life represented in the killings and incarceration, miseducation, and intergenerational poverty syndrome of postindustrial America. The three moments of our past-present situations, Dilemma, Exodus, and the Frying Pan, must be engaged from the place of the body-on-fire—the baptism of the Fire and the Holy Ghost. Fire represents a critical tool of the spirit that allows us to interrogate the ways the body, (black) subjectivity, and agency are continuously held in bondage to the political-cultural, theological-ethical, and existential-aesthetic gazes of the old ghost. Dilemma tells the body to "stand still and see the glory of God" while being torn asunder by competing ideals that signal doubleness, indecisiveness, anxiety, and stress. Exodus references a liberative event that has already happened and conspires with an alien force, an ideological/theological construct that engenders and sustains quietism in an imaginative escaped slave-body that awaits an eschaton. It points to a redemption beyond the world even as it posits a heteronormative epistemology and ethics that are attached to a trope of conquest and domination. The Frying Pan is indeed a lake of fire that burns day and night in the inner cities, in rural communities of our nation and around the world, and implies a state of existence in which African Americans are seen as damned souls subjected to the hellfires of social/political arrangements in a perpetual state of torment. It is for this reason that the Frying Pan seems the appropriate context in which to discuss the historic ways black churches have wrestled ambiguously in Dilemma and hoped in Exodus and continue to existentially and epistemologically *tussle*[24] amongst the plurality of diasporic and exilic communities and conversations without conscious appreciation of a new rhyme, rhythm, and time for the body.[25] *Turning from the Frying Pan to the Fire*, on the other hand, takes black churches to a deeper dimension of a discourse and practice that are currently ongoing and will continue. According to the formerly enslaved person quoted at the beginning of this chapter, "It is fire in the bones. Any time that fire touches a man [or woman], he [or she] will jump." This Fire is far more terrifying than the Frying Pan, far more dangerous, far more costly—but Fire is also purgative, empowering, and liberating as it *shape-shifts* toward something new and vital that is occurring in our midst, but we must be awakened to see and receive it. Before we discuss the Fire as a critical existential and aesthetic moment to which we must *turn*, let us take a look at what this *turning* might involve.

Turning

The problematized black body that bears the tropes of stigmata and dread is also a *locus of apparition*. This means that the body is not only a site of haunting, which implies the symbolic undertaking of mimetic, séanced ghostly ventriloquism in imputed narratives of conquest and domination; it is also a site of *conjuring*, a type of *embodied participation* in meaning-making that implies some measure of autonomy and grace, and hence the capacity to rename and *shape-shift*. One of the ways the body *conjures* is by *gesturing*. Bodily *gestures* are performances, dialogical tools that help us to make sense of the world and to communicate through cultural modeling what is meaningful, true, and beautiful; conversely, gesturing can communicate the demonic, destructive anguish of the spirit. Gestures are embodied, metaphorical actions, "kinesthetic schemas" that are culturally formed and defined, yet can be viewed as offerings to something else unseen, but present—in fact, the bodily gesture brings presences to us.[26] The body not only signs or points to something else, it consciously *gestures*—and through gesture it "fulfills a holy office"; it brings the sphere of holiness into profane existence; and in doing so, the gesturing body decenters space and time. Even more remarkably, the gesturing body is a *bricoleur*, a tool maker.[27] An illuminating passage from Albert Raboteau's essay "A Fire in the Bones" makes this point about African American liturgy and worship:

> "It ain't enough to talk about God, you got to feel Him moving on the altar of your heart" as one former slave explained. Ritual, in this liturgical perspective, is supposed to bring the divine tangibly into this world. The presence of God becomes manifest in the words, gestures, and the bodies of the believers. Their praying, singing, preaching and dancing occasion as well as signal the Spirit's arrival. In this form of African and African American ritual, the divine is embodied in the faithful. The emotional ecstasy of black Protestant worship symbolizes a profound religious truth: the preeminent place of God's presence in this world is the person. His

altar is the human heart. Moreover, it is the whole person, body as well as spirit, that makes God present. In a society chronically split between body and spirit, African American ritual exemplifies embodied spirit and inspirited body in gesture, dance, song, and performed word. In worship the human becomes an icon of God. A radically personal vision of life flows from this liturgical sensibility. Contrary to the depersonalizing pressures of slavery and racial oppression, the person is of ultimate value as the image of the divine. Anything, then, that defaces that image is sacrilegious.[28]

I pause to reflect on a picture placed on my altar of my mother in her church usher's uniform as a site for imaginative theological reflection on the somaesthetic and the place of narrative.[29] Stories that could be told ought not always be shared and certainly not filled with candor that makes suspect the telling, so I begin by simply saying that my mother's body bore the marks of bearing ten children, stigmata from work in the cotton fields of Mississippi and avoiding white men's gazes, and a mouthful of brown-sugary spit from dipping Garrett's snuff and chewing tobacco while performing "holy office" as an usher at Centennial Missionary Baptist Church. Arthritis and its accompanying ailments of stiffness, pain, and misery were part of her daily existence; and to add insult to injury, her epilepsy resulted in often contentious and disoriented behavior. But something happened when she put on her usher's uniform and took me to church. She would find her sacred space in that small side aisle in the packed little building that we called Centennial Missionary Baptist Church. She would greet the people of the Lord with her extended arm and swift turn as she escorted them to their seats. O, to see my mother's body *turn* heaven and earth in those simple, lithe, dance-like movements—*the extended arm* and *swift turn* were "gestures of immortality." Milan Kundera writes,

A gesture cannot be regarded as the expression of an individual, as his creation (because no individual is capable of creating a fully original gesture, belonging to nobody else), nor can it be regarded as that person's instrument; on the contrary, it is gestures that use us as instruments, as their bearers and incarnations.[30]

My mother's *body—the outstretched arm, the swift turn*, and the *ritualistic garment* of the usher extending hospitality to the other—is a site for reflection on the aesthetic sensibilities of religious experience and a human initiation of *global communitas.* Her gestures of immortality were moments of transfiguration where the intersectionality of history, race, gender, politics, and economic, cultural, and spiritual signs and meaning met and transgressed proscriptions on complex incarnate subjectivity bound in nation language—the language of empire that simultaneously binds U.S. black churches to the essentialism of cultural domination residing in worn-out, ineffective metaphors of the past that perpetuate the torment and horror of the Frying Pan. Is not my mother's *outstretched arm* an invitation to share in her humanity (if we follow Raboteau, her epiphany of divinity) by "facing the other" in all her/his strangeness, possibility, and hope? My mother's ritualistic performance as an usher provides entrée to a global picture of "recurring incarnations" and *shape-shifting* in *the swift turn* and *conjuring* acts of gesturing, touching, and facing the other as a greeter to diasporic bodies, lost and found in the Black Atlantic Middle Passage and the many plantations and boroughs and passages unknown and unremembered. This experience of *touching* and *facing* the other reveals the deep longing and yearning to be in unity with ourselves—our exiled and diasporic bodies—and with others from whom we are estranged, *home.*[31] In the complexity of that grand gesture of *the outstretched arm*, my mother, incarnated Black Madonna, not only faces and touches the other, she *turns.* The *turn* is from something fixed toward something beyond, new, *More*, and dynamic. She bids, "Come, *turn* with me in this strange, chaotic desert of human apathy where we no longer meet and speak to one another because in our diasporic and exilic conditions we do not understand one another's language." "How shall we begin to hear one another in his/her own language until we *turn*?" *Turning* is simultaneously defiance, repentance, and conversion—a *tussling* with God, self, and human structures of dominance, an act of *shape-shifting*, of leaving the old in order to embrace a newer dynamic, fluid self that includes *desire* for an Other.[32]

Anthony Pinn, in *Terror and Triumph*, suggests that conversion is

> based on a triadic structure of confrontation by historical identity, often presented in terms of existential pain and some type of terror; wrestling with the old consciousness and the possibility of regeneration, or in [William] James's language, a reconstitution of the soul; and the embrace of new consciousness and new modes of behavior affecting relationship with the community of believers.[33]

This conversion is a *turning* from death into new life, a yearning for complex subjectivity.[34] It is also a *crossing(s)*, a holy space where we are crossed by someone or something of which we may not be sure (Hark! Who goes there?)—yet we are called to decide, to shift with the shifting of the moment and to name and rename ourselves and our relation with others and the world.

At the *crossing(s)* we burn with fire. Elie Wiesel's interpretation of Jacob's wrestling with the midnight terror at the ford of the Jabbok associates the turning with a *tussling* with *fire*.[35] "*That night* Jacob got up and took his two wives, his two maidservants and his eleven sons and crossed the ford of the Jabbok" (Genesis 32:22–31, italics added). Wiesel says that we burn with the fire that issues not only from the world of creation and revelation but also from the silence of annihilation and nothingness. Above all, we burn with the longing for redemption. David Patterson's commentary on Wiesel's account of the story gives us a clue:

> A tale from the Midrash itself may provide a key. . . . It is about the night when Jacob wrestled his identity as a Jew—as Yisrael—from the Angel of Death. As the Angel wrestled with Jacob, it is written, "He put his fin-

ger to the earth, whereupon the earth began spurting fire. Said Jacob to him 'Would you terrify me with that stuff? Why, I am all together of that stuff!'" And thus it is written, "And the house of Jacob shall be a fire." (Obadiah 1:18; *Bereshit Rabbah* 77:2)[36]

That night in which Jacob is at a *crossing(s)*, he wrestles with God and himself in a time, a space, an encounter, an opportunity in which bodily identity or identification is *chosen*. It is not given; rather, it is wrenched from the clutches of nothingness and annihilation. He leaves *limping*— how could he not be damaged from such an ordeal? In his limping is his salvation, his heritage, and his renaming of himself and the world, and a sign of meeting God. Mystics call it the dark night of the soul. Howard Thurman calls it "marking the place that one calls one's own."[37] For African American liberatory practices and the question of the body as a site for aesthetic reflection on the birthing of new names and possibilities, it is always *that night*—always *crossing(s)*—for how else could we see our true selves, our truest and deepest selves, unless the fire of the soul is revealed against the night, in *luminous darkness*?[38] Are we not fire . . . is it not the holiest thing about us like fire shut up in our bones?

Martin Buber says that *turning, teshuvah*, is simultaneously an act of grace. Implied in this grace that strikes us in encounter with the stranger within us and outside us are also the acts of weeping, confession, and resistance.[39] It is a *turn* from Dilemma, Exodus, and the Frying Pan to the Fire! Moreover, my mother's ritualistic performance is a shape-shifting, signifying movement that calls us from the ghostly narratives of enslaved bodies and minds to the Fire of the Holy Ghost, who makes us *turn* and shift toward the other within and the other without. *Turning* to the Fire is a signification on black figuration of language and being—it is a "hermeneutics of style."[40] This hermeneutics of style is embedded in her body language; she is Madonna, the great trickster, a black interpreter god, signifying on culture and calling upon us to *turn*, a swirling dancer, incarnating the spirit of life, filled with the Holy Ghost and a Mighty Burning Fire!

"Baptized in the Holy Ghost and a Mighty Burning Fire"

In respect to the shape-shifting ghost of contested post-racial discourse, black church leaders and scholars must reimagine what it means to be bodily "baptized by the Holy Ghost and Fire" (Matthew 3:11–12 KJV)[41] as part of the task of retelling the story and revising race-based language and consciousness. As suggested in earlier chapters, all cultural performances involve the complex interlocking dimensions of cognition, affection, and behavior as domains of bodily existence. Leaders, in particular, must be aware of their "inner theaters," where internal dialogues regarding what constitutes beauty, truth, and justice are engaged *backstage*,[42] often unconsciously, and are preparatory for public presentations and cultural performances that are prefigured as characters in a larger social histori-cal narrative. Most narratives that are constructed backstage have their public analogue in the larger narratives that are culturally produced and arranged for the racialized, genderized, sexualized bodies before their appearance. This is the power of the old ghost that prefigures conscious-ness and provides complex cognitive schemas of self-perception as a consequence of the agent's adaptation to social structures.[43]

The Holy Ghost, as I am using the term, is the Spirit whom the agent discovers and encounters at *crossing(s)* and with whom the agent enters into an illuminating, reflexive fellowship so that the consciousness of their *somebodyness* and *possibles* are revealed.[44] From this perspective, the agent becomes aware of his or her power to resist and potentially transform her or his adaptations to social structures that have been in-ternalized as embodied history. The agent becomes aware, experiences an awakened consciousness, and through the internalization of new practices and rituals[45] available and indigenous to the agent's psycho-social environment, embarks on a new journey of identity and history toward *home*. To be baptized with the Holy Ghost and a Mighty Burning Fire, then, is to experience a "new birth" and a sense of autonomy, gifted through imaginative processes, and to envision new possibilities and pathways to human flourishing—it is to awaken from the dead. Such a project is not otherworldly, but decidedly material, human, and historical. To be saved from the ghostly hauntings of preconstructed narratives of bondage and alienation from the body is to be delivered and directed by the power of the Holy Ghost. In the language of the Sanctified Church, it is to cast out the devil—and to set the captive free. Howard Thurman reminds us, however, that "it is not enough to evict the devil, but something else must be put in his place and maintained there, or else he returns, refreshed and recharged, to deliver greater tyranny."[46] So this *turning* includes sanctification, "a sanctified spirit and sanctified mind," as a continuous spiraling—going deeper into the inner recesses of one's personal space and spiraling outward into the larger orbit of being and becoming in the world. I associate this *turning*, spiraling, counterclockwise movement of the Holy Ghost and Fire with *the fluid center(s)*, the innermost spaces of consciousness and being/becoming that ensure the dynamic quality of life and experience that remain unnameable and ineffable, yet it is these in-between spaces of the living/dead that give birth to *enfleshed* freedom and possibility.

As part of the sanctifying and turning of the body, the Holy Ghost is manifest as the refining Fire that separates "wheat from chaff" (Malachi 3:2–3). In other words, the counterclockwise spiral that reenters lost time (memory) and re-*turns* to the present (mission) through the future (vision), addresses and disrupts that which is counterproductive and destructive to human flourishing, and reorients the self and community to wholesome, fulfilling narrative quests that issue forth in disturbing theologies, disruptive ethics, and dangerous proclamations.[47] In this sense, I am also placing the Holy Ghost in counter-engagement with the ghost of post-racialism, which is an "unholy ghost." Through the power of the Holy Ghost, black church leaders are empowered to stand in new places of power and authority over the spirit of the ghost that holds them in captivity to the double consciousness of Dilemma, the dysfunctional dimensions of patriarchal, complicated narratives of Exodus, and the self-denigrating, disempowering, and destructive bodily aesthetics of the Frying Pan.

Fire, Nation Language, and Reimagining Global Possibilities

Fire, as a shape-shifting embodied metaphor, is global and local; consuming and purgative; fixed and fluid—it moves as it appears still. This image of Fire is akin to Diana L. Eck's experimentation with cross-cultural and religious themes associated with the Spirit. One of the common themes that bind traditional religious cosmologies is the element of Fire as denoting Spirit (also Breath, Wind).[48] In the Pentecost narrative, which we will discuss later, both Fire and Breath or Wind are present, denoting blessings, judgment, empowerment, movement, refinement, and purification. African American religious discourse is anchored in practices that seek the fullness of baptism in the Spirit that is like "fire shut in our bones."[49]

The metaphor of Fire also reminds us of the importance of the empowering, shape-shifting character of the Holy Ghost in constructing a global theology of Diaspora.[50] Allan Boesak's collection of sermons, an example of dangerous proclamations, *The Fire Within: Sermons from the Edge of Exile*, suggests that there is indeed a place for black Jeremiahs/jeremiads in Diasporas, whether in South Africa, the United States, or the United Kingdom. Preaching in exilic contexts where prophetic voices have been silenced, Boesak believes that black church leaders must confront their own "intensely personal" narratives, "framed within the perplexity of their own voicelessness," in order to answer the question, "How can the one made voiceless be speaking the Word of God to others?"[51] Fire, as representative of Spirit, has its bearings in diasporic and exilic possibilities and the reimagining of *home* not as a place elsewhere, but as a place of new life and healing, vibrant human flourishing, and the prophetic ministry of the Holy Ghost. "Home," writes bell hooks, "is a site where oppressed and disenfranchised people restore their spirits and continue the process of self-recovery."[52] In respect to the question raised earlier regarding the ghostly imagining of nation language that possesses the minds of many African American churches and their fidelity to the unfulfilled promise of equality, freedom, and justice,[53] might we explore how the Fire might lead us beyond the "dead space" into a new narrative of global citizenship as a site of *home*?

Fire, Globalization, and Global Citizenship

An interesting contemporaneous possibility inherent in the Fire metaphor, as an aesthetic/existential response to the diasporic and exilic situation of African Americans, is its correspondence to the language of globalization and global citizenship. On one hand, the term "globalization" has a pejorative connotation because of our experience of the voracious nature of the market economy; consequently, a type of existential angst has developed around the term. In fact, Amy Chua, the John M. Duff Jr. Professor of Law at Yale Law School, sees a correlation between "fire" and "globalization." In her monograph *World on Fire*, she argues that the exportation of free market democracy breeds ethnic hatred and global instability and caters to a new elite of "market-dominant minorities" who profit most from globalization rather than the ethnic poor and politically powerless in the world.[54] But on the other hand, according to Jochen Fried, director of education at the Salzburg Global Seminar, we need to pay close attention to what Karl Marx and Friedrich Engels in 1848 called "world-wide interconnectedness,"[55] which is a critical dimension of this sweeping phenomenon of which globalization is its most visible (and often tragic) consequence.[56] Fried proposes four criteria as starting points for providing a workable conceptual framework for mapping the transformations that characterize the *world-wide interconnectedness*: extension, intensification, velocity, and impact. *Extension* refers to the political and economic activities across borders on all levels that highlight the porous boundaries of nation-states and the widening of systems of global knowledge and the exchange of ideas. *Intensification* refers to cross-border flows of trade, investment, services, communication, people, migration, cultures, and so forth that are increasingly creating a dense global network of commerce and integration of cultures. *Velocity* references the rapid rate of the movement of globalized communication, fueled most by vast and complex digital systems and businesses, that travels at the speed of light.[57] Fried calls this phenomenon "the world on speed." Finally and most importantly is globalization's *impact*. The extension, intensification, and velocity of competition and cooperation of nation-states have already significantly impacted and shaped the future of the globe. Therefore, black churches, like other institutions, will need to rethink our understanding of global/local distinctions. In fact, such distinctions are contrived and misleading because we are all *glocal*.[58]

Connected to the economic, political, and cultural impact of globalization is the language of *citizenship*. As a philosophical and political signifier, the idea of global citizenship has been around for a long time, from ancient Stoic notions of being a *kosmon polites*—literally, a "world citizen"—to the more contemporary solidaristic approaches of Amartya Sen, who addresses "our inescapably plural identities," and Kwame Anthony Appiah's "cosmopolitanism." Global citizenship, as I am using the term in this context, "refers to a sense of belonging to a broader community and common humanity. It emphasizes political, economic, social and cultural interdependency and interconnectedness between the local, the national and the global."[59] For our purposes, this understanding of global citizenship is the pathway to larger and fuller diasporic and exilic conversations between black church leaders and scholars interested in strengthening black churches. Moreover, it is an indispensable ingredient in any ongoing task that strives for a sense of identity or identification of black churches as part of "world-wide interconnectedness" and serves as a corrective to the small house that race built. In respect to a global theological perspective for black churches, global citizenship is the deliberate and strategic claim to religiously orient, culturally educate, and politically engage its constituencies in "a world perspective"[60] that extends beyond the porous boundaries of nation-states and imagines itself as part of the global eruption of freedom seen in religious and political alliances around the world. Theologically, such a perspective will involve attention to critical pedagogical and kerygmatic dimensions of *turning* to the Fire of the Holy Ghost, who promises human and nonhuman flourishing,[61] and joining in a community of differences and creative languages[62] that expels the old ghost and evacuates it from the premises of what Martin Luther King Jr. called the "world house."

Fried's conceptual framework for thinking about global citizenship finds alignment with the possibilities inherent in the fire symbolism of global Pentecostalism (also called "Charismatic Christianity" and "Pneumatic religion"), which mirrors the larger picture of globalization and the movement's phenomenal growth as a religious, political, economic, and social movement in the past century. The critical indices of extension, intensification, velocity, and impact can also be viewed as cultural, political, economic, and religious markers of the global Pentecostal movement. The seismic shift in the character and look of Christianity in the latter half of the twentieth century is a statement about the global intensity, extension, velocity, and impact of Pentecostalism in the Southern Hemisphere. Nowhere is it more apparent than in Latin America and Africa.[63] Scholars of world religions have much to say about its concentrated, rapid growth and the cultural, political, social, and economic impact of its global reach. According to Lamin Sanneh, "Charismatic Christianity . . . is largely responsible for the dramatic shift in the religion's center of gravity." In 2007 Philip Jenkins asserted that Pentecostalism and independent African churches will soon "represent a far larger segment of global Christianity, and just conceivably, a majority, resulting in Pentecostalism being the most successful *social* movement in the past century" (italics added).[64] Indeed, the ground has shifted!

One of the reasons Pentecostalism has mushroomed in African and Latin American contexts is its adaptability to different cultures and societies and its ability to contextualize its expressions of Christianity. These are valuable lessons U.S. black churches might learn instead of mimicking traditional Christian liturgies and practices, especially when we are witnessing the opposite phenomenon in the decline of mainline denominations in the West. Attendant to this vast global movement is the ethical significance of the astronomical gap in wealth. A common concern is that certain prosperity gospel leaders gain "wealth and health" in a world of increasing globalization at the expense of the poor and powerless. This highly publicized and problematic social reality offers a lens through which to view the emerging scholarship, and the imaginative and constructive tasks of disturbing theological and disruptive ethical analyses of global capital, economics, money management, and larger questions of justice and fairness.[65]

Among theologians and Christian ethicists working on these important tasks is Nimi Wariboko, who identifies the new surge of religious, economic, and social fire with the "Pentecostal Principle," a theological perspective that emphasizes the possibility of novelty and change, especially in economic and political matters, against the forces of inertia and tradition backed by avarice and the relentless quest for power.[66] Wariboko utilizes the Pentecostal Principle as a critical method that provides a heuristic and hermeneutic tool with which to excavate and bring to light the complex intersections of *lifeworlds* and *systems* and the many different ways they function as apparatuses for cultural domination and late capitalism. Hence, his emphasis on inclusiveness, openness, novelty, excellence, and plurality is at once theological and ethical, but also decidedly political and economic, because the Pentecostal Principle aims to challenge all forms of normativity that have become encapsulated in power and that subjugate and disguise themselves as absolute or divine. In the latter sense, the Pentecostal Principle is therefore iconoclastic and anti-idolatrous. Wariboko insists that the Pentecostal Principle is not necessarily attached to Pentecostalism; rather, he defines it in the language of Hannah Arendt and Paul Tillich as the "capacity to begin":

> It encapsulates the notion that no finite or conditioned reality can claim to have reached its destiny. The movement of every existent to its destiny (full realization of its potentialities) remains forever incompletable because it remains "rooted" in the abyss of divine freedom. Every end has only one option: to be a new beginning.[67]

With this fundamental criterion for rethinking the theological and ethical dimensions of sociopolitical and economic apparatuses (read: the "preset ends of late capitalism"), Wariboko begins his deconstruction of normative claims of any religious, political, economic, or ideological belief, even his own Pentecostalism. In doing so, he makes available to a larger circle of public intellectuals, both religious and humanistic, a place for contentious debate about *excellence* (Greek, *areté*) as a "'depoliticized and destabilized' reading of the regnant genealogy and interpretation of virtue" that renders it disruptive and liberatory. For Wariboko, this particular conception of virtue conspires with "the pentecostal notion of grace as disruptive and as a gift given over and over again."[68]

This brief departure into the phenomenal growth of Pentecostalism is not meant as an endorsement of any of its doctrines and religiopolitical practices, but rather as an attempt to look at ways black bodies participate in complex interactions with global theological and ethical configurations that announce possibilities of finding *home*, the space of flourishing in encounter with other strangers who are seeking *common(s)* in a world where *the ground* has shifted.[69] Most importantly, theological and ethical reflection on the global Pentecostal movement accentuates the call to be baptized with the Holy Ghost and Fire for this time, and continues the long-standing traditions related to diasporic yearnings in exile in search of new language that extends beyond the narrow, confining language of nation.

A Scattered and Scattering People

The Pentecostal Principle, of course, is related to the "tongues of fire" that erupt on the Day of Pentecost described in Acts 2:1–13. I am interpreting the symbol of Pentecost and "the tongues of fire" as correctives to the consolidation of power through the facility of language and domination and as signs of blessings for plurality, novelty, diversity, and openness; and conversely, as judgment on structures that oppose plurality, novelty, and openness. In its most dramatic sense, Pentecost represents *dispersion* or the *scattering of the seed*.[70] In this perspective, the account of the Day of Pentecost recorded in the Book of Acts, where people speak in many languages and understand each other, is simultaneously a blessing and a reversal; it is a corrective of Babel—the confusion of the languages is a sign of judgment against the monolithic enterprise of hegemony.[71]

The story of Babel serves as a prologue, an introduction, to the complicated story of Abraham and Sarah, who represent the new faithfulness required by God in the extension of the human family, a family through which God will correct the damage of Babel and bless the nations of the earth through the scattering of his seed.[72] Scholars have also made a connection between the well-known stories of the Tower of Babel and Pentecost (the festival of the harvest). Normally the "tongues of fire" symbolism is interpreted primarily as a blessing upon the people at Pentecost, but Blaine Charette argues that the symbol of "tongues of fire" was also "divine judgment upon the disobedient."[73] Charette thinks that it is not a matter of small significance that Pentecost is celebrated along with the festival of the harvest, when all the seeds that were scattered in the early spring were collected and ready for harvest; he interprets this event as an allusion to Luke's narrative structure and his use of the Parable of the Sower.[74] Pentecost is harvest time, when all things come together for the next scattering, because the Lord of the harvest is always scattering seeds, collecting them, and making ready for harvest where the wheat and chaff are separated and the latter is thrown into the fire. As the narrative goes, on the Day of Pentecost, the festival of the harvest, those restless and fearful disciples who had scattered like seeds after the crucifixion were all in one place waiting on the harvest. Little did that trembling band know that soon they would become a scattering posse of apostles! Peter prophesies to all the ethnicities and nationalities gathered in that place—Parthians, Medes, and Elamites, residents of Mesopotamia, Judea, and Cappadocia, Pontus and Asia, Phrygia and Pamphylia, Egypt and the parts of Libya near Cyrene, visitors from Rome (both Jews and converts to Judaism), Cretans and Arabs! Soon through the scattering of Paul, Priscilla and Aquila, Lydia, and Barnabas, so many others would join the scattering of the Gospel. The Gospel *scatters and makes us a scattering people.* Soon Philip would baptize an Ethiopian—*scattered and scattering*! Peter would baptize a Roman centurion named Cornelius—*scattered and scattering*! Soon they were all on their way!

The point here is that according to Luke, the church of Jesus Christ is a *scattered and scattering people.* We gather and then we disperse like seeds in the hands of a sower who goes out to sow, whose seeds fall on shallow ground, among weeds and thickets and sometimes on good ground. The Holy Ghost *scatters us*! In this perspective, for black churches, one of the reasons we are scattered is that we are called to be new meaning makers for this historical passage in the lives of our respective peoples, nationalities, races, ethnicities, classes—to be and to create something more than the reformist, mainstream thinking of our rigid and rigor mortised dogma and doctrines that have become stale, lifeless, and ineffective. We need something more . . . a scattering of our complacency with our faith. We need a disturbing theology, a disruptive ethics, a prophetic preaching that moves us into this century like a rushing and violent wind where empires are working on a new Tower of Babel and speaking one language of *super-capitalism* based on money and power.

Walter Brueggemann sees the Hebrew story of the building of the city and the tower as an act of signification against Babylon, their oppressor. The oppressed, he suggests, find ways to signify on their oppressors. According to Brueggemann, the legend of the tower explained for the early Hebrew communities why Babylon fell; it is an explanation of the destruction of an oppressive civilization whose arrogance was interrupted by God's righteousness. The Babel story is a protest against every effort at oneness derived from idolatry and hegemony.[75] Howard Thurman suggests that this process of judgment attends to human arrogance and the will to dominate:

> The judgment of God appears again and again in the process of history, dramatized by the rise and fall of peoples who have neglected to build

their civilizations towards the higher ends of ethical responsibility. . . . The diabolical character of the enterprise itself destroys the vehicle so that finally the energies are scattered and dissipated.[76]

Indeed, Babel is a story about the concentration of power through the facility of language, but it is also a statement about the divine's will for diversity, openness, and hospitality to the stranger.[77] The builders proposed one language as the unifying form through which to organize power and to dominate. Frantz Fanon makes a poignant observation that connects the use of language and the status of citizenship. After a lecture in which he addressed "Negro and European poetry," one of his colleagues suggested that he was a "white man" because of his facility with language, which Fanon connects with "honorary citizenship."[78] I would like to suggest, therefore, that Babel is a metaphor, a symbol of sorts—a language that ascribes status and complicates the notion of citizenship in a global environment that has already happened. Moreover, the many languages of Pentecost speak to any human project that ignores the intended dynamism and diversity that is at the heart of the Holy Ghost's creative activity. The divine activity in creation was never a call to a sterile, monolithic world of uniformity; rather, God, as the text suggests, appreciates, and even mandates, the *many* over the *one*— *plurality* over *singularity*. An important reminder for black church leaders and scholars is the history of the Azusa Street Revival, led by William Seymour, which took place during other awakenings to the Spirit around the world, including the Welsh Revival and at Pandita Ramabai's orphanage in India. Interestingly, the evangelist Seymour fell from grace with his white former teacher, Charles Parham, over Seymour's call for multiracial assemblies and leadership. The biblical scholar Craig Keener references a testimony from Frank Bartleman, a white participant in the Azusa Street Revival, who proclaimed that "the color line had been washed away by the blood." We know that the experience of unity across the racial and color line was temporary.[79]

The following chapter further explores the themes of Exile and Diaspora, especially as they were embodied in the work of Martin Luther King Jr. and Malcolm X.[80] This discussion serves to prepare us to draw on the themes of remembering and retelling (memory/vision) as we begin to lay the groundwork for a revived mission for U.S. black churches. The next three chapters illuminate how the method of remembering and retelling our stories as black church leaders and scholars informs the reliving of our larger social-historical narrative for this time. The tripartite movement of memory (past) and vision (future) directs us to the mission (present). While there are many issues and challenges that could direct our mission, I focus on one of the most pressing matters of the present: the exilic condition of young black males. Chapter 9 will examine the cultural productions of black males as madmen, monkeys, and monsters and the ways these characterizations insinuate and imprison the minds and spirits of many of these young men, especially the poor. Chapters 8 and 10 will further develop the idea of "tools of the spirit" and ask which tools might be most appropriate to the quest for the liberation from madness through memory and counter-memory as practices for these young men. The final chapter will return to the questions with which we began regarding the haunting of black churches by the unholy ghost of race and provide some recommendations for the way(s) to *home*.

7

Just above Our Heads

A Meditation from the Middle

O Mother who sits by the fire
Make your self known to this small man
Who has forgotten, but now seeks his way home
Back to you and to those who dwell above and below.

Sweet Mother of God,
Life-giver, Womb before Time
Give birth now to a new consciousness that weeps with you
And prays with you for the souls of your children
Bereft, forlorned, and forgetful.
—Author's private journal

This chapter looks at, listens to, and learns from the shifts in the personal narratives of two martyrs of black faith, Martin Luther King Jr. and Malcolm X (later known as el-Hajj Malik el-Shabazz). We ask, Has hagiographic social reconstruction of their lives rid their history of the hauntings that plague all people of color in this society? The answer is yes and no, because it hovers just above our heads. Yes, because clinging to their memories makes us feel safe as their messianic tropes essentialize a path of salvation and freedom. They help us to believe that in Exodus someone in their *likeness* will rescue us and lead us to the Promised Land. No, because the strong, heroic imagery of these black male warriors has shifted in revelations of their fragility, their vulnerabilities, and our need to fashion new faces, images, and communal voices that hearken toward a new age in which heroes must share space with those *others* who gather in *common(s)*, at our *crossing(s)*, and *conjure* new narratives for a people negotiating safe spaces in the dark. Therefore, this meditation is placed in the middle (*mesa*) of this text, the in-between spaces, as a pause for recollection and reflection on memory/remembering and vision/retelling as we turn toward mission/reliving.

This chapter does not offer a critical examination of Martin's and Malcolm's theological and ethical perspectives; others have done that far better than I can.[1] Rather, it calls attention to the place of spirituality in their quests for social transformation and how their respective searches brought them to *crossing(s)*, especially at the end of their lives, to places where they were *turning*. In doing so, they signal to us that if we are to live into the visions of Diasporas, Exiles, and Fire, we, too, must *turn*.

An important aspect of their spiritual journeys is the men's relationships to their mothers, Louise Norton Little and Alberta Williams King. In fact, there can be no adequate understanding of their spiritual moorings without attending to the place and the role of their mothers in their early formation and in their quests for God. Both men were deeply influenced by their mothers, but in different ways, as biographers suggest. King was nurtured by the warmth and love of Alberta Williams King, especially during his difficult passages with his strong-willed, Baptist father, the Reverend Martin Luther King Sr. He writes in his "Autobiography of Religious Development" that his "Mother dear, . . . Alberta Williams King, has been behind the scene setting forth those motherly cares, the lack of which leaves a missing link in life. She is a very devout person with a deep commitment to the Christian faith. Unlike my father, she is soft-spoken and easygoing. Although possessed of a rather recessive personality, she is warm and easily approachable."[2]

Malcolm, on the other hand, witnessed early the death of his Garveyite father, the Reverend Earl Little, and the devastation wrought on his courageous but distraught mother. It appears that he never reconciled the traumatic experiences of her struggle to raise a family of eight children without a husband and her eventual institutionalization. Manning Marable observes, "As the winter of 1938 *turned* into spring, the Littles' slender hopes disintegrated. . . . A physician certified that she [Louise] was 'an insane person and her condition is such as to require care and treatment in an institution.'"[3] Alex Haley, who assisted Malcolm with the writing of his autobiography, reflected on the charismatic public leader's shyness, indeed, his difficulty in talking about himself, deferring rather to the Honorable Elijah Muhammad, leader of the Nation of Islam. Haley said that Malcolm would become testy whenever he delicately insisted that the autobiography was about him, not Mr. Muhammad. Finally, he asked one evening,

> "Mr. Malcolm, could you tell me something about your mother?" And I will never ever forget how he stopped, almost suspended like a marionette. And he said, "I remember the kind of dresses she used to wear. They were old and faded and gray." And then he walks some more and he said, "I remember how she was always bent over the stove, trying to stretch what little we had." And that was the beginning, that night, of his walking, and he walked that floor until just about daybreak.[4]

Clearly, Malcolm *tussled* and *turned* with those memories at *crossing(s)*.

This interval is not an attempt to psychoanalyze these figures; rather, I am imagining. Boldly and emphatically, I take imaginative license in this conjecture that in their quest for *home*, for wholeness and human flourishing, they were turning, re-turning to the Mother, to the womb/tomb of their existence.

Remembering Black Madonnas, Martin, and Malcolm

Remembering Martin and Malcolm is hard because they evoke dangerous memories. Oh, discussing their philosophies of self-defense versus nonviolence, black nationalism versus integration, Christianity versus Islam is really not hard. It does not cost us much. But to remember them, to enter into serious dialogue with these two shining princes of this nation, means embarking upon perilous paths into dangerous memories that shake the foundations upon which we rely for sanity, saintliness, and condescension. But it is only in *rememory*, as Toni Morrison calls it—reading the hieroglyphics of the flesh in trees carved on enslaved backs and touching the hollow places left by assassins' missiles—that our souls are given permission to rebirth a struggle for human community.

Situated on my family shrine, amidst messy concatenations of collected artifacts that help me to remember the *crossing(s)* of the years, there are three icons: two Madonnas with Child and a black crucifix (*corpus Christi nigrum*). On the left side, one of the Madonnas, from the Dominican Republic, is sculpted from a single piece of wood: the lines are rough and earthy. In her arms rests the Child, the eternal archetype of hope. The Mother and Child are one fluid sentence naming the mysterious beauty and harmony of human love: Mother and Child in embrace, lost in the wonder and nurture of the other. In the words of the late Audre Lorde, we are "forever with child."[5]

On the right is the Black Madonna of Częstochowa with Child: both wearing bejeweled crowns with arms extended to the beholder. The Madonna's eyes are fixed away from herself, following every move, every retreat from that which calls us to be human, while her right hand gestures toward the Child.

In his left hand, the Child holds the gospels like a treasure chest bearing his gift to the world, salvation (perhaps); with his right hand, he blesses. But salvation cannot be found in the bargain basements of a culture where the commodification of human souls still leaves a foul stench in the air. No—few are they who are willing to pay the price for an awakening from the deep sleep of polluted subterranean wells where consciousness dreams new dreams and spurns new realities.

The strong, stalwart Madonnas stir memories of Isis, the Mother of God and devoted sister-companion of Osiris, whom she found murdered and dismembered by their evil brother Seth. From his dismembered body, she took the generative organ and conceived the Child, Horus, who is the resurrected Osiris.[6] The Child is born from the dismembered parts, remembered in a gift of redemption.

Both mothers hold the Child in warning and wonder of the *crossing(s)* just above their heads. The broken and humiliated One, that dangerous memory from the past and that tragic-laden hope of the future, hangs just above our heads.

Underneath the icons is another, a photograph of my mother in her usher's uniform. She is standing in the front of our small storefront house of worship, the Centennial Missionary Baptist Church, *home* for generations of African American immigrants from the Deep South who "made a way out of no way."[7] She symbolizes the struggles of all of those saints who journeyed to Chicago looking for a city, a Promised Land flowing with milk and honey. Her story is the story of "many a thousands" who boarded the train called the City of New Orleans in hope of a better life for their children, and found instead a strange, intimidating urban environment far from the cotton fields back *home*. For her, the journey from *Frogbottom* to a *Bucket of Blood* was a tragic tale written on her black female body and inscribed in her soul like an ancient odyssey without the celebration of the hero's mythic return. But she treasured the lives of her children, holding them close and daring to *turn* in hope, because of the wretched, grotesque figure that hung just above her head. Is she not a (Black) Madonna as was Louise Norton Little, Alberta Williams King, and countless others whose children are crucified by the historical and political machinations of natal alienation? Are not Madonnas to be mourned and adored as much as the children whom they have lost?

This imaginative yearning for the Mother is not cast as a sign of reproduction, but as a sign of life (natality) that helps us to move away from death (mortality) and violence,[8] a *crossing(s)* marking the infinite cycle of turning and returning to *home*—the conscious decision to give birth in the midst of death. Is not the future in the Child, haunted, slain, remembered, and resurrected? Is this not the holiest of things?

I love to imagine and reimagine faces of the Madonnas. There are the long, strapping arms and firm frame of Sojourner Truth standing tall at the *crossing(s)* of the 1851 Women's Convention in Akron, Ohio, declaring,

> That man over there says that women need to be helped into carriages, and lifted over ditches, and to have the best place everywhere. Nobody ever helps me into carriages, or over mud-puddles, or gives me any best place! And ain't I a woman? Look at me! Look at my arm! I have ploughed and planted, and gathered into barns, and no man could head me! And ain't I a woman? I could work as much and eat as much as a man—when I could get it—and bear the lash as well! And ain't I a woman? I have borne thirteen children, and seen most all sold off to slavery, and when I cried out with my mother's grief, none but Jesus heard me! And ain't I a woman?[9]

And there is the stern face of Ella Baker standing at the *crossing(s)* on August 6, 1965, at the Democratic Freedom Party's Nominating Convention, adorned in her blue pillbox crown, saying to a grief-stricken crowd only two days after the killing of James Chaney, Andrew Goodman, and Michael Schwerner in Philadelphia, Mississippi, "Until the killing of black mothers' sons is as important as the killing of white mothers' sons, we who believe in freedom cannot rest";[10] and Fannie Lou Hamer standing at the *crossing(s)* with the Mississippi Freedom Democratic Party delegation in August 1965, her beautiful brown face and fleshly voice rocking, "This little light of mine, I'm goin'a let it shine, let it shine, let it shine, let it shine."[11] I like to see her many faces, hear her many songs and feel her many passions as I pay my debt at her altar:

> Dear Mother of mine
> Dear Mother of God
> Both you are
> And there is only one of me—
> Take this violent heart of mine
> And fasten it to yours

That I might live in you
And know even more love
More joy
Than time would allow and
Earthly space permit

You who swallow the seed
And give back to the earth
From your rich, dark womb
Trees and flowers
Flying creatures
Crying holy to the sky
Touch this simpleton
With joy

My heart I hold in my hand
Not a gift
But a promise to keep—
This hard stone
That will not thrive unless you bless it
Plant it in the ground, let it die
And kiss the place where it lies
Make it well, Mother
Make it laugh, Dear
Sing it a lullaby, Mommy please
So that I might know that I am
Alive in thee[12]

These figures of Madonna and Child evoke dangerous memories with redemptive possibilities. "Can we all get along?" they ask. The history of America and of humankind suggests not. But the deeper message of the Madonna and Child is that hope is coiled up in the heart of our struggles—that redemption rests in an infinite circle of birth, death, and rebirth and our willingness to *turn*.

Since the deaths of Martin and Malcolm, conversations within and beyond the African American community have focused on the political and social strategies of these two leaders as resources in articulating a new vision for the struggle against the jagged and complex congeries of race, gender, sexuality, and class and their impact on the plight of African Americans. The misogynist, patriarchal leadership of these men has been well-documented and will require even greater attention if they are to continue to serve as critical resources for reflection and formation of new ways of thinking, strategizing, and moving into the new times and rhythms of diasporic, exilic, and fire-filled journeys toward *home*. Yet they have much to teach us about *turning*.

A sorely neglected dimension of this exploration is the place of spirituality in their social and political thought and praxis. Beyond their respective approaches to the political and economic spheres of black existence is a more profound and relevant legacy. Malcolm and Martin leave living testaments of their *hope*: a tragic-laden hope searching in the luminous darkness that will not relinquish its hold on the redemptive possibilities inherent in human beings. Their searches for personal wholeness and transformation brought them to the forefront of a political movement that changed the direction of the nation and the world. But the crass and critical issues of our day demand that a new generation of leaders come on the scene, who, like Malcolm and Martin, are bold and courageous enough to journey through the dry, bone-filled valley of tradition and orthodoxy, and to wage battle with legions of Giants that stand guard over our entry into a future laden with ambiguity. Their lives and the dangerous memories they leave are summons for a new vanguard of visionaries who are spiritually disciplined and intellectually astute, able to interpret the present madness and hell that are upon us and to prescribe new formulas and possibilities for a people quickly losing hope. Out of their deaths they call us to find a third way, a new path *home*.

In Malcolm's and Martin's legacies, spirituality and social transformation are the dominant themes that define and make available the resources for this fragile, haunting hope of human community. For King, this theme is the basis for his articulation of the beloved community ideal, an extension of the moral reformist perspective articulated earlier. For Malcolm, spirituality and social transformation are the keys that decipher the sphinxlike riddle of his ironic quest for just relations among human beings, a diasporic, exilic perspective born of black nationalist and Pan-Africanist perspectives. In this sense, they represent the polarities and dilemmas that black churches have struggled with since their inception.

Make no mistake, Malcolm and Martin were different—one Muslim, the other Christian, from different sites of *crossing(s)*, but crossed, nonetheless. Attempts to create complementarities between the two where they do not exist are unproductive and futile. But while there are distinct differences in approaches to their respective goals, beyond (perhaps, beneath) their differences in methodology and ideology lies the common quest for personal wholeness and identity born of their brokenness, in a recalcitrant, racist society that militates against such possibility. The notion of transformation in both Malcolm and Martin is inextricably bound with their religious quests for self-understanding, human flourishing, and "defining moments" where they are called to turn at *crossing(s)*. Their personal quests, ultimately, involve searches for radical change in public policy and practice. One can hardly miss this truth in reviewing the spiritual developments of these black titans.

Turning from Montgomery to National Imaginary to the World House

Awakening to oneself and to justice is never a solitary, isolated event; it always involves *crossing(s)*, encounters with others, *facing and touching others*, and in *facing and touching others*—the trysting, tussling of death and birth—our faces and bodies are transformed. Faces and bodies tell stories and disclose mysteries of character and being.[13] Martin Luther King's development as a leader of the people can be viewed as a series of faces that were part of his transformative practice of justice. The faces of pre-Montgomery King, "Little Mike," "Tweed," and the "Philosopher King," do not readily lend themselves to the character that is disclosed in the moments of testing that follow his public ministry in Montgomery and thereafter. It is rather in his bodily engagement with the struggle for social justice that one begins to see the deep, furrowed glance of the preacher become leader of the people. The final face of King is the one we most remember—the somber, distant, almost melancholic look, a disfigured countenance that returns from the mountain. He has been *crossed*; he *limps* into history.[14] Nowhere is this face more vividly portrayed than in his bold excoriation of the Vietnam War and in his trials within the African American community around the political philosophy of black nationalism, articulated by Malcolm X. It was the Vietnam War, Malcolm, the activism of the young who could not accept anything less than full recognition of their humanity, and the global eruptions of freedom around the globe that caused King to *turn* from the national imaginary of dead space to the vision of the world house and global citizenship. At these *crossing(s)*, he was *crossed* by God.

The *scattered* and *scattering, diasporic, dispersing* ethical obligations of black church leadership will involve *crossing(s)* such as these, new and creative ways of communication and modeling global citizenship in exile. Martin Luther King's notion of the world house is an appropriate metaphor for the new moment to which black churches have been called by history and opportunity. Lewis V. Baldwin's examination of this possibility is a good place to begin. Baldwin argues that the distinctive contribution of King's vision of global citizenship is his deep commitment to justice that led him to condemn the United States for its complicity in "materialism, power and supremacy over other nations."[15] King called upon America, because of its unique democratic heritage and its great resources of wealth and technology, to be the leader in this revolution. King stressed, however, that a true revolution of values and priorities—a *turning*—would involve structural changes in the American economic and political system and in its foreign policy:

> I am convinced that if we are to get on the right side of the world revolu-
> tion we as a nation must undergo a radical revolution of values. A true
> revolution of values will soon cause us to question the fairness and jus-
> tice of many of our present and past policies. A true revolution of values
> will look uneasily on the glaring contrast between poverty and wealth.
> With righteous indignation, it will look across the seas and see individual
> capitalists of the West investing huge sums of money in Africa, Asia, and
> South America only to take the profits out with no concern for the social
> betterment of the countries, and say: "This is unjust." It will look at our
> alliances with the landed gentry of Latin America and say: "This is not
> just." The Western arrogance of feeling that it has everything to teach oth-
> ers and nothing to learn from them is not just.[16]

King's last speech is normally interpreted in light of the Exodus paradigm. In that speech, King stands on the summit of the mountaintop
and sees the "Promised Land." The "Promised Land" conjures images of
the conquest of Canaan by Joshua, but a "shift" in lenses would offer a
different reading. A closer examination of the substantive discourse in
the speech reveals several levels of meaning. One is that King speaks out
of a diasporic perspective. He begins his speech as a type of journey on
which he takes a panoramic view of Western history. He calls his listeners to remember with him the long journey of Western civilization. He
then locates himself in the latter half of the twentieth century, in which
there is a worldwide struggle for freedom. The Exodus event is included
as one instance in the long march of humanity toward freedom. The civil
rights movement is situated in the broader context of a world movement
that is taking place in America. This is a recurring theme throughout
King's thought, beginning in his initial public speech at Holt Baptist
Church in 1955. The primary discursive note throughout the speech is

the element of "hope." In the Exile motif, the dominant existential category is "hope." What are the source and direction of this hope for King? A reading from within the Exile paradigm favors the source of hope in the history of suffering peoples to create new meanings out of overwhelming oppression. The direction of the hope is toward a worldwide revolution guided by the ethic of suffering love. King viewed the strike of the garbage workers in Memphis as part of a worldwide struggle for equality and freedom. This *line of flight* points toward an exilic existence within the United States in the hope for a global eruption of freedom.

Before his tragic death in 1968, Martin Luther King reminded this nation that we no longer live in a small house; rather, we have inherited a world house of interrelatedness and interdependability. During his later years, King was acutely aware of the need for a broader interpretive framework for understanding what he perceived as a crucial passage in history. He wrote that

> the civil rights movement in the United States is a special American phenomenon which must be understood in the light of American history and dealt with in terms of the American situation. But on another and more important level, what is happening in the United States today is a significant part of a world development.[17]

He further suggested that the struggles of African Americans must be understood in light of a shifting of the West's basic outlooks and philosophical presuppositions about power:

> However deeply American Negroes are caught in the struggle to be at last home in our homeland of the United States, we cannot ignore the larger world house in which we are also dwellers. Equality with whites will not solve the problems of either whites or Negroes if it means equality in a world society stricken by poverty and in a universe doomed to extinction by war.

This understanding of the radical nature of the dream of the world house will make some ecclesiastical leaders uneasy, especially those who are content to see "business as usual" in America, in the ravaged countries of Africa, in Latin America, in Southeast Asia, in the Middle East, and in the core of our nation's inner cities. But if we are to be true to his vision, if we really believe that his dream continues, then it is important that we understand that King's dream is not one for sentimentalists and pop patriots. It is not an isolated episode in the chronicles of American history; rather, it is the continuing struggle against racism, economic injustice, and all forms of oppression that eat away at the heart of our body politic like an insidious cancer. It is a call for a new Pentecost. It is a summons to a scattered and scattering people who are willing to go into the no-trespassing zones of this world system and to declare boldly and courageously that the future of our communities, our nation, and indeed the world, hinges on moral foundations. To accept the radical implications of his dream means that we can no longer feign ignorance and invisibility in regard to the political and economic scenarios that determine our corporate destiny. A new world is being born. All around us there is evidence that a changing of the guard is taking place. In China, Africa, South America, the Middle East, Southeast Asia, Russia, Cuba, and even in the context of American society, significant changes are occurring that are having far-reaching effects on the way we do business. Business cannot go on as usual. We must make new beginnings.

Black church leaders must ask, What does this new season of worldwide struggle mean for us, for this nation, and for the world? *Can we all get along?* Dare we hope, or must we conclude that we are at the "end of history"? King did not think that we were at the end of history. King believed that what we are witnessing is a worldwide *turning* that challenges the very foundations of Eurowestern hegemony. In his last public sentences, King said that he was pleased to live during his chaotic and precarious era because beyond the despair and hopelessness that abounded, he believed that this was a great moment for the united struggles of people throughout the world:

I know, somehow, that only when it is dark enough, can you see the stars. And I see God working in this period of the twentieth century in a way that men, in some strange way, are responding—something is happening in our world. The masses of the people are rising up. And wherever they are assembled today, whether they are in Johannesburg, South Africa; Nairobi, Kenya; Accra, Ghana; New York City; Atlanta, Georgia; Jackson, Mississippi; or Memphis, Tennessee—the cry is always the same—"We want to be free."[18]

In his brief thirty-nine years, Martin Luther King Jr. did not witness the social freedom about which he prophesied nor the personal freedom for which he yearned, but his vision of *home*, the world house, seeded the hopes of millions of disenfranchised peoples of the world. In many respects, King's prophetic vision of the world house mirrors what we have in mind with the idea of the Fire of the Holy Ghost, who sees the interrelatedness and inherent value of all life. Indeed, Fire demands that our commitments to the nation and to institutionalized religion in a contested post-racial world be judged by a more inclusive and prophetic norm, not unlike the tongues of fire at Pentecost. Our commitments to the nation would be judged in the context of a greater loyalty to the world community, particularly to people of African descent and other oppressed peoples of the world. When Martin Luther King made that fateful decision to talk about a world house in which the triple affliction of war, poverty, and racism had to be removed, he was prophesying in tongues of fire. This courageous vision of world community cost him dearly. It was his sense of community that led him to identify the great new problem of humankind as the challenge of divided loyalties: loyalty to the particularized and local visions of race, ethnicity, and the state versus the demand for global community.[19] For King, the remedy for this problem of loyalty was a *turning*, a "revolution of values and priorities." "A genuine revolution of values means in the final analysis that our loyalties must become ecumenical rather than sectional. Every nation must now develop an overriding loyalty to mankind [*sic*] as a whole in order to preserve the best in our individual societies." King suggested that this *turning* would lift us beyond tribe, race, class, and nation to a worldwide fellowship of love.[20] At once, in this singular vision of reverence and possibility, King articulated the dream of the beloved community in which transformative civility was inspired and supported in the context of global communion. Many believe he was speaking in many languages as the Spirit gave utterance—languages that speak in loving and just ways to the agonizing, yet redemptive possibilities inherent in recognition, respect, and reverence for the other—a beloved community more grand than even the nation and the world can ever hope for—*a new heaven and a new earth*. At the time of his death, he was *turning*.

Turning from Hector's Hill to the Hole to the Holy City

Malcolm Little was born in exile and his basic philosophy of struggle until his death was based on a diasporic vision of African unity, but he was *turning*. At the close of his autobiography, the then-Malcolm X reflects, "My life has always been one of changes."[21] Malcolm's journey consists of shifts and turns, *crossing(s)* that inspire hope but also remind us of the jagged contours of transcendence and history in bodily time and social constructions of death. Robert Michael Franklin and others have suggested that there are at least three clear moments of *crossing(s)* in Malcolm's quest that shaped his ideological perspective. One is the early Malcolm Little, or "Detroit Red," the hustler, a product of the urban North. As a witness to the racial animosity meted out to his parents, siblings, and himself, he painfully fashioned an identity that enabled him to survive, in his words, as a ravenous animal preying on other members of the black underclass. Despite his early bondage to crime, drugs, and violence, Malcolm provides us with small glimpses into the spiritual moorings of his youth. In the Holy City of Mecca, Malcolm returned to his early childhood in an act of *rememory*:

In that peace of the Holy World . . . I lay awake surrounded by snoring brother pilgrims—my mind took me back to personal memories I would have thought were gone forever . . . as far back, even, as when I was just a little boy, eight or nine years old. Out behind our house, out in the country from Lansing, Michigan, there was an old, grassy "Hector's Hill," we called it—which may still be there. I remembered there in the Holy World how I used to lie on the top of Hector's Hill, and look up at the sky, at the clouds moving over me, and daydream, all kinds of things. And then, in a funny contrast of recollections, I remembered how years later, when I was in prison, I used to lie on my cell bunk—this would be especially when I was in solitary: what we convicts called "The Hole"—and I would picture myself talking to large crowds. I don't have any idea why such *previsions* came to me. But they did. To tell that to anyone then would have sounded crazy. Even I didn't have, myself, the slightest inkling.[22]

Although these memories were subjected to disillusionment and disappointment, especially from the Nation of Islam, they remained "residue of [an] unshakable conviction"[23] that could not be displaced. From the *crossing(s)* of the solitude of Hector's Hill to the solitary confinement of the Hole, to the stark silence of the black skies of the Holy City, Malcolm dreamed the dream of redemptive possibilities—"still as a cloud of windless sail horizon-hung" just above his head.[24]

His voluminous reading and self-education in Norfolk State Prison and his contact with the Honorable Elijah Muhammad shaped the second face of "Malcolm X." The dangerous memories of his early childhood and his time in the streets of Boston and Harlem had readied him for this encounter with the self-proclaimed Messenger of Allah. Malcolm's conversion to the Nation of Islam fits into the classical motif of mysticism reminiscent of other great spiritual leaders. In the readying, the prophet undergoes a trysting period—he or she wrestles with God, the demonic, and the divine. In the wilderness encounter, the initiate is acutely aware of promptings, clues, and messages that appear to be from the beyond, but indeed have been present all along in patterns of internal, psychological, and spiritual meaning. Often, there is an element of irony in the great surprise that he or she, being the most unworthy, would be chosen for such a revelation and gift. Confused and burdened by his brother Reginald's suspension from the Nation of Islam, Malcolm lay upon his bed, and in another *prevision*, as he called it, saw a man whom he later came to believe was Master W. D. Fard, the Messiah, whom Elijah Muhammad claimed had appointed him as His Last Messenger to the black people of North America. Malcolm remembers,

> As I lay on my bed, I suddenly, with a start, became aware of a man sitting beside me in my chair. He had on a dark suit. *I remember.* I could see him as I see anyone I look at. He wasn't black, and he wasn't white. He was light-browned-skinned, an Asiatic cast of countenance, and he had oily black hair.
>
> I looked right into his *face.* I didn't get frightened. I knew I wasn't dreaming. I couldn't move, I didn't speak, and he didn't. I couldn't place him racially—other than I knew he was non-European. I had no idea whatsoever who he was. He just sat there. Then suddenly as he had come, he was gone.[25]

As far as I know, Malcolm does not speak at any other place about this encounter, yet it is worth inquiring into the impact of this visitation on this spiritual leader and on his later pilgrimage to Mecca, where he underwent another transformation. I venture to suggest that this *prevision* is a pre-configuration of his eventual conversion to orthodox Islam, the third *crossing(s)*, a moment of transformation in his changing perspective on the possibility of just human community. The spiritual quest for meaning is always a dynamic process, ever changing in spirals of new insights and visions of possibilities. For leaders who choose to be directed by the deepest yearnings of the Spirit, there emerge critical junctures on the road where one is placed in candidacy for greater revelations of truth. This *prevision* explains, in part, Malcolm's eventual embrace of Islam as the most viable religious and social construction for the creation of a just community. After his visit to Mecca, where he met and prayed with Muslims of all colors and ethnic identities, he declares,

> I am in agreement one hundred per cent with those racists who say that no government laws ever can force brotherhood. The only true world solution today is governments guided by true religion—of the spirit. Here in race-torn America, I am convinced that the Islam religion is desperately needed, particularly by the American black man. The black man needs to reflect that he has been America's most fervent Christian—and where has it gotten him? In fact, in the white man's hands, in the white man's interpretation . . . where has Christianity brought this world?[26]

It is important to note here that after his trip to Mecca, the now el Hajj Malik el-Shabazz *did* believe in the possibility of a just human community, but not under Eurowestern interpretations of religion, politics, and culture. Rather, for him, Islam provided the paradigm for such a creative venture. He was convinced that Eurowestern culture was morally bankrupt and unable to provide the spiritual leadership to create such a world. His appeal to Islam was rooted in his own personal transformation and the potential for justly ordered public policy and law guided by the spiritual genius inherent in Islam. Christianity, in his thinking, had not only forfeited its right to make such an audacious claim, but was impeded by its parochial religious practices that conspired against a universal ethic. For el-Hajj Malik el-Shabazz, it was absolutely necessary that African Americans embrace a spirituality that was critical of and broader than the myopic vision of community perpetrated by Christian churches. He even suggested the imminent demise of Christianity as a rational and moral choice for the world's colored peoples:

> If the so-called "Christianity" now being practiced in America displays the best that world Christianity has left to offer—no one in his right mind

should need any much greater proof that very close at hand is the *end* of Christianity.

Are you aware that some Protestant theologians, in their writings, are using the phrase "post-Christian era"—and they mean *now*?

And what is the greatest single reason for this Christian church's failure? It is the failure to combat racism. It is the old "You sow, you reap" story. The Christian church sowed racism—blasphemously; now it reaps racism.[27]

These three faces of Detroit Red, Malcolm X, and el-Hajj Malik el-Shabazz are routinely interpreted in politico-cultural terms as movements from the apolitical criminal exploitation of his own people, to a black nationalistic perspective inherent in the political discourse of the Nation of Islam, to a Pan-Africanist cultural philosophy reflected in the Afro-American Organization of Unity. But my argument is that spirituality is the most significant variable in the broadening political and cultural perspectives articulated toward the end of his life—and that it was costly. Malcolm *limped* into these perspectives as he encountered deeper meanings and evaluations of himself and religious experience. While Pan-Africanism remained his social, political, and cultural position until his untimely death, and as the changing political context on the national scene contributed to his moderated position relative to whites, the impact of Islam on the potential unity of all peoples was the driving force that informed his post-Mecca political worldview. This last phase of Malcolm's spiritual transformation is representative of a dynamic spirituality rooted in a tragic hope and a prophetic vision of black America's future. While we might ask whether he was leaning toward an integrated society in the United States, his most important legacy is his post-Mecca vision that pointed toward a diasporic, global society built on respect for human rights and justice. Malcolm did not live long enough to see the actualization of this possibility. Until the day of his tragic death, the answer to the question remained just above his head.

How shall we *re-turn* to these visions of Martin and Malcolm and their yearnings for *home*, for global citizenship rooted in the inherent worth and dignity of human beings, without falling into the trap of universalizing our particularity and neglecting the specificity of our struggles of racialized identities imprisoned in the iron cages of modernity and the house that race built? How shall we return to the little house in which we lived and made do and imagine new possibilities of prophetic leadership that call us into mission that is rooted in memories of our past and visions of a new future? How shall we gather the fragments of this past—this endless struggle to achieve and confirm a human identity—without neglecting the larger world house in which we are also dwellers? The answer that we seek is not far from us, ever, but is there in the gaze of the Mother and the body of the innocent Child who is broken and in that brokenness offers its gift to the world. This grotesque figure and gift is just above our heads. *I remember each upon each / the swelling changed planes of my body / and how you first fluttered, then jumped / and I thought it was my heart.*[28]

PART III

Mission

Reliving Our Story

What a journey I have made, the things I have seen. I am but one of you. In my hand I grasp the sailing mast, while my left hand trails in the water. The trees are heavy with figs and olives. A coconut drops to the ground. I have separated myself from myself to sail again on the green Nile waters. I sail to the temple where the gods have gathered to gaze at their faces in deep pools. In my boat the souls of the years sail with me. The hair stands on my head in the wind. I hear the splashing of oars like the cracking of a thin blue shell. Horus keeps one hand on the rudder.

—"Giving Breath to Osiris," *The Egyptian Book of the Dead: The Book of Coming Forth by Day*

Returning to the Little House Where We Lived and Made Do

From my cabin window I look out on the full moon and the ghosts of my forefathers rise and fall with the undulating waves. Across the same waters, how many years ago they came! What were the inchoate mutterings locked tight within the circle of their hearts? In the deep, heavy darkness of the foul smelling hold of the ship, where they could not see the sky nor hear the night noises nor feel the warm compassion of the Tribe, they held their breath against the agony. How does the human spirit accommodate itself to desolation? How did they? *What tools of the spirit were in their hands with which to cut a path through the wilderness of their despair?* If only Death of the body would come to deliver the soul from dying. If some sacred taboo had been defiled and this extended terror was the consequence—there would be no panic in the paying. If some creature of the vast and pulsing jungle had snatched the life away—this would even in its wild fear be floated by the familiarity of the daily hazard. If Death had come being ushered into life by a terrible paroxysm of pain, all the assurance of the Way of the Tribe would have carried the spirit home on the wings of precious ceremony and holy ritual. But this! Nothing anywhere in all the myths, in all the stories in all the ancient memory of the race, had given hint of this torturous convulsion. There were no gods to hear, no magic spell of witch doctor to summon; even one's companion in chains muttered his quivering misery in a tongue unknown and a sound unfamiliar. . . . O my fathers what was it like to be stripped of all supports of life save the beating of the heart and the ebb and flow of fetid

air in the lungs? In a strange manner when you suddenly
caught your breath did some intimation from the future give
to your spirits a wink of promise? In the darkness did you
hear the distant silent feet of your children beating a melody
of freedom to words which you would never know, in a land
in which your bones would be warmed again in the depths
of the cold earth in which you will sleep, unknown, unrealized and alone?
—Howard Thurman, *With Head and Heart* [1]

I am the American heartbreak—
Rock on which Freedom
Stumps its toe—
The great mistake
That Jamestown
Made long ago.
—Langston Hughes, "American Heartbreak"[2]

Returning to the ruins of the little house in which we lived and made do
is a long, arduous journey from a past of wandering in the wilderness
in expectation of a Promised Land that never comes and "mourning
in lonely exile here until the Son of God appears."[3] But only through
remembering, retelling, and reliving our story, appropriating language,
signs, and symbols that conjure new practices for this new rhythm and
time in which we live, can we receive a glimpse of a hopeful future. In
the *meanwhile*, in the in-between-time of death and life, the present situation, the notions of Dilemma and Exodus, as we have portrayed them,
continue to trouble black churches like the old ghost in the house that
didn't die right. We must give ourselves permission to reimagine and
re-language ourselves in diasporic and exilic spaces that provide hospitality and sanctuary to strangers and those from whom we have been

estranged, especially those who are part of a larger global configuration of justice-seeking peoples who are constructing new roads to the future. Stacey Floyd-Thomas wisely reminds us that the black church is the

> fluid historical process in which Black Christians engage one another, invent, embrace, and inherit this tradition that they argue over and care deeply about, whether overtly or not. . . . The Black Church possesses distinctive characteristics and constitutive elements, including key questions, symbols, rituals, ideas, and beliefs that are always subject to adaptation, improvisation, reinterpretation, and even abandonment.[4]

As we attend to our little house where we "made a way out of no way,"[5] we must be aware that we are in a struggle not just for ourselves but for the soul of a nation and the world. There are legions of issues and challenges that threaten the future of our churches and communities, like veritable Goliaths standing on the mountainsides shouting profanities and mocking the powerlessness of the poor, but none is more important than attending to the habitation of the old ghost that is always present, even when it appears to have left, because it is an integral part of our national and cultural imaginaries. When in 2014 and 2015 the controversies and campaigns surrounding the Confederate flag and Black Lives Matter were at the center of public debate, they were really camouflages for a larger issue—a rupture in the soul of a nation and in the church, both signs of the habitation of the old ghost. As the author and critic John Jay Chapman wrote over a century ago, "There was never any moment in our history when slavery was not a sleeping serpent. It lay coiled up under the table during the deliberations of the Constitutional Convention. Owing to the cotton gin it was more than half awake. Thereafter, it was on everyone's mind though not always on his tongue."[6] We not only occupy the small house that race built, but the old ghost continues its occupation as a post-racial, post-9/11 manifestation of empire "coiled up under the table" at nearly every major national and foreign policy decision that is made by our government. As Democrats and Republicans continue to argue over the most appropriate strategies to maintain our geopolitical interests in sovereign nations like Iraq, Iran, and Afghanistan, and how best to respond to the "political terrorism" that has boomeranged into the American psyche since 9/11, black churches in America must be aware that we are witnessing, involved in, and implicated by every decision that is made by our political leaders. We must also recognize that the arrogance and confusion of some of America's top leadership is due to our failure to resolve what Mircea Eliade called the "terror of history." As a nation, we have unfinished business with the raped of the world; and we will not have peace and our children will not enjoy true prosperity until our incomplete story is resolved. Malidoma Patrice Somé has written that the great need in Western civilization is for *ritualized grief*:

> Modernism means *unemotionalism,* or that which owes emotion to the world. It also means loss of memory of the way of acting that encompasses both the body and the soul. To cleanse the modern world from its unresolved problems of the soul, there ought not to be a Memorial Day but a massive funeral day when everyone is expected to shed tears for the titanic loss wrecked by Progress on people's souls.[7]

The truth of the matter, however, is that there is a deeper and more fundamental ailment that plagues the American house than the issues being debated by its political leaders. Like the character in one of Jesus's parables, we have built a house on unsound foundations and the result is a veritable American Tower of Babel. Long before the recent concerns about terrorism, the founding fathers of this nation embarked upon their own campaign of terror that involved exclusion and rejection, genocide and slavery, jingoism and subjugation of the world's peoples. America experienced a "heartbreak," an identity crisis, a stumbling fall from grace: "the mistake that Jamestown made long ago," which renders our almost fanatical public conversations about "liberty" and "rights" contradictory and hypocritical.[8] If healing is to come to America and the world, it will not come from the children of the builders of the American

Tower of Babel (the children of the fathers who have eaten sour grapes and whose teeth are decayed); rather, it must come from "stones that the builders rejected." This is a strange statement, given the spiritual and moral eclipse that has occurred in the communities of the poor in our nation, but my fundamental premise is that God specializes in building new worlds with the stones that the builders rejected and dispersed; with the little ones who have nothing in their hands but slingshots and a few smooth stones. But these little ones, the rejected and dispersed, the scattered and scattering, must first have the courage to enter the valley and do battle with the Giants.[9]

This call for courage in the work of liberation begins with imaginative and analytical *bricolage*—excluding, including, and reconfiguring; conjuring new signs, symbols, and visions in new spaces and in new rhythms of time. It is what Morrison means by "willed creation"—taking the dispersed fragments of memory and creatively reordering, regrouping, reimagining, and reinterpreting them for this new moment. She quotes the Norwegian painter Edvard Munch: "It is not enough for a work of art to have ordered planes and lines. If a stone is tossed at a group of children, they hasten to scatter. A regrouping, an action has been accomplished. This is composition. This regrouping, presented by means of color, lines, and planes, is an artistic and painterly motif."[10] The reconfiguration need not mimic literality as in stoic realism, but is more like an artistic composition—like a painting, a gospel song, or a retold tale. What might this new configuration of space and time look like for black churches at this critical passage? I suggest three common (verbal) tasks that call us together into *common(s)*: congregating, conjuring, and conspiring. But first, we must *turn*.

Congregating, Conjuring, and Conspiring in the Common(s): Congregating in Diasporas and Exiles

Black churches in this century must learn the power of congregating among the diasporas and exiles of this new century as part of the

Pentecost discussed earlier. Pentecost represents the divine initiative and intent for diversity in creation and creating, in contrast to the effort to dominate and subject the other to an inscripted, monolithic code of empire where we speak only one language and pledge allegiance only to given signs. Pentecost, rather, is a warning and a call to be "bound up together" as a source of strength and a call to struggle for the inclusion of the powerless. Frances Harper, the eloquent educator and abolitionist, declared at the Eleventh Women's Rights Convention in 1866, "We are all bound up together in one great bundle of humanity, and society cannot trample upon the weakest and feeblest of its members without receiving the curse in its own soul."[11] This process of congregating, of being "bound up together," involves weeping, confession, and resistance, as suggested, but it also means speaking, acting, writing, dancing, and *turning* in the Fire of the Holy Ghost and listening and embracing others' many languages and histories. It means revisiting the questions of our identities and loyalties as scattered and scattering peoples. Occupying the haunted house of the national imaginary has cost us dearly and prevented many churches from realizing their power as global citizens of the world.

There are historical precedents for this new moment. We have witnessed this possibility through the living testimonies of figures from our past such as Martin Delany, Bishop Henry McNeal Turner, Bishop Daniel Payne, Marcus Garvey, Lott Carey, Ida B. Wells, Frances Harper, James Robinson, Pauli Murray, Samuel Dewitt Proctor, Martin Luther King, and el-Hajj Malik el-Shabazz. In the Fire of the Holy Ghost, black churches will receive power to cast out the old, unholy ghost that works relentlessly to prevent these diasporic and exilic conversations. Through conjuring and conspiring we can learn the power of celebrating difference and plurality of languages, voices, visions, and signs of a new age that is already within and upon us. It is only in the embrace of the dynamism of the Holy Ghost symbolized by the experience of Pentecost that we can see and prophesy deliverance for our people and oppressed peoples of the world.

Congregating (*congregare*)[12]—gathering, binding, and coming together—involves repenting by rethinking, regretting, *turning away*, and *turning to*.[13] Black church leadership and scholars have excellent opportunities to begin this work of repenting (*turning away* and *turning to*) by acknowledging and receiving the voices and visions of the new movements of the Spirit in our midst. The pastor and scholar Raphael Warnock has called for a *fifth moment*, the *flowering of a self-critical liberationist community*, which would integrate the preceding moments in the history of black churches and bring together black academic theologians and black church leaders in a broadening communal space for dialogue, risk taking, and testing reminiscent of the National Conference of Black Churchmen or the Black Theology Project.[14] While Warnock points to the *fifth moment* as an invitation and opportunity for black theologians and pastors to work together, the three critical shifts in black social/political, theological/ethical, and aesthetic/existential contexts discussed here complicate the conversation and ask complex questions about the ways black church institutional identity actually conspires with its oppression through language and praxis in a postracial era and makes recommendations for its healing and liberation. Like Warnock, I argue that this is the task of black theological scholars and church leaders (lay and pastoral), but it first involves repenting from acquiescence to the seductive powers of the old ghost that insinuates itself into nation language and surreptitiously designs liturgy, preaching, and engagement in antiquated metaphors that disguise the *glocal* challenges of leadership. The ghost ensnares its hosts in a moral language of utilitarian individualism that promotes prosperity as the province of the abstract, ahistorical individual who can magically summon wealth and health by speaking the word of faith, instead of challenging the structural and cultural forces that perpetuate the drama of the lake of fire that burns day and night in most of the communities that our churches serve. The deep sleep of black church leadership wrought by this possessive individualism and its embedded appetitive yearnings for capital, bourgeois lifestyles, and recognition breeds suspicion, resentment, and rejection of the poor. Therefore, even more must be done: repentance involves *turning to*, in this case by creating spaces of different forms and styles of leadership where the socially and politically disrespected, dismissed, excluded, "impure," and "grotesque" can gather in our diasporic and exilic quest for *home*.

Traditional formulations of power and the concomitant obligations that accrue from ecclesial authority have changed. Church leaders must assume a more humble posture and allow the "new wine" to construct and shape the "wineskins" and the new languages for this time. For example, the young activists who resisted the presence of traditional civil rights and religious leaders in the early days of the Ferguson movement signal to the church and the academy that a change has already taken place. "This movement was started by the young people," twenty-five-year-old Johnetta Elzie of St. Louis said at the December 13, 2014, march in Ferguson, Missouri. "We started this. There should be young people all over this stage. This should be young people all up here."[15] Some thought that this kind of public display of "disrespect" for elders meant that young activists had no sense of the great sacrifices made by the civil rights leaders who preceded them or the noble traditions of respectability that made much of the progress that we witness possible. Perhaps they were correct, but maybe the charged and impatient young folk had good reason. While many of our churches and civil rights organizations fell asleep in pursuit of the ghost's fantastic hegemonic treasure disguised in the radical egalitarian hypothesis, at least two to three generations of African Americans were born into cycles of poverty, incarceration, and miseducation not known since Reconstruction.[16] For the last fifty years, we have witnessed an accompanying deterioration of black civil society institutions that has left many black youth bereft of memory of the cultural narratives and procedural knowledge that preceded them. So when contemporary young activists not only question the "politics of respectability" but repudiate it as well, should we be surprised?

The debate over the "politics of respectability" has been raised from academics, ministers, and journalists regarding the boisterous and rude "take-no-prisoners" approach of many of the young activists. One of the outstanding critics is Harvard Law professor Randall Kennedy, who offered the "respectability perspective":

> As brutal and frustrating as our era can be, however, day by day it offers more racial decency than any previous era. At no point in American history has there been more overall freedom from antiblack racial impediments. At no point has there been more reason for young black men and women to be hopeful that investing in themselves will pay dividends in the future. At no point has a progressive black respectability politics made more sense.[17]

Similarly, Barbara Reynolds, an ordained minister and syndicated columnist in the *Washington Post*, raised the questions of respectability and strategy. She was also deeply concerned about the ways elders involved in the nonviolent movement have been dismissed as irrelevant and why moral suasion embodied in nonviolent resistance is not considered the most viable option for progress:

> The loving, nonviolent approach is what wins allies and mollifies enemies. But what we have seen come out of Black Lives Matter [BLM] is rage and anger—justifiable emotions, but questionable strategy. For months, it seemed that BLM hadn't thought beyond that raw emotion, hadn't questioned where it would all lead. I and other elders openly worried that, without a clear strategy and well-defined goals, BLM could soon crash and burn out.[18]

Kennedy and Reynolds responded not only to young activists but to the arguments of scholars who strongly identify with the strategy and tactics of the young leaders.[19] For instance, when the *Washington Post* journalist

Jonathan Capehart implicitly appealed to the politics of respectability in his lament of the Ferguson grand jury's decision clearing Officer Darren Wilson of charges associated with Michael Brown's death, the Africana studies professor Brittney Cooper at Rutgers University responded,

> Jonathan, surely you know a suit and tie won't protect you. So we're going to keep on marching, as you said. And we will keep holding aloft the banner of Michael Brown. We will do so, because Black folks have already tested out your theory of respectability. We've been trying to save our lives by dressing right, talking right and never, ever fucking up since about 1877. That shit has not worked.[20]

In some ways, reformist perspectives such as Kennedy's, Reynolds's, and Capehart's provide a broader lens through which to see respectability as a reasonable strategy for change. But what they do not seem to acknowledge is that the ground has shifted, and that while respectability was the politics of the past, it is now gone (forever), and if it is to have any role in the movements of the future it must be *revised*, not *revived*. The incredible pain and nihilism that have already possessed communities of poor, black, Latino, and disadvantaged youth must be taken into account in any serious response to what is being perceived as disrespectful, nonstrategic behavior in public spaces. Even scarier is that some young activists see many of the old guard as part of the problem, and perhaps *we* are—perhaps *we* are all ensnared by the trickery of the old ghost.

The disruptive behavior of some Black Lives Matter leaders is hardly the problem that we are facing in this nation at almost every level of social and political engagement, and they certainly should not be scapegoated for trying to be heard above all the cacophony and screaming that transpire in public spaces. As Black Lives Matter began its campaign after Michael Brown's death, there were other movements that had set the tone on the national scene, not the least being the Occupy movement.[21] Simultaneously we witnessed the escalation of the incendiary rhetoric of the U.S. Congress that began in the mid-1990s and the presidential campaigns of 2004, 2008, and 2015–2016. A "spirit of meanness" and incivility haunts American politics that spills over into other publics and touches our collective and personal lives.[22] Our universities and colleges are increasingly becoming sites of this haunting. The social psychologist Jonathan Haidt and Greg Lukianoff, president and CEO of the Foundation for Individual Rights in Education, suggest that we now have a new kind of extreme political correctness that is manifest in "microaggressions," "trigger warnings," and an overall climate of "protective vindictiveness." Issues at stake are freedom of speech, particularity, and a growing sense of individualism, which is not surprising given the larger cultural ethos that is played out dramatically on campuses around the nation and in political contests.[23]

There is an unspoken dilemma, therefore, in the respectability debate, because the focus on Black Lives Matter can easily obscure and downplay the dangers of the left-wing liberal/progressive and conservative/regressive combative discourse at all levels of society. The tendency of educational, religious, and public leaders to ignore the historical embodiment of race, class, gender, sexuality, and power in the discursive practices of American culture is a glaring concern not only for "Respectables" (to use Cooper's term) but for the question of American character. The larger question, therefore, is, How do we find a space in our civil society institutions where the battle over ideas does not descend into expulsion and exclusion from the debate? The political commentator Peter Beinart in the *Daily Beast* proposed a return to something that Arthur Schlesinger famously called a "vital center," that space in democratic contestation of ideas where the left and the right practice civility in speech and actions. In 1991 Schlesinger wrote,

Instead of a transformative nation with an identity of its own, America increasingly sees itself as preservative of old identities. Instead of a nation composed of individuals making their own free choices, America increasingly sees itself as composed of groups more or less indelible in their ethnic character. The national ideal had once been *e pluribus unum*. Are we now to belittle *unum* and glorify *pluribus*? Will the center hold? Or will the melting pot yield to the Tower of Babel?[24]

As suggested earlier, I think that the American Tower of Babel has already occurred, and that however our common spaces are reconfigured for this time, they will need to acknowledge their plural and temporal characters in light of the quickly changing demographics, globalization, and digitalization of the globe.

In addition, it is not of small significance that Black Lives Matter arose during an era of postmodernist claims of plurality of values in which asymmetry informs the ways we frame classical virtues like respect, truth, beauty, and excellence.[25] It is possible, therefore, to ask a more difficult question regarding youth and others who feel left out and forsaken by those in power or at least those perceived to be. Is the youthful activism in our communities only the response to the killing of black men and women by the police, or is it part of a larger resistance against institutionalized power in general that is perceived as disinterested, corrupt, and unjust—and are we, black church leaders and scholars, indicted by our own embrace and embodiment of the same? I think it is possible to frame the question in a way that seeks to respond to the overwhelming anger and rage—and yes, violence—that have swept across this nation like contagious diseases (which they are) and to the deeply felt concerns of many who remember the valorous sacrifices of the past, but we must have *conversations* in order to get there. Therefore, a critical task of *congregating* in a new *common(s)* will mean giving equal time and space for conversation and debate that is respectful of the disrespectful and patient with the impatient, and that probes the larger contextual issues of injustice, nihilism, and violence that are a part of our everyday worlds. This does not mean that elders completely forsake institutional roles and functions that empower and assist liberative efforts, but it does mean a new way of looking at, listening to, and learning from those young leaders in our midst. There is so much that can be taught and so much to learn if existing leaders dare listen and find ways to share power and visions of the possible.

In many ways Ferguson, Missouri, has become a symbol of what is on the rise among a growing and diverse cadre of new leaders. Here the conversation in black churches across denominational and religious lines becomes "up front and personal." In addition to finding ways to include the young and the restless, we must also include LGBTQIA (lesbian, gay, bisexual, transgender, queer, intersex, asexual, and allied) individuals,[26] crip and others in the vocabulary of leadership for the moment that has already arrived. While there are notable examples that have begun, there is still much to do.[27] In many ways, the strings of letters are incomplete and represent new methods by which our moral and theological grammar must be reconfigured and expanded to announce the advent of the Holy Ghost and Fire in our common tasks of speaking, listening, embodying, reading, and acting in and through diversity in creation.

Repenting insists that many of our black churches awaken from their apathetic slumber and join others, most notably the estranged and strangers in exile who sit in our pews, to transform the intersections of lifeworlds and systems on the *common(s)*. The language of *common(s)*, popularized by the scholars Michael Hardt and Antonio Negri, offers a new way of interpreting the role of empire in a post-9/11 world, where capital and democracy have become synonymous with biopolitical practices of conquest that play out in forms of production in the natural environment and in social interaction, which include "codes, languages, affects, information, and other forms of knowledge."[28] Religious scholars, for the most part, have identified the multifaceted ways empire has triumphed since 9/11 in preemptive strikes, hypersurveilling techniques, and the rapid growth of powerful corporations and transnational capital, and they have attended to calls for reconciliation and transformation.[29] For black churches and their leadership, I am emphasizing *common(s)* in the latter sense of social interaction, where coding, languages, affects, information, and forms of knowledge impact anemic African American lifeworlds, especially among our youth. The *common(s)* is a social/political/cultural space where black religious scholars and church leaders must congregate and ask themselves difficult questions about ways to reappropriate signs and symbols, and reinterpret them for the work of resurrecting the dead. It is also the space of work and engagement against empire, the principalities and powers, the spiritual wickedness of the ghost that has wrecked the lives of our children and thrown them in the fire that burns day and night—a natal alienation, a second death, before they have lived. As Jesus asked the father of the son who was seized by a demonic power, "How long has this been happening to him?" And he said, "From childhood. It has often thrown him both into the fire and into the water to destroy him. But if you can do anything, take pity on us and help us!" And Jesus said to him, "'If you can.' All things are possible to him who believes."[30]

Scholars of black church studies have an opportunity to provide curricular strategies and practices in these spaces, but they often encounter resistance at every *turn*. Yet repenting is a dynamic, ongoing practice of counter-resistance that continues to *turn* as in a spiraling dance, always in a space of *turning*, revolving, inwardly ingressing, and outwardly egressing—always *turning*. *Turning* involves repenting from singularity, hierarchy, patrilineality, from unhealthy language, signs, and symbols of the old ghost and the relentless struggle over power, capital, and the small trophies of recognition and respect over who are the *keepers of knowledge* (as the *author*-ity, first, the *archè*, the *archi*vist). Some of the most vicious struggles over power occur in black churches (the list is long and need not be revisited here). Likewise, scholars who come to the churches with their gifts must be as humble as the Magi, knowing that they come to serve and worship the Child whom the Madonna embraces—and to hold in tension the sharp analytical tools that deaden the spirit and the sincere adoration of the host who brings life to the dead. Therefore, the kind of rethinking that we must do involves nothing less than a revolution of values and priorities—that is, a critique of black churchly and theological cultures and of the ecclesiastical and academic practices of transacting and bargaining in the basements of globalized capital while so many people perish from lack of basic life needs like food, education, natural environmental resources, safety, and health.[31]

The very theological presuppositions and value assumptions upon which many of our churches exist must be *turned* around. We must repent all forms of idolatry, worship of the old ghost. "Every idea of [God] we form, [God] must in mercy shatter."[32] Many of the images of God that we worship are antithetical to the very mission that we are called to be and do in the world. The Jesus that many of our churches worship is not the liberator from Nazareth, but a false god created in the image of Euro-American oppressors. The late Ed Riddick was correct when he announced, "The white Jesus Christ is dead! He died somewhere between Hiroshima and Nagasaki and on the road to Selma, Alabama—and he must never be resurrected again as the Christ!"[33] Any church that does not view Jesus as the Crucified One from Golgotha, who died on a garbage heap outside Jerusalem for the sake of the poor and disenfranchised of the world, stands against the holy purposes of God. We must not teach our children to worship the ghost that haunts their young spirits and leads them into a future of inferiority and powerlessness. While we must engage the many public faces of evil, the most important revolution that we wage must first begin within our little houses that lie in ruins where the ground has shifted. It is in this *turning* that we encounter the Holy Ghost as the *Paraclete* (Gr. παράκλητος, Lat. *paracletus*), who is called alongside our reevaluation of ecclesiastical and theological authority to advocate annulling our orphanage and genealogical isolation, who empowers us to claim our citizenship as people of God. But even more is at stake in this critical moment that provides us entrée into a global conversation on what it means to be a cosmopolitan congregation sharing in the various diasporas and exiles of the world, which requires conjuring new narratives and signaling new possibilities for reimagining *home*.[34]

Conjuring in Diasporas and Exiles

Conjuring is a tool of the spirit that involves the critical task of remembering and retelling our stories as a reappropriation of the past, as history, and as long memory. *Conjuring* is a retelling and reliving of our many-layered and intertwined stories that garner a new sense of time—in and out of *Epiphenomenal time, negotiating transcendence*—in search of a livable and flourishing future. To use the language of the late Richard Iton, it is the "search of the black fantastic," "a genre that destabilizes, at least momentarily, our understandings of the distinctions between the reasonable and the unreasonable, and reason itself, the proper and the improper, and propriety itself, by bringing into the field of play those potentials we have forgotten, or did not believe accessible or feasible."[35] As such it signifies on modernist claims of knowledge and truth and revisits the quest for (black) subjectivity that is unsequestered by linguistic-legal-moral forms of bondage that are "immune to deep egalitarian reimagining and restructuring."[36] A key that helps us to gain access to this pragmatic theological approach is the African American genius of appropriation and bodily improvisation of mood.

My use of the term *conjure* is derived from several sources. One use of the term is rooted in its older, etymological meaning of swearing, taking an oath as a moral and legal act. Conjuration implies both a conjuring trick and the practice of swearing an oath.[37] Here my major concern is with "naming" the ghost, this apparition that appears/disappears, inhabits/inherits, and is untouchable/intangible because it does not really exist. It is ideology born of the rise of capital, according to Marx, which appears on the stage of history as a table séance, a levitating table that stands on its head and from its head generates innumerable phantoms; it simultaneously mutates, shape-shifts into other forms, though it is still that same ghost that has no material origin but exists in an imaginary space between body and idea, a ghostly chimera, a monster or demon that inhabits bodies. It is anachronous—it is out of time; it is out of joint because it does not abide by the constitution of time. It conjugates and conjures as in swearing an allegiance. So whence cometh this ghost? How might we seize it and make it speak and tell us its name—its identity—so that we can exorcise it? But alas, it does not give a name; it changes its name; it elides, escapes, appears, and disappears, because it is a ghost, the ephemeral and timeless; it is an ideology born in hell, of nothingness where being is born, recycled, resurrected, and returned to the Void.

The language of conjuration is also related to *mourning* (weeping, confession, and resistance) and *inheritance* (genealogical inheritance). It involves the swearing of an oath of fidelity to a covenant that rejects the ghost that possesses and protects itself (it projects itself into the sensuous activity of the agent but is not sensuous, but supersensible, i.e., transcendent, hence normative; it dictates speech, action, and counteraction). This *inheritance* that is the subject of *mourning* displaces human activity because it alienates sensuous action and thought from its subjugated vessel; it possesses the possessed and protects itself through the culturally produced actions and thoughts of the possessed. It creates an anachronous effect of dismemberment, forgetfulness, and hence alienation from history and time. Post-racialism, as I have argued, is a ghost, a chimera, a mutant shape-shifter, an ideological host for innumerable parasitic guests that feed on its victims; a haunt that inhabits its species and returns in multiple configurations and signs that distort meaning and eviscerates hope because hope requires memory. So the question is, How do we or can we *mourn* the titanic loss of memory, inheritance, the horror of human enslavement and desperation/despairing without falling into the clutches of the ghost that haunts, inhabits, and dictates meaning? What might be new ways (practices) of mourning the dead and the living dead and claiming a new inheritance as a people of God when the language of God is fraught and bound by the captivity of the ghost? Who frees God from the linguistic prison of the ghost? Might conjuration mean something else, something unheard of—which escapes the ghost's clutches, the ghost that exists in the ephemeral but is incarnate in the agent? How do we return, if possible, to the body, to *enfleshed life*—the sensuous activity of bodily existence, a sense of wholeness, a remembered self, an integral, integrated sense of self that does not pay homage to the greedy, grinning gods of modernity? Is the body the site of this emancipation? How might we reread the Pauline injunction, "Be transformed by the renewal of your body so that you might approve what is good, perfect, and noble"? A return to the body, I am arguing, is transformative praxis, a redistillation, reconstitution of material life, a return of origins-creations-reactivation of *fluid center(s)* that are manipulative, ever at the disposal of reforming, transforming of consciousness of the body and spirit—that exorcises, evacuates the ghost—a return to bodily knowing, intelligence, and wisdom; not to ontology, theology, or abstract reasoning, which is the domain of the ghost, but sensuous, organic materiality ("the smell of life," to use Anderson's apt interpretation of Howard Thurman's phraseology),[38] where we are bodily baptized by Fire and the Holy Ghost. This is the work of the artist, the *bricoleur*, the refashioner, the shift-shaping agency of the trickster who exists in contradiction and parody and paradox. (See our earlier discussion of Stuckey, where the trickster plays a tune, sound, breath, wind that wakes the dead/living dead.)

So, as African American church leaders and scholars congregate in *common(s)* with others, young and old, *Respectables* and disrepectables, gay and straight, cis- and trans-gender, we must *conjurate*, swear an oath that is binding, pledge allegiance to each other in all of our differences and to the God of Pentecost who creates and celebrates diversity, that we will remain bound together until the work of building a new world house is done. Our conjuring in the *common(s)* implores us to see beyond the narrow, fixated, restricted agency that leaves us orphanaged in the old house that was built by the ghost that taught us the language of singularity and capital. Moreover, it means that we must create from the linguistic debris of this past, a new "word house" in which to live and to bequeath to our children as our inheritance.

The other way of thinking about conjure is its use in African American religio-magical practices (Voodoo/Hoodoo) in the Deep South.

According to Albert Raboteau, *conjure* arose out of slave culture as a response to "irrational suffering": "not only was conjure a theory for explaining the mystery of evil, but it was also a practice for doing something about it."[39] In other words, *conjure* has a pragmatic function: it is a tool that allows revisability and reformulation of materiality and the perceived purposes of given phenomena that can be changed, mixed, and remixed to accommodate other presenting needs.

Several years ago, I discovered firsthand the level of skill and dexterity associated with *conjuring* as a practical, material act. I was rushing to a meeting and discovered that someone had left the back door of my car ajar and the battery had died. In my desperation, I began dialing my emergency road service. As I was dialing, a huge red truck with its motors roaring appeared in my driveway. Inside was a rugged but smiling angelic face. I asked what I could do for him. He explained that he was there at my wife's request to cut down an ailing tree in the backyard. Seizing an opportunity to get my car started, I asked if he had jumper cables. He replied that he did not, but he seemed surprised that I did not have any in my garage. Embarrassed, I told him that it had been years since I needed jumper cables. As I was talking, he interrupted me and pointed to an old set of cables on a shelf in the back of the garage. He took a look at the cables, placed one set of clamps on my battery and the rather worn set on his. He asked me to turn the motor on—but nothing happened. My stomach dropped and I resigned myself to fate—but not this handyman! He immediately looked for a knife in the garage, found an old blunted excuse for the same, and began stripping the plastic covering and calcium deposits until he had a clean sliver of bright copper wire. He reconnected the cable to our respective vehicles, and like magic, my engine turned over. For that moment, he was a *conjurer*, a *bricoleur*, a handyman who constructed a solution from the materials at hand.

This pragmatic use of *conjure* is also related to what Theophus Smith calls "conjuring culture," the imaginative art of taking that which is at hand, that which experience gives us, and imaginatively refashioning it into creative tools, which is a part of a *"pharmacopeic tradition of practices."*[40] Hence, I am using *conjuring* as a type of "spiritual alchemy" related to "bricolage," the process of inclusion, exclusion, and reconfiguration of experience through an internal locus that seeks vindication and wholeness in material and cultural space.[41] *Conjuring* also has a trickster quality—it insinuates as it signifies on consciousness by releasing it into a domain of freedom before it realizes that it is free.[42]

Tools of the spirit refer to the different ways spirituality and forms of cultural imagination (cultural narratives, myths, rituals, and aesthetic triggers) can be used to activate and inform experiential and reflective learning, critical thinking, and moral judgment. After participating in a collective act of aesthetic creation, agents view the world differently. Black preaching, as a collective antiphonal, call-and-response event, is an example of one of the marvelous ways imagination is triggered through cultural narratives and becomes a medium through which one is translated into a space of hearing the first-order, primal utterance of speech that is revelatory, eventful, and liberating. "Preaching the Word" as an eventful narration of the-past-come-alive is to experience the body-heat intimacy of revelation. The liberating word is near and calling us, writes the Apostle, intimately connected and configured into our very existences; it is *in* our faces, in our minds and hearts like a champion fighting for the silenced, daring us to hear, see, believe, and speak, and to act on their behalf. We are transformed by a word that comes our way and that "liberates us from the frightening restrictions that bind us to what is present—and from the anxiety of our hearts." In fact, we "need the Word more for hearing than speaking, for believing than acting."[43] One has only to listen to the legendary orators of the black preaching tradition to find an example of *conjuring* along these lines. C. L. Franklin's sermon "The Valley of Dry Bones" reveals the conjuring of cultural narratives of Euro-American interpretations of the Promised Land and the ways African American interpreters subverted the narrative as part of their liberatory praxis. Franklin extracts what Ray L. Hart calls *linguistic debris* to "raise a word house for first-order language."[44] Similarly, contemporary scholar/preachers like Renita J. Weems take the unwanted scrapings (*linguistic debris*) of biblical traditions and *conjure* polyvalent potions that challenge, correct, and comfort while opening new ways of reading, thinking, healing, and acting in the church and society.[45] Such are the pragmatic, cultural, and spiritual usages of conjuring that I am espousing, but this sense of conjuring also includes a theological task of re-creating.

Conjuring Creation

In theological terms, *conjuring* is keenly related to our understandings of creation and the fall. Willie James Jennings has identified the renarrating of the Christian doctrine of creation as an urgent and critical work of contemporary scholars who are concerned with the insidious ways racial ontology both confers and wheedles itself into nationalistic and cultural imaginaries. He suggests that in the hegemonic project of colonialism, Europeans "performed a deeply theological act that mirrored the identity and action of God in creating."[46] In assuming the role of a divine creative council, they not only defined and subjugated races, but also transitioned and reconfigured land and territory as part of the domain of the project of whiteness. He argues, "Theorists and theories of race will not touch the ground until they reckon with the foundations of racial imaginings in the deployment of an altered theological vision of creation. We must narrate not only the alteration of bodies, but of space itself." Reconfiguring or *conjuring* space as a creative and energetic domain of the Holy Ghost, who leads us into truth, is both an exploration in the interiority of religious experience and a call to bear witness in the various public spaces occupied by the dominating forces of the ghost. Haunted houses and captive spaces of black life are areas of this focus. The conjuring of common spaces or common(s), in this respect, finds affinity with what Howard Thurman called the *search for common ground.*[47] Thurman was a *conjurer*, an opener of the way whose prophetic imagination provides us with "tools of the spirit" that interrogate and implicate the ghostly masquerades of race and postcolonial fascism.[48]

Thurman's reinterpretation of the creation and the fall as a way of reclaiming a sense of space in black bodies is a helpful point of entry into the larger project of black churches and scholars in remembering, retelling, and reliving their stories. *Common ground*, for Thurman, is a conjured space of consciousness, which seeks intersubjective connectedness with the other. I am aware of the criticisms of his essentialist, onto-eschatological perspective, and I am reconstructing his notion to speak to pluralities, temporalities, and allegiances to work together in *common(s)*, which are conjured spaces where agents congregate, disperse, and return again in acts of "willed creation."[49] In order to gain a sense of Thurman's project along these lines, we may find it helpful to follow the movement from his initial inquiry in *The Search for Common Ground*, which interrogates mythological memory as part of remembering the story of creation. He first asks, "What is there that seems to be implicit, or inherent in [human] racial memory that is on the side of community?"[50] Second, he examines sources of imagined futures (*utopias*), or what he calls "the prophet's dream" as a way of retelling or re-visioning the story of creation.[51] He then returns with his application to his contemporary setting in the midst of the fading modern civil rights movement and the ascendency of Black Power, and asks new ambassadors of freedom to relive the story of creation, which involves renarrating and remaking the world, finding *common ground*, or, in my reconstructed sense, *common(s)*.

For Thurman, creation and the fall are neither metaphysical nor doctrinal in any fixed sense; rather, they are mythological constructions with existential and psychosocial implications that correspond to the ontological categories of *innocence* (*that which is untested*) and *brokenness* (*dismemberment*). Thurman examined the creation myths of the Hebrew and Christian traditions and the Hopi Indians and maintained that a consistent theme in both accounts is the association of *"creation with the harmony of innocence; the loss of innocence with the disintegra-*

tion of harmony."[52] In each account, he opines, the remembered original experience of community by humans is both *potential and actualized potential within the framework of innocence.* In this hypothesized original state of innocence, the things that work against community are dormant or unactualized, but once they are actualized by knowledge and the agency of human free will, dismemberment results and innocence is lost.[53] I am suggesting that the loss of innocence in the colonization of (black) subjects has affinity with what Jennings called the "conference and creation of whiteness,"[54] in that this act of idolatry both transitions and marks the fall as a loss of innocence within persons, in interpersonal relationships, in divine-human relationships, in nature and the body— and most importantly, in the alteration of a sense of space and time.

Once innocence as a mythological space is lost it can never be restored; it can be refashioned or reimagined, but not restored to its original state. The religious imagination posits innocence as a state of being untested, untouched, undisturbed, undefiled, and pure; but after the "fall from innocence" (the interruption and sequester of bodies and land through colonial conquest), the divine-human project toward a "sense of wholeness" (*integrity*) becomes the goal toward which human endeavor must be directed. Unlike innocence, *integrity* must be achieved through free, responsible actions. Integrity, therefore, as self-actualized potential, is predicated on human agency, as in *negotiated transcendence*, to make conscious, deliberate choices to strive for wholeness, harmony, and integration within the *enfleshed* self, in relations with others, and in the world. A consistent theme, therefore, is that *innocence is given without knowledge (experience); integrity, or a sense of wholeness, however, is achieved through knowledge, freedom, and responsibility. Integrity,* as it relates to (black) *enfleshed* existence, is achieved through acts of freedom, defiance, and resistance against the cauterizing assaults of racial constructions of the self. As Thurman writes,

> When the quality of goodness has been reestablished, a great change has taken place. Eyes are opened, knowledge is defined, and what results is

the triumph of the quality of innocence over the quality of discord; a new synthesis is achieved that has in it the element of triumph. That is, a child is innocent, but a man who has learned how to winnow beauty out of ugliness, purity out of stain, tranquility out of tempest, joy out of sorrow, life out of death—only such a man may be said to be good. But he is no longer innocent.[55]

Hence *innocence* and *brokenness* (creation and fall) sit side by side in dialectical relation within the agent; and a *sense of wholeness* (*integrated* or *remembered*) is actualized (or synthesized) through sustained spiritual practices that are "tools of the spirit." Creation is not a static notion, but an ongoing, dynamic process of innocence, brokenness, and wholeness being relived in a continuing, spiraling narrative of enfleshed life.

Thurman's response to first seeing the coasts of Africa was not unlike many African Americans' response to finally seeing the motherland,[56] but what is most striking about the meditation at the beginning of this chapter is the question that informs this discussion: "How does the human spirit accommodate itself to desolation? How did they? What *tools of the spirit* were in their hands with which to cut a path through the wilderness of their despair?"[57] Thurman's thinking and experience with mysticism as a resource for personal and social transformation, and most importantly, for his own struggle with problematized racial identity give us some insight into his probing query. His personal quest for a sense of wholeness and his theological project address the profoundly human issue of "feeling like a problem," the overriding sense of guilt and shame, and the need to imagine a new sense of space and time for black diasporic bodies. What then might the *tools of the spirit* offered to us by Thurman's *conjuring* of race, religion, and culture in the Deep South, the cosmopolitan centers of San Francisco, Boston, and his revelation aboard a ship, a *chronotope*, that reverses and rehearses his ancestor's journey to here from there, say to black churches in the twenty-first century as we negotiate our journey from Dilemma to Diasporas, from Exodus to Exiles, and from the Frying Pan to the Fire?

Common ground, or in my language, *common(s)*, therefore, as a *conjured* space of consciousness is the product of disciplined, intentional acts of intersubjectivity in quest of a *sense of wholeness* within material, historical, and psychosocial configurations of space and time. It is also an active, ongoing, unfinished, spiraling, self-reflexive, narrated project of remembering, retelling, and reliving between the human and divine—in sum, a conversation with God. (Thurman's early work on these themes finds creative affinity with Du Bois's *blue sky* and with Morrison's *other (livable) place*, which will be discussed in a later chapter, both of which function as correlates of innocence and as antitheses to *habitus*, which I will refer to as the *implanted jungle*, a site of *brokenness*.)[58] *Common ground* involves a tussling of negotiated transcendence to name a space *called one's own*, a finding of *home* in one's body and in the world regardless of place or context.

> To be known, to be called by one's name, is to find one's place and hold it against all the hordes of hell. This is to know one's value, for one's self alone. It is to honor an act as one's very own, it is to live a life that is one's very own, it is to bow before an altar that is one's very own, it is to worship a God who is one's very own.[59]

This space is also a *fluid center* or *fluid area of consent*, a core of possibility, resilience, and resistance that will not yield even in the severest of circumstances, *le point le verge*.[60]

There is, therefore, in the process of becoming whole or establishing a sense of at-home-ness, a *debt* to be paid to history and time, a sacrifice at *crossing(s)*, if you will, to enter the holy of holies, which is one's own sacred space, one's own belonging to self and to God. It is not given, but must be taken, wrested from the hands of fate, a fate designed and maintained by the trickery, artifices, and strategies of the ghost. Beyond the accidents of birth, family heritage, and social location that are given by virtue of being in the world, one's destiny is carved through the thick existential thickets of one's becoming.[61] *Historical debt*, as I am calling it, is the price exacted for knowledge, freedom, and possibility; it is the condition of the birthing of conscious existence: the movement from imagined primal innocence to new awareness of human possibility and freedom. "The transition from innocence to knowledge is always perilous and fraught with hazard."[62] The "order, continuities, and cooperative processes of life" as potential are wrecked by the ravages of human consciousness coming to itself and struggling to wrest goodness, a sense of flourishing, from the clutches of fatedness by the continuing conferences and creations of post-racial masquerades. These are not mere binary, oppositional forces, but *fluid center(s)* out of which opposition appears, *fluid center(s)* of consciousness manifesting in varied and myriad forms of creative vitality and intelligence.

The task of creating and claiming (black) subjectivity—that is, achieving and confirming a human identity—then, is the journey to *home*, the quest for meaning, understanding, and purpose in the midst of tragic existence, and it is this quest that marks *fluid center(s)* of innocence and becoming. To use Terrence Johnson's expression, it is "tragic soul-life."[63] As an analytical tool, tragic black soul-life provides a comprehensive means for critically engaging black churches' national imaginary of "dead space" or an "unaccomplished imaginative shift from enslaved to freed subjectivity and the marked gap between genealogical isolation and the ancestral past";[64] it is also a means for examining the institutions and systems (religion, politics, economics, etc.) that help to perpetuate injustice. Furthermore, tragic soul-life decenters the oppressive realities of the black experience in America, and posits black cultural aesthetics as a bulwark against oppression and a necessary aid to the development of a sense of wholeness. As indicated earlier, the black body as a site of *somaesthetics* is a vital dimension of this imaginative and creative struggle to achieve and maintain a sense of self and flourishing in the world. In fact, the character of the aesthetic and moral struggle is shaped by the frustration experienced when the ends one seeks to fulfill are limited by ambiguity, contingency, difference, and structural and cultural constraints. Frustration, moral angst, is always tied to private and personal outreach; but when private and personal ends are extended beyond self, the struggle ensues. There is no escape from the vicissitudes of history and the moral struggle that must be worked out in public life. This understanding of the *enfleshed* spiritual, aesthetic, and moral struggle is of inestimable value for the exilic conditions of black churches and the quest for a liberative space to prophesy and resurrect the dead. As Holland notes,

> Speaking from the site of familiarity, from the place reserved for the dead, disturbs the static categories of black/white, oppressor/oppressed, creating a plethora of tensions *within* and *without* existing cultures. Embracing the subjectivity of death allows marginalized peoples to speak about the unspoken—to name the places *within* and *without* their cultural milieu where . . . they have slipped between the cracks of language.[65]

But what is going on here? What is a *fluid center* or *fluid area of consent*? What is this inner sense of wholeness that is a synthesis of innocence and brokenness—resilient, unyielding, and able to bend and return to a center that is turning? And how might it assist us in prophesying from this *dead space*, the intergenerational habitus and cultural production of evil that haunt black churches and condemn our children to a second death of natal alienation? It is appropriated through encounter that begins in the woof and warp of one's own self-reflexive, narrated personal and social-historical experience—an interiority that is *enfleshed* with the "smell of life" and bearing the weight of existence— and it is discovered through struggle, a *tussle* with the complex, tragic dimensions of human strivings.[66] *Becoming whole* is a process, a *tussle* that begins in the intensely personal experience of remembering and reclaiming the soul as a psychosocial and embodied subject. This *tussle* is emblematic of my father's reappropriation of the song that he heard from the white woman evangelist in the Mississippi Delta:

> Me and the Devil had a tussle, but I won.
> Me and the Devil had a tussle, but I won.

> I hate the Devil, he hates me.
>
> Me and the Devil cannot agree.
>
> Me and the Devil had a tussle, but I won.

In encounter with self, other, and the world, we are called to undergo this process of remembering and reclaiming subjectivity from the subjugated axis of symbolic, historical, and social possession by an alien ghostly force. It is here that we meet the *Angel with the flaming sword*, the in-between, spectral space of life and death where we choose to go forward into the freedom of destiny or suffer the bondage of fate as defined.[67] To pass through the Angel is to encounter the Devil, the *diablo*, the ghost, and to discover one's deepest fears and yearnings in an endless struggle to become whole, and to assign to oneself a new name. In doing so, one establishes a new space and a *new sense of time* and *identity*.

A New Sense of Time

The sense of wholeness, a *fluid center* or the "place one calls one's own," is appropriated through the retrieval of personal and collective memory as an initial step in deconstructing *habitus* and history and developing a new rhythm of time. It is precisely the *tussling* with the African American past through the agency of religious or spiritual experience that bequeaths to our present concern of (black) subjectivity a key to the meaning of its continuing horror, and *maybe* its healing. The creation of African American spirituals is an example of the act of conjuring that provided enslaved Africans with a tool of the spirit to make sense of the irrationality of evil and to preserve some modicum of sanity and wholeness in a strange land where they had to reconstruct a new rhythm of time and meaning for their bodies that were "a long ways from home." Stripped from the land of their birth and the rituals and ceremonies that gave them a sense of place and identity, they sought a new land in the inner territorial soul-scape of the body in a space called one's own. Charles Long, for instance, argues that Thurman's early investigations of the spirituals "resituates the problematic [of race] within the structures of inwardness as the locus for a new rhythm of time."[68] Long suggests that Thurman's exploration represented the appropriation of a *mythos* that provided meaning and affirmation of human dignity to an otherwise hopeless existence:

> The slaves who lived both within and outside of history, created historical structures but having no power to determine the locus of their meaning found a spiritual locus outside the body of historical time in which to save their bodies and to give meaning to their communities. The spirituals were their myths, and . . . the "affirmation of a historicity is an affirmation of the non-modern, [non-Western] peoples."[69]

In other words, through the inward journey, Thurman teaches us how to remember, to reenter time in order to address the loss of space, "forgetfulness," and "learned ignorance." Thurman's theological project of reimagining creation addresses the profoundly spiritual issue of "*feeling* like a problem," the overriding sense of guilt and shame, of falling into space and time constructed by a ghostly alien narrative; and offers tools of the spirit needed to address the questions of identity, otherness, and human flourishing in captivity to *exilic rhythms*. In other words, he teaches us how to *conjure* anew space *and* time. Thurman suggests, in *Deep River and The Negro Spiritual Speaks of Life and Death*, that this is what the enslaved African did with the experience of political suffering. These African singers not only *experienced suffering*, but actually gained entrée into the heart of the experience and there performed the art of *conjure*—they created from the toxic intentionality of the master's grand narrative to enslave black bodies and to transition space, new *possibles* that signified freedom and hope. For him, this art of *conjure* is precisely what is at work in the thematic bent of the spirituals:

> And this is the miracle of their achievement causing them to take their place alongside the great creative religious thinkers of the human race.

They made a worthless life, the life of chattel property, a mere thing, a body, *worth living!* They yielded with abiding enthusiasm to a view of life which included all the events of their experience without exhausting themselves in those experiences. To them this quality of life was insistent fact because of that which deep within them, they discovered was God, and his far-flung purposes. God was not through with them. And He was not, nor could He be, exhausted by any single experience or any series of experiences. To know Him was to live a life worthy of the loftiest meaning of life. Men in all ages and climes, slave or free, trained or untutored, who have sensed the same values, are their fellow-pilgrims who journey together with them in increasing self-realization in the quest for the city that hath foundations, whose Builder and Maker is God.[70]

Thurman's creative mythological and existential *conjuring* of creation and the fall is an example of the task of conjuring for black scholars and churches who must renarrate: remember, retell, and relive their stories in a new rhythm and time as we reconstruct and reimagine possibilities for mission in the twenty-first century. What might this idea of *conjuring* mean for dismantling hierarchies of power within our churches and the academy, and how is it related to *crossing(s)* as a sign of becoming whole in the jagged and sharp contours of difference and *the fifth moment of the flowering of a self-critical liberationist community*? The Answer is just above our heads.

Conspiring in the Haunted House

What might conspiring look like in a haunted house where there are memories without habitation? Conspiring means to literally breathe together, to plot and to do together as one;[71] only in its more modern sense does it connote something sinister or evil. I am using "conspire" here in the sense of "to do as one," to swear an oath against the ghost, to literally breathe and move together toward common goals and purposes that inspire and guide leaders, scholars, activists, and others to aspire into new *common(s)*. Those *common(s)* may well expire over time, and new strategies for that moment will of necessity be constructed. The challenges to black life in the United States and throughout the many diasporas of which we are a part are so multitudinous that one could resign oneself to fatedness and despair, as many of our churches have done in this era of contested post-racialism; or we can choose to congregate in this *fifth moment* and begin (for some, continue) the work of conjuring new narratives and new strategies for struggle by building on the gifts and tools of the past that have been handed down to us from so many of our prophets and seers whose lives bear witness to the Broken One whose dangerous memory rests just above our heads.

One such *common(s)* where we must congregate, conjure, and conspire is around the plight of black youth, particularly black men. The most disproportionately impacted group in the United States that suffers from diasporic and exilic wandering in the small house that race built is black and poor urban youth, particularly black males. Their plight, however, is hardly limited to the United States, but to a larger global matrix of capital driven by enormous shifts in the meaning of work and prescribed social identities.[72] By nearly every statistical measure of success, including demographics pertaining to health, education, income, and overall life chances, black youth (male and female) are woefully underrepresented.[73] By nearly every negative indicator in American society (high school dropouts, arrests, homicides, incarcerations), black males are overrepresented, and the toll on black families, especially black females faced with the tasks of child-rearing, is staggering.[74] In the next chapter, we will examine the cultural production of a postindustrial exilic characterization of black men as madmen, monkeys, and monsters as we explore the continued utilization of Dilemma, Exodus, and the Frying Pan by black churches. It will be necessary to inquire about the relevance and applicability of the proposed metaphors of Diaspora, Exile, and Fire and how they might point to solution-driven strategies for the issues and challenges associated with the problematized identity of black male subjects; but most important for this work, how do these metaphors sign and gesture toward home for black churches in the United States? In our continued discussion on mission in chapter 9, we will examine the exilic condition of young black men in *cultural asylums* and *jungles* and the accompanying cultural productions of black men as monkeys, monsters, and madmen. Chapter 10 outlines a modest proposal for black churches in this area.

9

Cultural Asylums and the Jungles They Planted in Them

In memory of my nephew and niece, murdered in cultural asylums: Charles Lee Godbold (May 9, 1969–found February 9, 2007) and Charlestein May Godbold (May 9, 1969–May 2, 2007).

The day Stamp Paid saw the two backs through the window and then hurried down the steps, he believed *the undecipherable language clamoring around the house was the mumbling of the black and angry dead*. Very few had died in bed, like Baby Suggs, and none that he knew of, including Baby, had lived a livable life. Even the educated colored: the long-school people, the doctors, the teachers, the paper-writers and businessmen had a hard row to hoe. In addition to having to use their heads to get ahead, they had the weight of the whole race sitting there. *You needed two heads for that*. Whitepeople believed that whatever the manners, under every dark skin was a jungle. Swift unnavigable waters, swinging screaming baboons, sleeping snakes, red gums ready for sweet white blood. *In a way, he thought, they were right*. The more coloredpeople spent their strength trying to convince them how gentle they were, *how clever and loving, how human*, the more they used themselves up to persuade whites of something *Negroes believed could not be questioned*, the deeper and more tangled the jungle grew inside. But it wasn't the jungle blacks brought with them to this place from the other (livable) place. It was the jungle whitefolks planted in them. And it grew. It spread. In, through and after life, *it spread, until it invaded the whites who had made it. Touched them everyone. Changed and altered them. Made them bloody, silly, worse than even they wanted to be, so scared were they of the jungle they had made*. The screaming baboon lived

under their own white skin; the red gums were their own. . . .
Meantime, the secret spread of this new kind of whitefolks'
jungle was hidden, silent, except once in a while when you
could hear its mumbling in places like 124.
—Toni Morrison, *Beloved*[1]

Between me and the other world there is ever an unasked question: unasked by some through feelings of delicacy; by others
through the difficulty of rightly framing it. All, nevertheless,
flutter round it. They approach me in a half-hesitant sort of way,
eye me curiously or compassionately, and then, instead of saying directly, How does it feel to be a problem? they say, I know
an excellent colored man in my town; or, I fought at Mechan-
icsville; or, Do not these Southern outrages make your blood
boil? At these I smile, or am interested, or reduce the boiling
to a simmer, as the occasion may require. To the real question,
How does it feel to be a problem? I answer seldom a word.
—W. E. B. Du Bois, "Of Our Spiritual Strivings"[2]

Searchin for Black Jesus
It's hard, it's hard
We need help out here
So we searchin for Black Jesus
It's like a Saint, that we pray to in the ghetto, to get us through
Somebody that understand our pain
You know maybe not too perfect, you know
Somebody that hurt like we hurt
Somebody that smoke like we smoke
Drink like we drink
That understand where we coming from
That's who we pray to
We need help y'all.
—Tupac Shakur, "Black Jesus"[3]

We begin the discussion of the plight of black youth, particularly young black men, as a *common(s)* where black churches and their many and varied interlocutors must congregate, conjure, and conspire. At the outset, I want to be clear that this focus on young black males is not meant to ignore, erase, or make nonspecific the incredible toll of systemic violence against black female, lesbian, transgender, and queer bodies. The focus on black males in this chapter grows out of long-standing work in this area and is offered as one of the many challenges that churches and their leadership should address together.

W. E. B. Du Bois put a question to his readers in 1903: "What does it *feel* like to be a problem?" Or more precisely, as suggested earlier during our discussion on Dilemma, Du Bois's question asks, What does this mean for the social life and personal sanity of today's young black men? As we have seen, this is not simply a sociological or historical problem, but a religious/theological problem that demands historical, sociological, and cultural analysis. Du Bois's famous question is an existential query denoting the angst of *doubleness* in African American life in the quest for citizenship at the dawn of twentieth-century America. It is also a response to a *wasted, bitter cry* of dereliction and abandonment that arises from the deep processes of social alienation and estrangement in a world constructed in the image of whiteness. The discursive features of the problem, of course, precede Du Bois and have received wide scholarly attention.[4]

Cultural Asylums

The *cultural asylum* is a metaphor for the various institutions of social control created to maintain the child/savage imagery of African Americans and other marginalized groups in a market economy. In the words of Michel Foucault, these institutions (asylums for the insane, penitentiaries for criminals, and almshouses for the poor) imposed a universal form, a morality that would prevail from "within" upon those who were "strangers" to it. "These institutions [also] helped to discipline white indigent, delinquent, and lower working classes, and to inculcate Protestant and republican values."[5] After the long and difficult history relating to the struggle for full citizenship in the United States, interpreted mainly as electoral options, African Americans still must deal with the complex challenges of psychological and intersubjective dynamics that impact our responses to notions of citizenship and what it means to be an American. Michelle Obama's controversial remark that the election of her husband was the first time she felt proud of being an American is an example of this ambivalence and doubleness.[6] The implications for the exilic existence of contemporary young black males are far more destructive and nihilistic. In many ways these young men are not recognized as citizens; instead their legal and political status is at best dubious, and tends to be more closely aligned with the notion of denizens, persons with rights between those of a citizen and a resident alien, essentially, a "free Negro" without full citizenship rights.[7]

The *asylum* also exiled and punished the madman and taught him to watch, punish, and brutalize himself. In the midst of justified protests against police killings of young black people, there continues to be an ongoing story of black-on-black homicide, especially among young men.[8] As a public spectacle and cultural scandal, black men have been taught to be public performers of the guilt, shame, and dread that characterize their dilemmalistic, exilic existence of torment in a perpetual lake of fire that destroys hope. The *cultural asylum* reproduces its patients, distorting and repressing their histories and memories in the service of the status quo. Foucault writes,

> The asylum no longer punished the madman's guilt; it is true; but it did more, it organized that guilt; it organized it for the madman as a consciousness of himself, and as a non-reciprocal relation to a keeper; it organized it for the man of reason as an awareness of the Other, a therapeutic intervention in the madman's existence. In other words, by this guilt the madman became an object of punishment always vulnerable to himself and the Other; and, from the acknowledgement of his status as

object, from the awareness of his guilt, the madman was to return to his awareness of himself as a free and responsible subject, and consequently to reason. This movement, by which, objectifying himself for the Other, the madman thus returned to his liberty, was to be found as much in Work as in Observation."[9]

The liberty that accompanies reason, as Foucault insinuates above, is related to a socially constructed *habitus* that guarantees the madman's allegiance to a form of liberty that serves a common purpose, the perpetuation of the status quo. The one considered mad by him/herself and others happily conforms to the rules and matrices of culture for its benefits and rewards associated with social recognition and respect, but still is not free to claim an identity and autonomy that are his or her own. On the question of the racialized house to which black churches continue to pledge allegiance, this peculiar notion of liberty becomes even more problematic. We have identified the liberty of the "race house" with the "freedom of the Christian," which has had deleterious effects on our ability to restore prophetic voices to public space. The questions before us are, Why is this so? Why do we continue to look for the living among the dead spaces "haunted by the old ghost"? "A Christian is a perfectly free lord of all, subject to none. A Christian is a perfectly dutiful servant of all, subject to all," writes Martin Luther in his *Treatise on Christian Liberty* (1520).[10] But our churches, for the most part, are hesitant to claim the freedom that is subject to none; rather, we emphasize the latter, insisting that our children do not disturb the peace of the house that race built. We fear for their safety and we fear that disruptive behavior is not in accordance with good Christian practices, as evidenced in some critiques of Black Lives Matter. The duality of the spiritual inner self and bodily, lustful, carnal self also creates a schizoid frame of reference for ways churches deal with the question of young black males. Looming large in this perspective is a spurious concept of salvation that places a premium on saving the souls of black youth to the neglect of their bodies. It is a curious dynamic that supports established structures and practices that are antithetical to the materiality of black lives and that perpetuate the cycle of death. Is it possible to congregate, conjure, and conspire in these dead spaces as a common theological and political task that inspires hope and resurrects the dead? Perhaps a closer look at the inner life of the asylum will help us to better understand this obsession with the ghost and why it continues to haunt and prevent us from congregating, conjuring, and conspiring in *common(s)* on behalf of our young men—and in fact, all of our youth.

The Jungles That They Planted in Them

The passage quoted above from Toni Morrison's award-winning novel *Beloved* provides a view of the inner life of the discourse and practices of these asylums. An intriguing minor character, Stamp Paid, looks through the window in the little house at 124 Bluestone Road and *overhears* the "mumbling," "undecipherable language," "the voices of the black and angry dead" of Sethe and Beloved, two women, mother and child, murderer and murdered, guilty and innocent—and is struck by the fact that "Negroes" are indeed *mad. Mad* because of the horrors of their history, yes, but also *mad* because *whitefolk* had to perceive them that way in order to assure their own sanity. Morrison's literary sample of the house at 124 Bluestone Road functions as an analytic window that allows us to outline the anatomy of the problem and resituate it in the context of African American male agency.[11] Stamp Paid's voyeurism is a movement from *image* to *text* that frames and juxtaposes the historical and material situation of Sethe and Beloved and allows us to examine the implantation of the *jungle*. In order to delve into this territory—*cultural asylums* and the *jungles that were planted in them*—this chapter provides an analysis of the cultural production of these representations relative to black males and their psychosocial implantations as a form of cultural domination.[12] As a subsidiary but no less salient feature of this oppression, this chapter explores the ways the ideas of the *cultural asylum* and *jungles* as structural problems inform institutional life, policies, and practices that perpetuate the existence of these characterizations. What I hope to achieve through this approach is a creative balance and interplay between the claims of structuralists and culturalists, the latter of which are often unfairly and categorically lumped with conservative behaviorist interpretations that have skewed the possibility of more accurate interpretations of context and agency.

Generally, structuralists argue that the political and economic structures of American society have been framed in such a way as to ensure that black and poor people of this nation will never be on an equal playing field with elite whites and other privileged groups.[13] Through the enactment of public policy, judicial appointments, and legislation, the powerful and the privileged make the rules, enforce the rules, and sentence the black and poor to lives of poverty and second-class citizenship. Therefore, structuralists contend that in order to change our political and economic situation, we must become actively engaged in the political and economic struggle to transform recalcitrant systems that work against the life chances of the black and poor of this country. This perspective has been the long-standing staple of many of our civil rights organizations, churches, and other civil society groups. The other side of the argument, which is increasingly gaining momentum, is the behaviorist argument, born of the "culture of pathology" theme that began in the early sixties,[14] which says that instead of claiming to be victims of the system, individuals must change their habits and practices so that they can participate fully in the democratic practices that reward hard work, personal virtue, and strong family values.[15] The public debate regarding structural versus behavioral causes of the plight of black youth has proven unhelpful in resolving the deep-seated psychological, social, and spiritual issues of young black people. More to the point, a more balanced approach helps us to appreciate how intricately connected are the *outer* and *inner jungles* and the ways their public performances are impacted in a *postindustrial, postmodernist* society that orders meaning in their *exilic existence.*

In respect to structural arguments, *postindustrial* refers to a period in the development of an economy or nation in which "the enhancement of instrumental powers, powers over nature, and powers even, over people" significantly minimizes the role of manufacturing while services, information, and research intensifies. This means that the "deindustrialized" economy is "characterized by more casual forms of work, marked especially by part-time working hours, fixed-term contracts, more 'flexible' patterns of employment and pay scales that can dip below the adult minimum wage," creating an almost impossible environment for unskilled, uneducated, and displaced laborers to find meaningful work.[16] Over the past two centuries in the United States, for instance, we have seen significant shifts from an agricultural age characterized by production of food and goods through farming to an industrial age characterized by mechanistic or machine culture, mass production that relied on physical strength and personal fortitude. Black migrations from the South to the northern, southwestern, and western regions of this nation had much to do with the escape from segregation, but also with the promise of jobs in factories, slaughterhouses, and automobile industries.

Over the past thirty years, however, there has been a significant shift to an information age that requires high skill sets in technology and specialized work that fuels a knowledge-based economy. Simultaneously with the rise of the information age have come the social dislocation and disconnection of many African Americans and other groups, especially males, from some of our most basic institutions—families, schools, churches, and other religious and civic institutions that historically provided personal and social capital for mobility in American society. A significant challenge for the present state of many black people is the increasing promotion and advancement of science, technology, and corporations. The changes produced by this triumvirate have already resulted in a significant upheaval in all of American society, impacting the meaning of life, intelligence, and work and, most importantly, anemic black civil society institutions that have been the mainstays of our social, spiritual, and moral development.[17]

What this means for black males in the twenty-first century, as William Julius Wilson poignantly argued in his celebrated 1996 book, is that "when work disappears," the impact of growing joblessness and dwindling work opportunities on inner-city areas in America is devastating. The lack of low-skilled manual work in the inner city is linked to poverty, crime, incarceration, family dissolution, and the deterioration of the social life of neighborhoods. It is a new form of the ghostly appearance of race in a post-racial society. Black people become disproportionately represented in neighborhoods where there is a high ratio of joblessness and very few work opportunities.[18] This new segregation, plus its interaction with other changes in society, escalates rates of neighborhood joblessness and compounds existing problems in our communities. Most importantly, it strips men and women of personal agency and the dignity that comes from work; and since work is no longer available for large and distinct populations of black men, they seek other ways of finding what I describe as *recognition*, *respect*, and maintaining *a sense of reverence* through practices related to the attainment of capital. Mainly, it ill-prepares them to become effective members of civil society.

An examination of the effects of postindustrialism and postmodernism among black males is helpful for understanding how they impact and help to explain the following questions: (1) If there is no essential or absolute self that endures over time—then who am I, and how do I understand my purpose and destiny?; (2) Who is the *other*? How do I understand *difference* and my relation and responsibility to the *other*? For instance, why should I care about the *other* if there is no *absolute* or morally legitimating reason or connection that tells me that I should care about the *other*?; and (3) How can we reflect upon our situation of hopelessness, despair, and deep alienation in a postindustrial society and in an exilic existence?

For African Americans, our collective condition prior to the advent of postmodernism (and perhaps more tragically expressed under current postindustrial conditions) has been and is characterized by continued displacement, profound alienation, and despair.[19] Interestingly, there are some parallels that can be drawn between postmodernism and what is now called the post–civil rights era. During the modern civil rights era, our struggle was primarily a struggle for equality and justice under the law. We witnessed some successes in political rights—the passage of landmark legislation in voting rights and public accommodations—but the question of economic rights and parity under the law has been far more problematic. During the decline of the civil rights era, we witnessed a heightened movement of black consciousness that favored the postmodernist claims of self-definition and critical questions regarding truth and morality ensconced in master narratives that defined the place and role of blacks and other historically marginalized groups in American society. Before the rise of the black consciousness movement, blacks—for the most part—participated in civil society institutions that transmitted our narratives of self-understanding and group understandings (the church being a primary institution), but with the rise in black consciousness, the main narratives that defined black *manhood* (responsibility to family and community, the dignity of work and citizenship) became less central to our self-understanding and moral responsibility. During the civil rights era and before, certain roles and responsibilities to the community were assumed. There were certain moral scripts that defined, in large part, how one was to behave and perform in public space. These ideological and cultural scripts, which I have written about elsewhere, had to do with certain understandings of character, civility, and a sense of community, but this has dramatically changed.[20] Consequently, two to three generations of young African Americans (from the late 1960s to the present day) have arrived on the scene without a clearly defined "moral script." Some might argue, and should, that some of those scripts were worth losing. I agree, but when you appear on the stage of history without your lines, in most cases you appear either as an anxious stutterer or as a highly improvisational actor.[21] What we are witnessing today among many of our youth, especially young black males, is the absence of well-articulated moral scripts and the lack of clear definitions on what role they should play in a larger historical narrative—

and the consequences have been danger, death, destructiveness, and madness in the streets of our inner cities.

The analysis of the problem of black youth requires a structural approach like Wilson's, but should also include a sustained cultural analysis that takes seriously the meaning and methodologies associated with cultural knowledge. Orlando Patterson argues that cultural knowledge is constituted collectively and intergenerationally and provides a sense of stability and order about the world in which we dwell. Cultural knowledge is also produced through pragmatic usage, the ongoing exchange and interaction of ideas. The former pertains to the latter in ways analogous to language and speech. It is in language's most practical relationship with speech that humans learn, and are consequently shaped by, the language world of which they are a part. Analogously, culture, in its more formal aspects, constitutes a shared knowledge base, explicit and implicit rules that govern the ways we respond, proceed, and evaluate our place in the world and understand who we are in relation to others. *Procedural cultural knowledge*, that is, how we proceed, consists of routines or scripts and distributed knowledge that informs social interaction. Patterson thinks that this function of constituted cultural knowledge is most important for understanding ethnoracial inequities, especially as they pertain to black youth.[22] This is true, in part, because procedural knowledge introduces youth to mainstream American society and instructs them on how to act, react, and interact in formal and informal situations with others; and most importantly I would add, how to perform as citizens.

On the other hand, the pragmatic dimension of culture is concerned with "rules of practice" that have implications for the limited autonomy of agents, because in order to achieve desired outcomes in interactions with others, one tends, often unconsciously, to rely upon the constituted order of things. In other words, one could easily imagine oneself in an undesirable social situation where the rules of etiquette were overdone, but in order to make the necessary overture for the contract, one chooses to hold one's nose. The rules of practice are often unconsciously adhered to, as they are habits of the mind, and one responds and interacts without discernment and deliberation, but through routinized behavior. Patterson calls these "performative strategies" because structure, even if opposed internally, is understood as necessary to achieve one's private goals. Cultural knowledge, however, is impeded among many black youth because of inadequate social institutions that have traditionally educated them for mobility in society. Rather, they "must rely on inadequate schools, segregated role models (themselves with limited knowledge of the constituted culture), and popular media to acquire what they know about dominant mainstream middle-class knowledge domains." Moreover, this limitation is further exacerbated because many of these youth are left completely devoid of the "acquisition of vital procedural knowledge." In ways similar to Pierre Bourdieu, Patterson thinks that "the concepts of *habitus* and *cultural capital* are grounded on the principle of procedural knowledge acquisition" and are helpful in the analysis of cultural productions of domination among young African Americans and for understanding their creativity, improvisation, and sociocultural configural performances like hip-hop.[23]

For our purposes, we emphasize the dynamic and interrelated concepts in Bourdieu's work of *habitus*, *field*, and *capital*. According to Bourdieu, the agent is socialized in a "field" (an evolving set of roles and relationships in a social domain, where various forms of "capital" such as prestige or financial resources are at stake). As the agent accommodates to roles and relationships in the context of his or her position in the field, the agent internalizes relationships and expectations for operating in that domain. These internalized relationships and habitual expectations form, over time, the *habitus*. Bourdieu's work, therefore, attempts to reconcile structure and agency, as external structures are internalized into the *habitus* while the actions of the agent externalize interactions between actors into the social relations in the field. Bourdieu's theory, therefore, is a complex, multilayered dialectic between *externalizing the internal* and *internalizing the external*. The social spaces or fields in which social actors perform, live, and struggle are largely structured by the logic of the legitimizing symbols (*symbolic capital*) of a given society. These legitimizing symbols inform the laws and embody the institutions that regulate the distribution of goods and services to members of the population. They also inform the cognitive structures (schemas) of individual and group agents who tend to unconsciously reproduce the social order, in the service of the status quo. To understand a particular cultural production, we must examine the founding historical events and symbols of that particular historical formation.

Historically, in the American context, there are several dominant representations of black masculinity (for instance, the *Tom*, the *Coon*, *Sambo*, and the *Brutal Black Buck*) that shape our normative perceptions of black men. The historical cultural presentations that continue to view young black men in this century as dangerous madmen, monkey men, and monsters are vivid reminders of the challenges that confront the mission and praxis of black churches and their exilic condition.

Meet *King Kong*: Cultural Representations of Black Males

In the director Antoine Fuqua's 2001 film *Training Day*, starring Denzel Washington (who won the Academy Award for best actor for his performance), there is a revealing scene that speaks to these caricatures of black masculinity.[24] In the final scene, Alonzo, Washington's character, staggers and braces himself against the car to maintain his balance as his bullet-riddled body jerks and contorts. A madman pushed to the extremity of his animality finds himself surrounded by his executioners and defenseless in a world that he once ruled through fear and violence. Like the monster/monkey/madman of a trail of movies depicting the black outlaw, he cries out in agony and defeat:

I'm the police, I run shit here. You just live here. Yeah, that's right, you better walk away . . . 'cause I'm gonna burn this motherfucker down. King Kong ain't got shit on me. That's right. . . . Yeah, you can shoot me, but you can't kill me.[25]

In this quote, the character Alonzo effectively captures the cultural portrayal of the postindustrial, postmodern, post-racial, exilic existence of the black male as the tragic madman, monkey, and monster, represented by his allusion to King Kong. There were three versions of the movie *King Kong*. In the 1933 version, a similar scene of helplessness and defiance is depicted when Kong has climbed the phallic Empire State Building and is wounded, surrounded, and still rebelliously fighting for his life. Although Kong is pummeled with artillery from the airplanes circling about him, he refuses to die. *King Kong* was such a cinematic triumph that the movie was remade twice—in 1976 and 2005—and is the subject of numerous spin-offs and spoofs. More significantly, Denzel Washington's acclaimed lines from *Training Day* are meant to juxtapose the racial troubles of black men in white society and the perceived racist imagery that is apparent in the iconic figure of King Kong. Alonzo is a "madman," a "beast," a "monkey man," a "monster" who simultaneously represents a public spectacle and a cultural scandal, stimulated and controlled by economic interests that perpetuate the ongoing negative stereotypes of black males.[26]

Equally important to our discussion is how the King Kong archetype has historically governed black male portrayal in movies. In his book *Toms, Coons, Mulattoes, Mammies, and Bucks*, Donald Bogle argues that only three traditional roles were available to black males in early twentieth-century cinema: the *Tom*, the *Coon*, and the *Brutal Black Buck*. Historically, the *Tom* caricature represents "the socially acceptable negro," and the *Coon* is associated with the "black buffoon."[27] Both of these roles are nonthreatening; the black male character is either subservient to white power (the *Tom*) or stupid (the *Coon*). In other words, these caricatures overwhelmingly depict black masculinity through public—therefore normative—perceptions as dumb and emasculated. However, the *Brutal Black Buck* is a different character entirely. The *Buck* is threatening to the normative gaze—strong, hypersexualized, instinctual, and lusting for white women—and feeds public perceptions associated with rage, violence, and rape. The character Gus, played by a white man in blackface in *The Birth of a Nation*, is an oversexualized *Buck*; "the mere presence of a White woman in the same room could bring him to a sexual climax."[28] The classic portrayal of the *Buck* is that he is unable to control his urges to have sex with white women; therefore, the *Buck* "is easily assimilated into a rapist."[29] Bogle also argues that the animal metaphor implies that "the sexual desire attributed to Black males by this representation is more appropriate to savage beasts rather than to civilized human beings," which easily flows into the depiction of the savage, transgressive, nonhuman monster.[30]

> The sexuality attributed to Black males through this stereotype is monstrous, then, because this sexuality is represented as abnormal. Black males are represented as possessing a sex drive that is animalistic—and, thus, not appropriate to human beings—and that drive is represented as focused upon white women, thus breaking the norm against miscegenation. Unlike civilized white males, Black men are depicted as monsters rather than persons because their sexual impulses are savage and transgressive.[31]

White obsession with racial purity and hatred toward black people took many forms at the turn of the twentieth century. The film *The Birth of a Nation*, released in 1915, may be taken as emblematic of that obsession. *Birth* is certainly the most cinematically influential and racially controversial film in American history. The movie is marked by black male desire to rape white women and the reemergence of the Ku Klux Klan to protect white ideals, white purity, and white women. In that same year, there was also a surge in membership in the Ku Klux Klan, which "boasted some three to four million members nationwide by its mid-1920's peak."[32] As a historical correlate, the public lynching of black men and women rose in the 1920s. Lynchings were popular pastimes for excited crowds of white people, who would gather to watch the emaciated black body hang in the open air. White Christian religious services were not exempt from the entertaining spectacle of lynching. Services were routinely dismissed for these holiday festivities. Billie Holiday's rendition of Abel Meeropol's 1936 poem "Strange Fruit" captures in lyric tone the sense of terror and the tragic character of black male exilic existence in America; it is "rememoried" by Kanye West:

> Southern trees bear strange fruit,
> Blood on the leaves and blood at the root,
> Black body swinging in the Southern breeze,
> Strange fruit hanging from the poplar trees.[33]

Almost three thousand lynchings took place in the United States between 1889 and 1933. Moreover, "rumors of rape were almost always circulated to vindicate, if not any particular act, then the more general need for lynching as a means of keeping the savage sexuality of the black 'buck' in check."[34] The lynching tree, a symbol of terror and trauma, revisits and haunts every attempt by American Christians to reconcile the cross with sacrifice and redemption. Young black men, generations removed from the scourge of lynching, are still haunted by this ghost, which elides, obscures, and obfuscates the terrible scandal of American Christianity while it silences those who remain—all the while maintaining order, symmetry, and epistemic foundations that justify innocent suffering. According to Professor James Cone, "Until we can see the cross and the lynching tree together, until we can identify Christ with a 'recrucifed' black body hanging from a lynching tree, there can be no genuine understanding of Christian identity in America, and no deliverance from the brutal legacy of slavery and white supremacy."[35] What might be possible in reimagining the cross and the lynching tree in this time of mass black incarceration and the killing of young black men? Might the fatal shooting of seventeen-year-old Laquan McDonald by Officer Jason Van Dyke in October 2014 and the systemic cover-up by the Chicago police department become a site of dangerous memory?[36] "Dried up, like a raisin in the sun. Where young black men are prone to lynching—mostly by gun. Some by police. But mostly by our own black sons. Still, I can never forget: Fred Hampton and Mark Clark executed by police while they slept."[37] Has the lynching tree shape-shifted into police crucifixion of young black bodies and the evisceration of safe spaces in the exilic lives of poor and black communities all over this country? Might it be through the lens of this continuing trauma, *the wound that cries*, that these young witnesses are the hinge between shattering and remaking of the world; between life and death; between despair and hope, perhaps a *crossing(s)* where we return and repay our *historical debt* to memory and time?[38] Might the lynching-tree-cross-prison-gun-violence that still frightens and torments us in its strident grotesquery and ignominious shadow become a space where we, with these young witnesses, reimagine our world?

Bestiality and Madness

Integrally related to the notion of the cultural asylum are the conjoined notions of bestiality and madness. In Western history, the cultural production of the bestiality of the black monkey man was also linked to *madness* (as in uncivilized) and to public spectacle. As Michel Foucault discussed in his classic work *Madness and Civilization: A History of Insanity in the Age of Reason* (1964), madness during the Middle Ages and well into the Renaissance was equated with animality or bestiality; the "animality of madness" is linked with the public performance of the monkey. The display of the insane was one of the favorite pastimes and distractions of the French bourgeoisie up until the French Revolution of 1848. "One went to see the keeper display the mad men the way the trainer at The Fair of St. Germain put the monkeys through their tricks."[39] In addition, the mad were allowed to exhibit the other madmen "as if it were the responsibility of madness to testify to its own nature."[40] "The insane who appeared in these theatricals were the object of the attention of a frivolous, irresponsible, and often vicious public. The bizarre attitudes of these unfortunates and their condition provoked the mocking laughter and the insulting pity of spectators" and became a public spectacle.[41] "Madness had become a thing to look at: no longer a monster inside oneself, but an animal with strange mechanisms, a bestiality from which man had long since been suppressed,"[42] which must be punished and brutalized; but it is also a public scandal "for the general delight,"[43] as Foucault's analysis of the Ship of Fools and its human cargo illustrates.[44]

Richard Wright's construction of the troubled character Bigger Thomas was greatly influenced by a 1938 *Chicago Tribune* article that described a black male accused of the rape and murder of a white woman (who becomes Wright's character Mary Dalton). In one scene in *Native Son* (1940), Chicago's citizens direct all their racial hatred directly at Bigger Thomas. They shout, "Kill him! Lynch him! That black sonofabitch! Kill that black ape!"

> "He looks exactly like an Ape!" exclaimed a terrified young white girl who watched the black slayer. . . . Though the Negro Killer's body does not seem compactly built, he gives the impression of possessing abnormal physical strength. . . . [H]is lower jaw protrudes obnoxiously, reminding one of a jungle beast. His arms are long, hanging in dangling fashion to his knees. It is easy to imagine how this man, in the grip of a brain-numbing sex passion, overpowered little Mary Dalton, raped her, murdered her. . . . All in all, *he seems a beast utterly untouched by the softening influences of modern civilization.*[45]

According to Foucault and Wright, bestiality was a vital dimension of madness (as in *unreason*), which gave rise to the incarceration of the madman in order to civilize him. Civilization had both external and internal mechanisms: not only was the madman forced to yield to the civilizing influences of his environment, he also was taught to watch himself and to internalize the virtues of civilization. For his failure to do so, he was punished by the society and *by himself*, often more brutally than the society that imposed its sanctions and penalties. Consequently, he was exiled from society and, most significantly, from himself. Simultaneously he was a public spectacle to be laughed at and derided—since it was also a cultural scandal—but he also laughed at and derided himself in personal shame. What happens to a soul over time who is the object of laughter and derision and who internalizes his own derision and spectacle? He becomes the derision and the spectacle; at the same time, he becomes alienated and alienating, ambiguous and frightening, marginalized and dangerous—*a monster*. Is he to be confined and pitied, mocked and ridiculed, hunted down and destroyed; or liberated and set free—and if set free, how?

Legitimizing Symbols

Symbolic forms such as King Kong shape cultural perceptions and behavior toward black men as mad, monkey-like, and monstrous. This symbol functions as an authoritative cultural idea, partly organizing and embodying the social structures and institutions that shape our "social relations, distribution of goods and services, and legal practices of dispensing justice."[46] The killings of young African American men illustrate how symbolic forms shape perceptions of these men as bestial and monstrous entities, perceptions that are reinforced by law and custom. Emilie Townes comments on the subtle ways symbolic cultural forms such as King Kong "legitimize structural violence, rationalize institutional violence, and impersonalize personal violence."[47] She combines Michel Foucault's notion of *fantasia* and imagination[48] with Antonio Gramsci's concept of hegemony[49] to construct the concept of the "fantastic hegemonic imagination."[50] These caricatures "ooze from the pores of videos and magazines and television and radio and music and the pulpit" to seep into all major American institutions, especially our laws, religious beliefs, and behaviors.[51]

The case of Michael Brown, an unarmed black teenager who was shot and killed on August 9, 2014, by Darren Wilson, a white police officer, in Ferguson, Missouri, is illustrative of the ways media and legal systems support and sustain the "fantastic hegemonic imagination." While there were many conflicting accounts of what occurred, the St. Louis County prosecutor said that the most credible witnesses reported that Michael Brown charged toward the officer. Officer Wilson said that Brown was making "*a grunting, like aggravated sound.*" "*The only way I can describe it, it looks like a demon, that's how angry he looked. He comes back towards me again with his hands up.*"[52] Michael Brown's death was part of a succession of highly suspect killings of young black males, killings that were subjected to intense media scrutiny and public debate. Nearly all of the cases, with few exceptions, involved men who were unemployed, with multiple arrest records and living in toxic environments that perpetuate a vicious cycle of cultural caricatures of black men as madmen, monkeys, and monsters—*demons* who deserve execution.

For the educator and author Joy DeGruy, the social effects of racist images, mass lynchings, and the public shootings of African American men can be understood in the context of trauma studies and post-traumatic stress disorder (PTSD). Originally studied to understand and treat the debilitating effects of war in World War II veterans, PTSD occurs when a person has "experienced, witnessed, or was confronted with an event or events that involved actual or threatened death or serious injury or a threat to the physical integrity of self or others."[53] If a person's PTSD is untreated, these threatening events often lead to persistent reexperiencing of aspects of the horrible event, almost as if it were occurring or could potentially occur in the present. DeGruy suggests that racist imagery, slavery, and the multigenerational violence that followed (slave whippings, lynching, police brutality, mass imprisonment) have created a social form of PTSD in American culture, *Post-Traumatic Stress Slave Syndrome*, in which painful and dangerous memories of the past continue to haunt our collective consciousness and intra-communal behaviors.[54] The unconscious desire to deny these painful memories leads to "forgetfulness" of important events, to set up racial, class, sexual, and gender barriers that avoid people and places that remind us of our terrible past, and to cut off feelings for members of other groups and even among African Americans. Thus, the vertical violence of the dominant group and of history is unconsciously reproduced in the horizontal everyday relations between communities and among black people. Both forms of violence remain buried from American consciousness as unacknowledged memories and contribute to a never-ending cycle of pain and oppression. Some scholars suggest that one of the major unresolved issues related to black-on-black violence in the inner cities, especially among youth, can be linked to long-standing codes of honor inherited from enduring cultural memory embodied in social practices of the Deep South.[55]

Habitus, History, and Memory

The interrelated concepts of "*habitus*," "history," and "memory" provide an analytic aperture through which we can glimpse the intergenerational impact of these cultural presentations on contemporary social situations and black male agency. The set of cognitive schemas and internalized dispositions that persons or groups inherit as a result of their ongoing historical adaptations to the social world "ensures the active presence of past experiences, which, deposited in each organism in the form of schemes of perception, thought and action, tend to guarantee the 'correctness' of practices and their constancy over time, more reliably than all formal rules and explicit norms."[56] Analytically, *habitus* can be understood as the *implant of symbolic power* in the individual mind, and it helps us to appreciate the ways the psyches of oppressed peoples, especially young black males, become sites of cultural domination, containing repressed *memories and embodied histories* that inform and structure behavior. In other words, in order to survive in the dominant group's world, oppressed peoples exercise adaptive functions or performative strategies that tend to avoid or forget the painful truths of their history and memories, helping them to accept the unequal arrangement of the social order as something natural and therefore, livable—*a jungle planted in them*.

Commenting on the power of history and memory as sites of domination and hope, Townes, as discussed earlier, argues that the traditional distinction between history as objective fact and memory as subjective opinion is unhelpful for an analysis of cultural productions of domination. For Townes, history and memory are both ideologically constructed in order to reinforce "the order of things." She writes, "The imagination of U.S. culture must be deconstructed and understood for the awful impact they [cultural productions] have on how a stereotype is shaped into 'truth' in memory and in history."[57] On the other hand, Townes also speaks of "counter-memory," in which memory may also "serve as a corrective to dominant sociocultural and theological portrayals of history."[58] Townes proposes that if we listen to *particular* African American narratives in depth as sites of counter-memory, the "truth of proceedings that may have been too terrible to relate may nevertheless be heard."[59]

Bourdieu's *habitus*, like Townes's *memory*, is a dialectical concept. It is culturally constructed by dominant groups, and unconsciously embodied by social actors. However, the *habitus* of social actors is not entirely fixed or static. Human beings are capable of reimagining themselves beyond dominant narratives and determinative social orders (again, much as Patterson's performative strategies combined with sociocultural configurations allow for some measure of autonomy).[60] Bourdieu asserts that "only in imaginary experience [in the folk tale, hip-hop, preaching, somaesthetic activities], which neutralizes the sense of social realities, does the social world take the form of a universe of *possibles* equally possible for any possible subject."[61] Bourdieu and Townes, therefore, lead us not only to appreciate how young African American men embody the "fantastic hegemonic imagination" of American slavery and its continuing legacy of violence, perpetuating racial stereotypes through self-debilitating behaviors, but also to consider them as potential agents of counter-memory and personal forms of knowledge in which it is possible to overhear and observe, to become self-reflexive in rediscovering their own truth and agency. As such, African American men (as well as all human beings) embody a type of "dangerous memory" and what Howard Thurman calls an "unconscious autonomy" that must be brought to the surface of awareness.[62] Cornel West concurs that the struggle for liberation must occur at the deeper levels of memory and meaning. West cites the foibles of structuralist and behaviorist interpretations and recommendations for those at the bottom of the social ladder. He argues that this debate "conceals the most basic issue now facing black America: *the nihilistic threat to its very existence.*" Beyond political and economic remedies, while significant, the threat of personal meaninglessness and worthlessness, brought about in large part by unbridled market forces and political chicanery, is the real challenge that confronts African Americans and the national community. West recommends a "politics of conversion" fueled by a love ethic that has historically sustained the African American community. Important for our purpose is the identification of memory and hope as key resources in the politics of conversion. According to West, "these modes of valuation and resistance are rooted in *subversive memory*—the best of one's past without romantic nostalgia—and guided by a universal ethic of love."[63]

Liberating Madness through Memory and Counter-Memory: The Inner and Outer Jungles

How might we liberate "madness" through memory and counter-memory? What are the *possibles* (to use Bourdieu's term)? Let us return for a moment to this question of madness, bestiality, and the symbolic implant of the jungle as a site for subversive memory. The *inner jungle* is socially constructed and implanted through the processes of symbolic power, *habitus*, and practices serving as psychosocial modes of domination and alienation from self, "the other (livable) place." At stake is more than the captivity of consciousness of black subjectivity, but the full range of the subjugating *habitus*, according to Morrison, of everyone who is "touched" by it—*And it grew. It spread. In, through and after life, it spread, until it invaded the whites who had made it. Touched them everyone. Changed and altered them. Made them bloody, silly, worse than even they wanted to be, so scared were they of the jungle they had made.*[64]

Morrison resituates the problematic: it is not merely a "Negro problem" or the "problem of blackness," but an insinuation and signification on the elevation of cultural symbols to the ontological status of divine creation (the jungles within, culturally produced by the project of whiteness) with images of demonic and fallen monsters predestined to exilic existence, a veritable hell, an eternal damnation—a lake of fire. Hence, *monsters* see *monsters* in their victims—a type of scapegoat, *pharmakos*, *homo sacer*, the object of a biopolitical gaze,[65] "the screaming baboon [that] lived under their own White skin" as a consciousness shaped and altered over time by habits, practices, and dispositions embodied in institutions and public policy, and as a cultural production that secretes itself into history as a form of righteousness and judgment. Religion plays a legitimizing role here as guarantor and preserver of a certain morality imposed from without and internalized by the object of its gaze. The *jungles*, therefore, are not only historical and social but also religious and spiritual sites of memory that demand analysis, reflection, and interpretation.[66]

To Achieve, Reveal, and Confirm a Human Identity

No one begins the arduous task of liberating black souls without first asking the hard questions of the past. Literary artists, like Morrison and Wright, have been helpful in deciphering these hidden transcripts and black codes of black male suffering and misery. Few have done this better than James Baldwin, who offered a clue into this past of terror and the *endless struggle to achieve and reveal and confirm a human identity*, as suggested in chapter 2. Du Bois's reflections on his early childhood offer a material sample of Morrison's literary idea of *rememory*,[67] which addresses the analytic relation of *habitus*, memory, and history in the endless quest for human identity, a sense of space and time in which one is *at-home* in one's own body:

> It is in the early days of rollicking boyhood that the revelation first bursts upon one, all in a day, as it were. I remember well when the shadow swept

across me. . . . Then it dawned upon me with a certain suddenness that I was different from the others; or like, mayhap, in heart and life and long-ing, but shut out from their world by a vast veil. I had thereafter no desire to tear down that veil, to creep through; I held all beyond it in common contempt, and *lived above it in a region of blue sky and great wander-ing shadows* . . . . With other black boys the strife was not so fiercely sunny: their youth shrunk into tasteless sycophancy or into silent hatred of the pale world about them and mocking distrust of everything white; or wasted itself in a bitter cry, *Why did God make me an outcast and a stranger in mine own house?* The shades of the prison-house closed round about us all: walls strait and stubborn to the whitest, but relentlessly nar-row, tall, and unscalable to sons of night who must plod darkly on in resignation, or beat unavailing palms against the stone, or steadily, half hopelessly, *watch the streak of blue above.* (italics added)[68]

Du Bois's *rememory* of the disruption of childhood innocence is an example of what is at stake for theological investigations of suffering and evil in black life. His remembering, however, must be situated alongside his registered parody on the lament, *Why did God make me an outcast and a stranger in mine own house?* This *wasted bitter cry of dereliction*, captured in his other writings as well, is an appeal born of great suffer-ing and sorrow, a petition to the idealization of a creative intent directed to the structure of consciousness that is *innocent* and *guiltless*; it is an imagined innocence that has encountered the experience of defilement and rejection, yet fixes its gaze on *(watches) the blue sky*. In his commen-tary on the question of "What does it feel like to be a problem," Du Bois returns to memory, to the moment of the shattering of innocence, his fall into the world of difference and dissemblance, blackness and misery.

The desire, indeed the necessity, to return to the *blue sky* is finally a petition for salvation (but alas, a *wasted bitter cry*) and an eschatological yearning for identity, relationality, and human flourishing—a return, to use Morrison's artistic stroke, to *that other (livable) place—home.* But the *sons of night* must wrest this identity through a negotiated transcendence, a fragile and dissembled hope while *watching the streak of blue above*. The struggle is rooted in an interior life that seeks confirmation in a material world; it is at once emphatically spiritual (of our *spiritual strivings*) and political—and it is a struggle against nihilism and despair.

How do churches and faith-based institutions positively and con-structively intervene on behalf of young African American men with-out further jeopardizing their agency and humanity? And what are the critical resources and methods at our disposal to address the exilic exis-tence of young men trapped in *cultural asylums and the jungles that were planted in them*? An important point of departure for exploring answers to these questions revolves around our discussion of Du Bois's memories of early childhood and his shattered sense of innocence on realizing that he was different from his schoolmates. In these reflections, he captures the deep alienation and torment of being created as *an outcast and a stranger in one's own house*, which is a statement of theodicy and a cry of dereliction, *a wasted bitter cry*. His musings also bring to the fore a desperate and friable petition for salvation, by living above in a fantasti-cal home in the *blue sky*; in fact, he and other black boys *watch the streak of blue above* as a means of maintaining sanity, a sort of compensatory salvation, while existing as bondsmen in the *shades of the prison-house* that was constructed for them. These ruminations are akin to Morrison's discussion of *that other (livable) place*, which is a yearning for a return to a type of innocence, a state of purity, a mythical home where identity, re-lationality, and human flourishing are fulfilled. Morrison's and Du Bois's longings are not for some great eschatological interruption, a breaking into history and time; rather, they are the inverse: both desire a new sense of space, time, and history, *rememory*, a return to a *home* uninhab-ited by the ghost. Finding home in the body, in relationship with others, and in the world is at once a psychosocial and political, theological and ethical, aesthetic and existential endeavor that requires certain *tools of the spirit*, which we will address in the next chapter.

10

Waking Up the Dead

I find you, Lord, in all Things and in all
my fellow creatures, pulsing with your life;
as a tiny seed you sleep in what is small
and in the vast you vastly yield yourself.

The wondrous game that power plays with Things
is to move in such submission through the world:
groping in roots and growing thick in trunks
and in treetops like a rising from the dead.
—Rainer Maria Rilke, "I Find You, Lord"

Behold, I show you a mystery: We shall not all sleep; but we
shall all be changed in a moment, in the twinkling of an eye,
at the last trumpet. For the trumpet shall sound, and the
dead shall be raised incorruptible, and we shall be changed.
—1 Corinthians 15:51–52

Slowly I walk into this narrow space
Carefully maneuvering until
I am able to negotiate the terrain

Quietly I wonder into this open space
Mindfully charting until
I am able to see up close

Surely I feel into this lonely space
Breath-fully motioning until
I am able to clear the path

Daring-ly I unfold into blooming dandelions
Opening-ly inviting until
I become the Wind
—Author's private journal

My mother and father never returned to Mississippi. Their bones lie in a cemetery in Chicago that I do not visit often enough. I sometimes think they must be so lonely and wonder whether they are at rest. I also wonder what it would take to awaken them, and us, from our long sleep. As I stand at their gravesides, an ancient text comes to mind: "What a journey we have made, the things we have seen. We are but one of you. . . . Give us air to breathe and a strong sailing wind when we rise from the underworld."[1] But how shall we prophesy to the wind and call forth the breath so that your bones might live again? What will it take to rekindle, re-create, reenact a movement of presence in a contested post-racial era dominated by the impersonal forces of vast and complex systems that exchange information and capital at the speed of light? As the world is tip-tilted toward a global crisis beyond any conventional understanding of political violence, is there a place for our little house where we lived and made do? How and where shall we *turn* to find answers to these and many other questions that confront our churches in this era of contested post-racialism?

We can begin by returning to the problem associated with the *falling* from innocence to brokenness, described in Du Bois's eloquent meditative discourse, to ask what tools of the spirit might be available to black church leaders and scholars to address the madness, bestiality, and monstrosities that plague the twenty-first-century lifeworlds of African American youth and, by full implication, the ongoing mission of black churches. How do we wake up the dead? Waking the dead in black churches in the United States will mean bringing to the fore of our collective consciousness the possibility that we can claim agency and responsibility for our own lives, especially for the future of our youth. To *congregate, conjure,* and *conspire* in *common(s)* in the early decades of the twenty-first century is a dangerous and costly proposition because it demands that we confess our complicity with the very systems and values that have eviscerated the memory and sacred stories of our traditions. Waking the dead will also mean that we mourn the incredible toll that our forgetfulness has taken on generations of our young who have had to create new meanings and identities from the fragmented discourses of a past that has been neglected, ruptured, and cast aside in our pursuit of recognition, prestige, and power. It also means that we must pay a *historical debt* to time and memory. The *crossing(s)* in this century will be those in-between spaces where we will remember, retell, and re-live our stories. In doing so we will leave nothing less than our own lives as sacrifices for the path that must be constructed for those in search of home. In other words, in order to wake up the dead, we must be willing to die so that our youth might live. Such a provocative endeavor necessarily means engaging youth in naming and shaping their own destiny and ours as well. Perhaps we must now let them take the lead. Callie Crossley, host and moderator of *Basic Black*, a Boston Public Television (WGBH) series, quotes one young activist as saying, "It's our time. The Revs have had their turn!"[2]

A Proposal

I am proposing that we provide opportunity for a new generation of black church leaders, scholars, and, importantly, youth activists to reflect upon tools of the spirit that might assist us in liberating madness through conjuring practices of culture and religious experience. To paraphrase Thurman, we must make a careful survey of our situation and work out a method, a way of life that will yield growth and development for us despite the contradictions under which we must eke out our days. I here suggest a path to home in the attempt to secure understanding and closure. This multi-part proposal assumes that the key to entering the infinitesimal space of black subjectivity, the realization and articulation of our agency, rests within the centermost place of the will, a politicized and fractured yearning for home, a new sense of space and time that finds its locus in a new appreciation of the body. In fact, it is in our commitment and embrace of our own freedom and its concomitant spheres of responsibility for own embodied lives that we will discover the God whom we meet at the *crossing(s)*, who is with us in the struggle to achieve and affirm our humanity. We need not zigzag between transcendence and immanence; rather, both must be negotiated from the middle, the in-between space where we meet the "Angel with the flaming sword" and where we chart a path toward home.

Our Personal and Collective Task

First, it is our personal and collective task to assist those trapped in cultural asylums to fashion a way of life that is resilient, praiseworthy, and liberating as we also free ourselves. Everyone committed to this dream must find his or her own way of challenging and transforming the inner and outer jungles of which we are all a part into places of justice and peace. How might black churches, in particular, bring these tools of the spirit to the twenty-first-century exilic existence of young black American youth where the ground has shifted? I propose a model for developing emerging leaders in local communities that would entail public and private agencies sponsoring and working alongside civil society organizations, including religious institutions (churches, mosques, synagogues, and other establishments of faith communities), schools, media, philanthropic and public health institutions, and others who *congregate, conjure,* and *conspire* in *common(s)*. This model of leadership revolves around three concepts: morally anchored character, subversive civility, and a sense of community. Each concept represents a corresponding dimension of the personal (character), society (civility), and spirit (community), which combines principles and practices for a transformative model that I call "ethical leadership." A critical

dimension of this work is the education and training of a new generation of leaders who will share leadership with existing leaders, with the
goal of creating communities of discourse and practices that dismantle
and transform the cultural asylums and jungles of twenty-first-century
America.[3] This is an imaginative and visionary project fraught with
the challenges and difficulties we have already discussed, but it is a
necessary step in creating a (livable) future for emerging leaders and
generations yet unborn.

Public Policy and Public and Private Partnerships

My proposal includes a second simple but yet complex postulate: black
youth need to have knowledge and skills to earn a living. The cultural
asylums and jungles that have been planted in all of us, especially in
many of our youth, are largely related to social and economic situations,
though not all black youth are economically disconnected.[4] Cultural
configurations and media play a large part in the licentious caricatures of black youth as *homo sacers*, scapegoats, and denizens.[5] Society
requires citizens with a variety of knowledge and skills if it is to have an
adequately productive economy. The wasted lives of these young people
are not only their problem and responsibility or the problem of black
churches and communities; ultimately they are the problem of society.
Therefore, black youth need to possess the cultural knowledge, procedural skills, and values required if they are to be citizens of a liberal
democratic society. The development and implementation of ennobling
and participatory public policy in the areas of education, industry, the
criminal justice system, health care, media, and other civil society institutions is paramount. Black churches and the academy have already
done considerable work in this area, but going forward it will take a
monumental effort of collaboration with the youth themselves, and public and private partnerships alongside other civil society institutions.
Leadership, in this respect, must be construed as communities of discourse and practices where all parties *congregate, conjure,* and *conspire*

in *common(s)* that are constructed for strategic purposes, addressing public policy and aligning with public and private partners.

Citizenship training that is local, national, and global is necessary to ensure that the futures of young people and the future of this society are not limited by narrow, nostalgic, and exclusive visions of statehood. My own work and experience with educating and training young men and women in leadership has convinced me of the efficacy of global citizenship training in stimulating consciousness beyond the boundaries and territorialism of national imaginaries. One such initiative began through a grant from the Oprah Winfrey Foundation to Morehouse College, where we engaged with students in learning the culture and sharing with fellow youth from South Africa. The students lived among youth in that country and worked with health workers tending to the challenges of poverty and HIV-AIDS. Likewise, South African youth came to the United States and shared in our culture and learned of the challenges associated with black youth in America, including poverty and HIV-AIDS.[6] Similar programs took place, and continue, in partnership with the Salzburg Global Seminar and the Andrew Mellon Foundation in "creating sites for global citizenship." More recently, we have begun conversations with Global Friends and other groups in Hong Kong and other parts of Asia.[7] An integral part of these programs is the visitation of "sites of memory," where young people have opportunities to learn from both sides of the globe, and the power of memory connects them with the long embodied history of diasporas and exiles and provides a source of hope in their solidarity.

I am recommending that black church leaders and scholars engage youth in the inner cities and rural areas of this nation with initiatives aimed at local, national, and global citizenship as part of the new Pentecostal "worldwide interconnectedness" addressed in a previous chapter. These programs and contexts can provide black church leaders and scholars with excellent opportunities to *congregate, conjure*, and *conspire* in *common(s)* that raise the consciousness of youth as they elevate their own. Moreover, they fulfill the great commission to be a scattered and scattering people. Prophetic leadership of the future will increasingly arise from those *common(s)* where fellow exiles and strangers meet in spaces that are not confined to the restricted logic of nationalisms and territories.[8]

The Good Life

My proposal involves a third postulate: young black people need a praiseworthy view of good living and the cognitive skills (related to the processes of acquiring knowledge by the use of experience, reasoning, intuition, or perception) to lead such a life. This good life in its most basic formulation includes the interrelated concepts of morally anchored character, transforming acts of civility, and a sense of community. But black churches and scholars will need to address a more difficult challenge. If young black people are not to be cognitive captives in cultural asylums and the jungles they planted in them, they need the ability to reflect on their own lives. Religious and cultural institutions, in partnership with other mediating institutions, can have a very positive impact in creating spaces where young people can reflect on the questions of identity, otherness, and human and nonhuman flourishing as we have outlined them. Much like an author, one can rewrite, edit, and manage one's script by reimagining one's place in the world and how one chooses to perform. This self-reflexive activity is an invitation to find one's *fluid center*—that space which is profoundly spiritual, elusive, and undefined. It is also here that one comes in touch with one's spectrality, residing in the in-between space of death and life, between material and spiritual— the shadowy third where binaries no longer exist, but merge as part of conscious existence in exilic prophetic speech.[9] It is in this space that commitment as a *tool of the spirit* begins.

Commitment, or singleness of mind, is rooted in this "fluid characteristic in life" that makes it possible to reimagine and revise one's internal environment.[10] For those who live in toxic environments that have been culturally produced and implanted into mental and spiritual processes, this notion of commitment is of paramount importance. On the one hand, as stated earlier, a *fluid center* is unnameable precisely because it belongs to no territory or homeland—it points to *home*. On the other hand, it is the space of imagination where one hears and chooses how one is named: "To be known, to be called by one's name, is to find one's place and hold it against all the hordes of hell. This is to know one's value, for one's self alone. It is to honor an act as one's very own, it is to live a life that is one's very own, it is to bow before an altar that is one's very own, it is to worship a God who is one's very own."[11] This exaltation can be realized only by a demanding self-examination and discipline of the spirit. Only this powerful potion, this pharmacopoeic mixing and remixing of materiality and spirit, can defeat the old ghost, because it provides the space for reimagining one's self and making conscious commitments to the same. Hence the *tools of the spirit*—disciplines or practices and rituals of religious/spiritual experience—are subjected to rigorous observation and analysis and are tested in the context of observed experience in *common(s)* where we *congregate, conjure,* and *conspire*. This is an ongoing, dynamic, spiraling process that is constantly decentering and calling forth new tools, practices, and strategies of engagement and liberation.

Remembering, Retelling, and Reliving Stories

Fourth, for black youth trapped in cultural asylums and struggling with the traumatizing effects of racialized identity, it is crucial that they first become aware of the history of social and cultural productions that have helped to create the *shades of the prison-house* and the *jungles that were planted in them*. This is no small task. To claim responsibility for one's existence presupposes a certain authorial positionality that requires the discovery of *tools of the spirit* and ongoing practices of self-reading, self-revising, and self-authoring of one's own story.[12] Accordingly, there are three concepts/questions that must be self-consciously engaged with that serve as indicators or targets for "tools of the spirit" (identity, otherness, and human and nonhuman flourishing). These questions are (1) Who am I, really? How do I understand and construct my purpose and destiny? (identity); (2) Who is the other and what is my relation and responsibility to the other? (otherness); and (3) What does it feel like to be human and to embrace the power and beauty of my humanity in nature and creation? (human flourishing and nonhuman flourishing). In this last question, regarding what it feels like to be human and to embrace the power and beauty of my humanity, we have much to learn from our religious humanist brothers and sisters and ecological investigations about freedom and claiming responsibility for own lives and the world of nature of which we are a part. For young black women and men, many of whom must daily deal with the humiliating indignity of being treated as the perennial other, the question of human flourishing specifically asks, What does it mean to feel and be human and to reflect upon my situation of hopelessness, despair, and deep alienation in a postindustrial, contested, post-racial world? But to work on the inner life alone is not sufficient. Black church leaders and scholars must congregate in those institutional spaces of power and address the structural and cultural captivity of our youth (e.g., mass incarceration, the perverse availability of guns and drugs, deteriorating urban and rural schools, unemployment, mental and physical health care).

The Black Lives Matter movement that began in 2013 is a hopeful sign of this new moment to which we are called. As a grassroots movement it bears similarities with the prophetic cadence of an earlier era when young black activists, many of them college and university students, were able to produce a critical tension among the black leadership of the civil rights movement and the larger society. In doing so, they elevated the struggle for freedom and jobs to a cultural revolution of black consciousness and political awareness. This new movement, in its embryonic stages, incorporates some of the same logic but within a very different historical context and therefore agenda—particularly evidenced in the leadership of youth, women, and LGBTQIA activists.[13] It struggles not so much with the ghostly apparition of Jim Crow (though he does exist in the residual remains of growing white resentment), but with the ghost of contested post-racialism that has reconfigured the radical egalitarian hypothesis into an assertion that since all lives matter, slogans like "black lives matter" dismiss the many others in our society who also have legitimate claims to identity, difference, and equal justice. In doing so, the ghost disguises itself yet again by minimizing the particularity and the disproportionate vulnerability of black youth in American society over and against the majority of other youth. This universalizing tendency invokes a thin description of what's really going on in America rather than providing a thick description of the situation of black lives and why they matter in this context. Most importantly, the youth of this movement have placed their bodies on the line—they have put some flesh in the game; "This is flesh we're talking about here. Flesh that needs to be loved." Every church leader and scholar who is involved in the work of social and political transformation should follow the lead of these youth in being committed to placing his or her body on the line and putting some flesh in the game in new ways. In doing so, we will continue the legacies of those sainted martyrs whose broken bodies and dangerous memories rest just above our heads.

Reimagining and Resurrecting Identities

Fifth, reimagining and resurrecting identities begins with the acknowledgment that there is a consortium of many internalized others who must come together and cast a unanimous vote for a sense of wholeness and integrity within the self, society, and the world. A critical question for black churches is how we assist and empower youth to rename and re-language their world, beginning with their own black, bestialized, sexualized, and criminalized bodies. In light of the preceding discussion about creation, black churches must help youth to understand what it means to *fall* into a world that was not designed with their humanity and flourishing in mind and to equip them with tools to choose between fantastical notions of success and the dangerous existence in cultural asylums. Moreover, as pastors, educators, and youth workers in the church, we should inquire about the multiple constructions of identity that youth must negotiate daily and that inform their judgment and behavior. Church leaders and scholars have excellent opportunities here to begin to assist young men and women in a revised and long process of salvation and sanctification by interrogating how race as a cultural and social ghost shape-shifts and reinvents itself in myriad figurations in theological and aesthetic expressions. In this respect, theological constructions that address young black men and women have formal affinity with post-blackness as a quest for identity, authenticity, and agency.[14] As the artist William Pope.L says, "Blackness is limited only by the courage to imagine it differently."[15]

Reimagining a sense of self is necessarily related to the others with whom one shares the world. Thurman refers to this sense of authenticity of identity as the "sound of the genuine."[16] But what might the sound of the genuine mean for a new generation of young men and women who live daily with noisy intersections of market-stimulated media and surreptitious sound-games and stereotypes? A remarkable feat of conjuring that black church leaders and scholars can learn from our youth is their ability to exist, negotiate transcendence, and create new aesthetic and spiritual practices from the noise. Contemporary artistic expressions speak to a spiritual striving, an endless struggle to achieve and reveal and confirm a human identity. The religious studies scholar Anthony Pinn posits, for example, that "at its best, perhaps rap music is a continuation of the creative manner in which meaning is made out of an absurd world by promoting a style of living through which a sense of self and community is forged in a hostile environment."[17] Rap music, carrying forward elements of the earlier traditions of the sorrow songs and the blues, with complex polyrhythmic layering, repeated scratching, breaks, and pauses in the beat, is meant to create a sense of suspension and surprise in listeners, rupturing their regimented styles of being within the cultural matrices of power to which we are all adapted. This deep dialectic in rap music between the expected and unexpected, the beat and multiple silences and rhythmic layering, between the regimented habitus of subjugated black mentalities and the physical, breathing black body, may open up new spaces and experiences in the expansion of African American identities and consciousness. Rap music may represent an aesthetic struggle for the "sound of the genuine" in listeners seeking to reveal and confirm a new human identity that is more than the sum of its parts. Moreover, musical expressions like rap are expressions of conjure that reconfigure meaning and language—and offer to the believer a new sense of space, time, rhythm, and possibility, an encounter with the Holy Ghost that stimulates consciousness and returns to memory, but also spurs new narratives about self and the world. According to Mark Lewis Taylor, rap

> awakens certain spiritual functions. When it brings noise, then, rap music also conjures spirit. . . . Even the definition of conjure that most dictionaries describe as obsolete—"to conspire," from conspirare ("to breathe together")—may be appropriate given rap music's capacity to encode the winds of resistance that blow and sometimes swirl among people struggling to survive and flourish amid states of disorder and deadly regimentation.[18]

The recommendation here is not to simply host a concert or incorporate rap and hip-hop into regular worship (which a growing number of churches are doing), but to become aware, to awaken as it were from the long sleep, from a death that has entranced black churches and their communities and to hear, maybe for the first time, a new movement of the Holy Ghost that blows among us like a noisy, rushing, and mighty wind calling upon us to resurrect the dead. Much like an old song that my father sang in the mornings while he made coffee, the noisy and loud clamoring of our youth is meant "to wake up the dead."

> O where shall I be when the first trumpet sounds,
> O where shall I be when it sounds so loud?

When it sounds so loud as to wake up the dead?
O where shall I be when it sounds?[19]

The apocalyptic, eschatological meaning of trumpet sound is evident in this old hymn and is reminiscent of James Weldon Johnson's sermon/poem "The Judgment Day,"[20] but the question *Where shall I be?* is also a signal, a summons of sorts to locate oneself, or better, to identify where and with whom one is standing, or will choose to take a stand. What is suggested here is not a return to binary oppositions like black and white, but a summons to decide where and with whom one chooses to identify—because it matters. Reimagining, if we take William Pope.L's suggestion seriously, begins with remembering, retelling, and reliving our stories and determining which characters we will play in the larger drama. The many legions of unaffiliated and unnamed apparitions that masquerade in the spaces between the living and the dead can be named and renamed in ways that bring healing and support to disconnected youth. But first, black churches must awaken from the dead spaces where we lie entombed in a past imaginary that has not reckoned with its future, which lies coiled up in the chaos and noise of the present. In order to do this, we must take seriously our exilic and diasporic situations as possibilities of reimagining ourselves for this new surge of the Holy Ghost that is making a lot of noise around the globe.

Remembering the Dead

Finally, a critical task in waking up the dead is remembering the dead. Amidst the continuing incarceration and killing of young black people in this country, it is appropriate that we find ways to remember them because as we memorialize them, we also call our own souls into life and action on their behalf. In many ways our task as it relates to the killing of young black men, women, and transgender people by police and black-on-black homicide is to wake up the dead and allow them to speak through us. In these liminal spaces, between bondage and freedom, black churches must explore new ways to erect sites of memory where we can weep, confess, and resist. This would involve a reframing of religious education that insists on the place of memory, vision, and mission, which are correlates to remembering, retelling, and reliving our stories. The violence against young black people in this country that often results in their deaths does indeed bring about shock and grief—but mourning must also be connected to confession and resistance.

This book has argued that black churches in the United States have much to confess regarding their complicity with the ghosts of utilitarian individualism masquerading as prosperity gospels and the social-political narcolepsy that perpetuates forgetfulness and narcissism. Our confessions must be the beginning of our resistance to social, political, and economic plantations that have become our diasporic and exilic homes in the nation's inner cities and the neglected rural areas of this country. Resistance must also be the beginning of the resurrection from the dead that Eddie Glaude calls for in his epistle to black churches in America. But resistance without weeping and confession is empty and bereft of memory—and to exist without long memory is to wander in the graveyards of post-racial sentimentality haunted by legions of names but without a space to call one's own, a long ways from home.

We return to the central question of our initial concern, the Du Boisian query, What does it feel like to be a problem? This question is a *crossing(s)* of African American existence. We did not choose these *crossing(s)*, but to answer the question at the beginning of this century is to bear it in the hope that beyond the space of death that we continue to occupy is the possibility of resurrection. The resurrection from the dead is a negotiated transcendence; it follows the gaze of the Madonna who knows that even though we never truly achieve the blessed life of fulfillment, we continue in struggle because of the figure of the broken child who is just above our heads. And this is holy—madly, wonderfully, and courageously holy. For the holiness (wholeness and integrity) that we seek in our yearnings for salvation, sanctification, and glorification is born of our longing for home. In those in-between spaces—between feces and urine[21]—where life is born out of death, we find hope and home. "The birth of the child—life's most dramatic answer to death— this is the growing edge incarnate."[22] To accentuate the holy that is found in this in-between space is also to discover where love flourishes, where justice is sought, and where the desire for being at-home within one's body and one's self and with the other does not end in pessimism and hopelessness, but with the positive assertion of identity and relationality. The daring to speak in one's own voice as a signature of the sound of the genuine is the freedom to act out of a *fluid space* where one is no longer captive to the ghost. The creative intent of human flourishing, of becoming—or better, reclaiming one's humanity through the integrity of the act—means that the *blue sky* and the *other (livable) place* are not beyond but within. This sphere of negotiated transcendence that we never quite achieve, but experience as hope within the confines of the tragic, is where we are mapping our trajectories toward home. Hence, the inward journey into cultural asylums and the implanted jungles is a continual dialogue with self and world, "between the world and me";[23] it is a tool of the spirit that demands the rigorous discipline of self-criticism and self-reflexive agency that empowers one to engage culture and its many productions of evil and domination. For churches, this will mean more emphasis on religious education without diminishing the place of empowering, spirit-filled worship and preaching. The challenge of developing strategies of infusion of character, civility, and community is part of the educational task of the church. Religious education will require the development of innovative and imaginative curricular strategies, pedagogies, and practices that address the questions of cultural production of images and patterns of unconscious behaviors that are rooted in trauma, as well as courageous institutional leadership and support.[24]

In closing, the future of black churches in the United States will depend largely on how we minister to the most disproportionately impacted group in our communities, black youth of all sorts (poor and middle-class, male, female, lesbian, gay, bisexual, transgender, and queer). What should appear so obvious often eludes us because of the manifestations of the ghost, "the mistake made in Jamestown long ago" and our own preoccupations with religious personalities and paraphernalia. In the shifting and turning metaphors of black churches' institutional and theological identities, it will be well to remember that without our youth, we no longer have churches nor a reason for their existence. As we engage in the hard work of reimagining, discerning, and deliberating, repenting, rethinking, and refashioning signs, symbols, and metaphors for this time, let us listen for the sound. Are we able, do we have the courage, to put ourselves in that space—to be in the in-between when the Sound, like a mighty and rushing wind, fills the room and we hear ourselves and the many others long-gone and yet-unborn in their own language—the many voices that herald the New Age? I am hopeful that this future will yield for us new ways of *congregating, conjuring*, and *conspiring* with the Holy Ghost who brings to us the fire, the wind, the noise, and the sound of the genuine in new languages that speak to the diversity of creation and the resurrection of the dead.

NOTES

CHAPTER 1. FROM FROGBOTTOM TO A BUCKET OF BLOOD

1 Fluker, Louisiana, is located between the villages of Tangipahoa and Arcola on U.S. Highway 51 at the junction (on the west side of U.S. 51) with Louisiana Highway 10. See "About Tangipahoa Parish," USGenWeb Project, www.rootsweb. ancestry.com, accessed July 1, 2015; see also "Tangipahoa Tourism," Tangipahoa Parish Convention and Visitors Bureau, www.tangi-cvb.org, accessed July 1, 2015.

2 David Rubel, *Fannie Lou Hamer: From Sharecropping to Politics* (Englewood Cliffs, NJ: Silver Burdett, 1990), 73; Kay Mills, *This Little Light of Mine: The Life of Fannie Lou Hamer* (New York: Dutton, 1993), 56–77. The role of the FBI in this bloody massacre was even more insidious. Kenneth O'Reilly, *Racial Matters: The FBI's Secret File on Black America, 1960–1972* (New York: Free Press, 1989), 1–7.

3 See "Old Lem," in *The Collected Poems of Sterling A. Brown*, ed. Michael S. Harper (New York: Harper and Row, 1980), 180–81.

4 See Nicholas Leman, *The Promised Land: The Great Black Migration and How It Changed America* (New York: Vintage, 1992); and Neil R. McMillen, *Dark Journey: Black Mississippians in the Age of Jim Crow* (Chicago: University of Illinois Press, 1989).

5 See Wallace D. Best, *Passionately Human, No Less Divine: Religion and Culture in Black Chicago, 1915–1952* (Princeton: Princeton University Press, 2005), 63–65.

6 Ibid., 48, 208, n. 40.

7 Anthony B. Pinn, introduction to *Loving the Body: Black Religious Studies and the Erotic*, ed. Anthony B. Pinn and Dwight N. Hopkins (New York: Palgrave Macmillan, 2004), 2.

8 Milan Kundera, *Immortality* (New York: HarperCollins, 1991), 7.

9 Isaiah 48:10 (NIV).

10 See Albert J. Raboteau, *Slave Religion: The "Invisible Institution" in the Antebellum South* (New Haven: Yale University Press, 1978), 275–88; see also Mechal Sobel, *Trabelin' On: The Slave Journey to an Afro-Baptist Faith* (Princeton: Princeton University Press, 1988).

11 Some of the material in this section is adapted from Walter Earl Fluker, "Old Songs and Strong Arms: Remembering Daddy," in *Father Songs: Testimonies by African-American Sons and Daughters*, ed. Gloria Wade-Gayles (Boston: Beacon, 1997).

12 Howard Thurman, "A Strange Freedom," in *The Inward Journey* (Richmond, IN: Friends United Press, 1961), 38.

13 Arna Wendell Bontemps, *Black Thunder: Gabriel's Revolt, Virginia, 1800* (New York: Macmillan, 1936; repr., Boston: Beacon, 1992), 53.

14 Toni Morrison, *Beloved* (New York: Knopf, 1987), 198–99.

15 See W. E. B. Du Bois, *The Gift of Black Folks: The Negro in the Making of America*, intro. Edward F. McSweeney (Boston: Stratford, 1924), 320; Clifton L. Taulbert, *Once upon a Time When We Were Colored* (Tulsa, OK: Council Oak Books, 1989); Jimmy Lewis Franklin, "Black Southerners, Shared Experience, and Place: A Reflection," *Journal of Southern History* 60, no. 1 (February 1994); and Henry Louis Gates, *Colored People: A Memoir* (New York: Knopf, 1994).

16 Pierre Nora, "Between Memory and History: *Les Lieux de Memoire*," *Representations* 26 (Spring 1989): 7–25.

17 Toni Morrison, "Memory, Creation, and Writing," *Thought* 59, no. 235 (December 1984): 385.

CHAPTER 2. HAUNTED HOUSES

1 James Baldwin, *The Fire Next Time* (1963; repr., New York: Vintage International, 1993), 98.

2 The black church is a lot like love—it is a many-splendored and many-splintered thing. The phrases "the black church" and "black churches" are used interchangeably throughout the book, but for the most part, I reference "black churches" to denote the plurality of institutional beliefs and practices of black churches alongside different denominational and cultural configurations of meaning. For instance, the plethora of definitions on what constitutes the black church or black churches is long and changing, as it should be. See the following as examples: Victor Anderson, *Creative Exchange: A Constructive Theology of African American Religious Experience* (Minneapolis: Fortress, 2008), 162; Michael Battle, *The Black Church in America: African American Christian Spirituality* (Malden, MA: Blackwell, 2006); Allan Aubrey Boesak, *Black and Reformed: Apartheid, Liberation, and the Calvinist Tradition*, ed. Leonard Sweetman (Maryknoll, NY: Orbis, 1984); and C. Eric Lincoln and Lawrence H. Mamiya, *The Black Church in the African-American Experience* (Durham: Duke University Press, 1990.) See also Anne H. Pinn and Anthony B. Pinn, *Fortress Introduction to Black Church History* (Minneapolis: Fortress, 2002); Henry H. Mitchell, *Black Church Beginnings* (Grand Rapids: Eerdmans, 2004); Iva E. Carruthers, Frederick D Haynes III, and Jeremiah A Wright Jr., eds., *Blow the Trumpet in Zion* (Minneapolis: Fortress, 2005); and Stacey Floyd-Thomas, Juan Floyd-Thomas, Carol B. Duncan, Stephen G. Ray Jr., and Nancy Lynne Westfield, *Black Church Studies: An Introduction* (Nashville: Abingdon, 2007).

3 Baldwin, *The Fire Next Time*, 81.

4 Ta-Nehisi Coates, "There Is No Post-Racial America," *Atlantic*, July/August 2015, www.theatlantic.com; "The Paradigm Shift: The Origins of the Post-Racial Fantasy," *Forty Acres and a Cubicle: The Official Blog of Post-Racial America*, August 9, 2012, http://40acresandacubicle.com.

5 For references to *crip*, see Robert McRuer, *Crip Theory: Cultural Signs of Queerness and Disability* (New York: New York University Press, 2006); see also Sharon Betcher, *Spirit and the Politics of Disablement* (Minneapolis: Fortress, 2007); and Sharon Betcher, *Spirit and the Obligation of Social Flesh: A Secular Theology for the Global City* (New York: Fordham University Press, 2013).

6 Eddie Glaude Jr., "The Black Church Is Dead," *Huffington Post*, February 24, 2010, www.huffingtonpost.com.

7 Ibid.

8 Ibid.

9 Eddie S. Glaude Jr., "Updated with Response: The Black Church Is Dead—Long Live the Black Church," ReligionDispatches.org, March 15, 2010, http://religion-dispatches.org.

10 Ibid.

11 Pew Research Center, "A Religious Portrait of African-Americans," January 30, 2009, www.pewforum.org. For technical definitions of religiousness and spirituality, see also Peter C. Hill, Kenneth I. Pargament, Ralph W. Hood Jr., Michael E. McCullough, James P. Swyers, David B. Larson, and Brian J. Zinnbauer, "Conceptualizing Religion and Spirituality: Points of Commonality, Points of Departure," *Journal for the Theory of Social Behaviour* 30, no. 1 (2000): 51–77, www.psy.miami.edu.

12 Glaude, "Updated with Response."

13 Benedict Anderson, *Imagined Communities: Reflections on the Origin and Spread of Nationalism*, rev. ed. (London: Verso, 1991), 9–36, quoted in Sharon Patricia Holland, *Raising the Dead: Readings of Death and (Black) Subjectivity* (Durham: Duke University Press, 2000), 22.

14 Genealogical isolation is a concept related to "social death." Orlando Patterson, *Slavery and Social Death: A Comparative Study* (Cambridge: Harvard University Press, 1982), 5, quoted in Holland, *Raising the Dead*, 13; see also 5.

15 Luke 24:5.

16 Robert Bellah et al., *Habits of the Heart: Individualism and Commitment in American Life* (New York: Harper and Row, 1986), 33. See Vincent Harding, "Toward a Darkly Radiant Vision of America's Truth," *Crosscurrents* 37, no. 1 (Spring 1987); C. B. MacPherson, *The Political Theory of Individualism: Hobbes to Locke* (New York: Oxford University Press, 1962); and C. B. MacPherson, *The Life and Times of Liberal Democracy* (New York: Oxford University Press, 1977).

17 My idea of the "unholy ghost" came initially from informal remarks by Pastor Jay Johnson, Union UMC, Boston, September 30, 2012.

18 Peter J. Paris, *The Social Teaching of the Black Churches* (Philadelphia: Fortress, 1985), 8–12.

19 See Cornel West, *Prophesy Deliverance! An Afro-American Revolutionary Christianity* (Philadelphia: Westminster, 1982), 47–65. In "The Will to Believe," William James quotes Sir James Fitzjames Stephen:

> We stand on a mountain pass in the midst of whirling snow and blinding mist, through which we get glimpses now and then of paths which may be deceptive. If we stand still we shall be frozen to death. If we take the wrong road we shall be dashed to pieces. We do not certainly know whether there is any right one. What must we do? "Be strong and of a good courage." Act for the best, hope for the best, and take what comes . . . If death ends all we cannot meet death better.

Sir James Fitzjames Stephen, *Liberty, Equality, Fraternity* (London, 1874), 353, quoted in William James, "The Will to Believe," *The New World: A Quarterly Review of Religion, Ethics And Theology* 5 (1896): 846. See Eddie S. Glaude's discussion of the "American Idea," that spurious, abstract claim that denies the congenital condition of race in the American conception of democracy, founded on what he calls the "value gap," which is fundamentally the belief that white people are more valuable than others. Eddie S. Glaude, *Democracy in Black: How Race Still Enslaves the American Soul* (New York: Crown, 2016), 29–50.

20 For instance, nineteenth-century emigrationists like Paul Cuffee, Edward Wilmot Blyden, and Henry Highland Garnet, though advocates of black nationalism and colonization, still embraced a cultural and national imaginary of America that expressed an inherent contradiction in their vision of free Africans. Viscount Nelson sums up the issues at stake in his reference to Garnet:

> While he toyed at one time with the idea of emigration, Garnet spoke for generations of future black leaders and African Americans when he said: "America is my home, my country, and I have no other. I love whatever good there may be in her institutions. . . . I love the green hills which my eyes first beheld in my infancy. I love every inch of soil which my feet pressed in my youth. . . . I love my country's flag, and I hope soon it will be cleansed of its stains."

Viscount "Berky" Nelson, *The Rise and Fall of Black Leadership: Chronicle of a Twentieth Century Tragedy* (Lanham, MD: University Press of America, 2003), 10.

21 See Emmanuel Chukwudi Eze's ethnographic critique of modern philosophy's historical complicity with racialism and post-racial postmodernism's continuing dilemma with the "everyday life-and-death events of race." Emmanuel Chukwudi Eze, *Achieving Our Humanity: The Idea of the Post-Racial Future* (New York: Routledge, 2001), ix–xvii; Lucius T. Outlaw Jr., *On Race and Philosophy* (New York: Routledge, 1996), 159–82. A good example of how race continues to

determine social, political, and legal deliberations is the debate on affirmative action, which has been ongoing since the 1964 Civil Rights Act. For a summary of the arguments surrounding race and gender, see Robert Fullinwider, "Affirmative Action," in *The Stanford Encyclopedia of Philosophy*, ed. Edward N. Zalta (Stanford: Stanford University Metaphysics Research Lab, 2014), http://plato.stanford.edu.

22 R. Drew Smith, William Ackah, Anthony G. Reddie, and Rothney S. Tshaka, eds., *Contesting Post-Racialism: Conflicted Churches in the United States and South Africa* (Jackson: University Press of Mississippi, 2015); Raphael G. Warnock, *The Divided Mind of the Black Church: Theology, Piety and Public Witness* (New York: New York University Press, 2013); Anthony B. Pinn, *Understanding and Transforming the Black Church* (Eugene, OR: Cascade, 2010); Anthony G. Reddie, *Working against the Grain: Re-Imaging Black Theology in the 21st Century* (New York: Routledge, 2008).

23 Jacques Derrida, *Specters of Marx: The State of the Debt, the Work of Mourning, and the New International*, trans. Peggy Kamuf (New York: Routledge, 1994). See especially his discussion in "What Is Ideology?" Derrida's use of *hauntology* was in response to the neoliberal conversations that followed the fall of the Berlin Wall and the alleged death of communism or Marxism as viable political alternatives to democratic liberalism. Derrida takes issue with this perspective, especially Francis Fukuyama's *End of History and the Last Man* (New York: Avon, 1992), which for him was an example of the messianic, eschatological yearning of neoliberal claims that the moment marked a period of "post-history," the triumph of Western democratic idealism as the final form of human government. This means that with the apparent demise of other viable systematic alternatives to Western democratic liberalism and the ineluctable spread of consumeristic Western culture, the stage is set for a nihilistic, utilitarian world culture that sees the human self as a rational, profit-maximizing individual. Derrida argues otherwise, asserting that the West is haunted by ghosts, the specters of Marx or Marxism (as was Marx himself). According to Derrida, Marx perceived the rise of capital as an eerie visitation of ideology supported by religious-theological haunts of Christendom that announced themselves in the "sensuous non-sensuous, sensuously supersensible" apparition of a *thing* (commodity):

> The commodity is a "thing" without phenomenon, a thing in flight that surpasses the senses (it is invisible, intangible, inaudible, and odourless); but this transcendence is not altogether spiritual, it retains that bodiless body which we have recognised as making the difference between spectre and spirit. What surpasses the senses still passes before us in the silhouette of the sensuous body that it nevertheless lacks or that remains inaccessible to us. Marx does not say sensuous and non-sensuous, or sensuous but non-sensuous. He says: sensuous non-sensuous, sensuously supersensible. *Transcendence, the movement of super-, the step beyond (über, epekeina), is*

made sensuous in that very excess. It renders the non-sensuous sensuous. One touches there on what one does not touch, one feels there where one does not feel, one even suffers there where suffering does not take place, when at least it does not take place where one suffers (which is also, let us not forget, what is said about phantom limbs, that phenomenon marked with an X for any phenomenology of perception). The commodity thus haunts the thing, its spectre is at work in use-value. (189, italics added)

24 For classical readings, see John Rawls, *A Theory of Justice* (Cambridge, MA: Belknap, 1971, 1999); Robert Nozick, *Anarchy, State, and Utopia* (New York: Basic Books, 2013); Michael Walzer, *Spheres of Justice: A Defense of Pluralism and Equality* (New York: Basic Books, 1983); and Michael Sandel, *Liberalism and the Limits of Justice* (Cambridge: Cambridge University Press, 1982, 1998). For the debate surrounding desert and fairness in race and affirmative action, see Stephen L. Carter, *Reflections of an Affirmative Action Baby* (New York: Basic Books: 1991); Terry Eastland, *Ending Affirmative Action: The Case for Colorblind Justice* (New York: Basic Books, 1996); Terry Eastland and William J. Bennett, *Counting by Race: Equality from the Founding Fathers to Bakke and Weber* (New York: Basic Books, 1979); Christopher Edley Jr., *Not All Black and White: Affirmative Action and American Values* (New York: Hill and Wang, 1996); Kenneth Einar Himma, "Discrimination and Disidentification: The Fair-Start Defense of Affirmative Action," *Journal of Business Ethics* 30 (April 2001): 277–89; and Kenneth Einar Himma, "Desert, Entitlement, and Affirmative Action: A Response to Francis Beckwith," *Social Theory and Practice* 28 (January 2002): 157–66. For an interesting ethical reading, see Jonathan Haidt, *The Righteous Mind: Why Good People Are Divided by Politics and Religion* (New York: Random House, 2013).

25 Derrida interrogates the ghost and the temporality of being, as well as our ways of thinking about being: "The time is out of joint, O cursed spite that ever I was set to put it right" (*Hamlet*). Thus, his deconstructive task identifies *spectrality* as an abstract space that is not a space, a thing that is not a thing, with the disjuncture of time and the pluralization of temporalities so that the ghost signifies on all notions of being and justice. Most importantly, for our purposes, *hauntology* displaces ontology, a schema of movement that proceeds from the metaphysical to the historical, to the ethical-political, which is the question of justice. See Christopher Prendergast, "Derrida's Hamlet," *Substance* 34, no. 1 (2005): 44–47.

26 A key term for Derrida is the "visor effect" (sometimes, "ghostly effect"), which points to the phenomenology of the specter who sees but cannot be seen:

This spectral someone other looks at us, we feel ourselves being looked at by it, outside of any synchrony, even before and beyond any look on our part, according to any absolute anteriority (which may be on the order of generation, of more than one generation) and asymmetry, according to an absolutely unmasterable proportion. Here anachrony makes the law. To feel ourselves seen by a look which it will always be impossible to cross, that is the *visor effect* on the basis in which we inherit the law. Since we do not see the one who sees us, and who makes the law, who delivers the injunction (which is, moreover, a contradictory injunction), since we do not see the one who orders "swear," we cannot identify it in all certainty, we must fall back on its voice. The one who says, "I am thy Father's Spirit" can only be taken at his word. An essentially blind submission to his secret, to the secret of his origin: this is a first obedience to the injunction. It will condition all others. It may always be a case of still someone else. Another can always lie, he can disguise himself as a ghost, another ghost may also be passing himself off for this one. . . . The armor, this "costume," . . . we see it cover from head to foot, in Hamlet's eyes, the supposed body of the father. We do not know whether it is or is not part of the spectral apparition. This perception is rigorously *problematic* (*problema* is also a shield) for it prevents perception from deciding on the identity that it wraps so solidly in its carapace. The armor may be but the body of a real artifact, . . . a spectral body that it dresses, dissimulates and protects, masking even its identity The armor lets one see nothing of the spectral body.

Derrida, *Specters of Marx*, 7, italics in original.

27 For there is no ghost, there is never any becoming-spectre of the spirit without at least an appearance of flesh, in a space of invisible visibility, like the dis-appearing of an apparition. For there to be a ghost, there must be a return to the body, but to the body that is more abstract than ever. The spectrogenic process corresponds to a paradoxical incorporation. (ibid., 157–58)

28 As of the writing of this book, a number of church leaders and theologians have engaged in the Black Lives Matter campaign, but hardly a sufficient mass of churchly and scholarly manifestos that could be called prophetic. For exceptions, see Pamela R. Lightsey, *Our Lives Matter: A Womanist Queer Theology* (Eugene, OR: Pickwick, 2015); and Leah Gunning Francis, *Ferguson and Faith: Sparking Leadership and Awakening Community* (Atlanta: Chalice, 2015).

29 Touré, *Who's Afraid of Post-Blackness? What It Means to Be Black Now* (New York: Simon and Schuster, 2011).

30 Henry Louis Gates Jr., "The 'Blackness of Blackness': A Critique of the Sign and the Signifying Monkey," *Critical Inquiry* 9, no. 4 (June 1983): 686–93, 723; see also Henry Louis Gates Jr., *The Signifying Monkey: A Theory of African-American Literary Criticism* (New York: Oxford University Press, 1988). See Sterling Stuckey's discussion of Brer Rabbit in *Slave Culture: Nationalist Theory and the Foundations of Black America* (New York: Oxford University Press, 1987), 17–26; and Robert D. Pelton, *The Trickster in West Africa: A Study of Mythic Irony and Sacred Delight* (Oakland: University of California Press, 1989).

31 Sallie McFague, *Metaphorical Theology: Models of God in Religious Language* (Minneapolis: Fortress, 1982); Sallie McFague TeSelle, *Speaking in Parables*

(Philadelphia: Fortress, 1975); and *Models of God: Theology for an Ecological, Nuclear Age* (Minneapolis: Fortress, 1987). See also Robert Cummings Neville, *The Truth of Broken Symbols* (Albany: State University of New York Press, 1996).

32 Theodore Walker Jr., *Mothership Connections: A Black Atlantic Synthesis of Neoclassical Metaphysics and Black Theology* (Albany: State University of New York Press, 2004).

33 A fuller explication of this idea is in chapter 4 of this volume; see also Walter Earl Fluker, *Ethical Leadership: The Quest for Character, Civility, and Community* (Minneapolis: Fortress, 2009), chaps. 2 and 6, where I employ this narrative methodology in understanding leaders.

34 For black churches and their leadership, *common(s)* refers to the conjured spaces of common loyalties, common responsibilities, and social interaction where coding, languages, affects, information, and forms of knowledge impact African American lifeworlds nationally and globally. It is in these spaces that the work of remembering, retelling, and reliving the story is executed. See chapter 8 in this volume; and Warnock, *Divided Mind of the Black Church*, 185–89.

35 Cornel West, *Prophetic Fragments: Illuminations of the Crisis in American Religion and Culture* (Grand Rapids: Eerdmans, 1993), 3.

36 Pierre Bourdieu, *The Logic of Practice* (Stanford: Stanford University Press, 1990), 19.

37　Our interest in *lieux de mémoire* [sites of memory] where memory crystal-lizes and secretes itself has occurred at a particular historical moment, a turning point where consciousness of a break with the past is bound up with the sense that memory has been torn—but torn in such a way as to pose the problem of the embodiment of memory in certain sites where a sense of historical continuity persists. There are *lieux de mémoire* . . . because there are no longer *milieux de mémoire*, real environments of memory.
Dereck Daschke, *City of Ruins: Mourning the Destruction of Jerusalem through Jewish Apocalypse* (Leiden: Brill, 2010), 50, quoting Nora, "Between Memory and History," 7 (brackets and ellipses in original).

38 Baldwin, *Fire Next Time*.

39 See quote at the beginning of this chapter. "The notion that black people are human beings is a relatively new discovery in the modern West. The idea of black equality in beauty, culture, and intellectual capacity remains problematic." West, *Prophesy Deliverance!*, 47.

40 An important concept to which we will return throughout the book is the analytic tool of *habitus*. Suffice it to say for now, the idea of *habitus*, in the sense used by the sociologist Pierre Bourdieu, as "the logic of practice: [the] ordinary invisible operations by which a society perpetuates itself," is helpful in the analysis of cultural productions of domination for black churches in an era of post-racialism. Jennifer Glancy, *Corporal Knowledge: Early Christian Bodies* (New York: Oxford University Press, 2010), 146. Drawing upon classical and modern philosophical

and sociological notions of the term, Bourdieu defines *habitus* as the cognitive schema that is internalized by agents as a result of their adaptations to the social structure. "It ensures the active presence of past experiences, which, deposited in each organism in the form of schemes of perception, thought and action, tend to guarantee the 'correctness' of practices and their constancy over time, more reliably than all formal rules and explicit norms." Bourdieu, *Logic of Practice*, 54. Bourdieu defines social structure as a

> system of cognitive and motivating structures, . . . a world of already realized ends—procedures to follow, paths to take—and of objects endowed with a "permanent teleological character," in Husserl's phrase, tools or institutions. This is because the regularities inherent in an arbitrary condition . . . tend to appear as necessary, even natural, since they are the basis of the schemes of perception and appreciation through which they are apprehended. (ibid., 53–54)

In other words, *habitus* is both *structured and structuring* in respect to the everyday lifeworlds of agents. It is the "product of structure, producer of practice, and the reproducer of structure." Bourdieu, cited by Loïc Wacquant, in *Key Sociological Thinkers*, ed. Rob Stones (New York: Palgrave Macmillan, 2007), 221. This means that class location relative to means of production is not the only social determinant for agents, but self-identity and how others perceive one are shaped by a common, shared *habitus* that is culturally produced. It is the "immediate adherence . . . to the tastes and distastes, sympathies and aversions, fantasies and phobias, which more than declared opinions, forges the unconscious unity of a class." Pierre Bourdieu, *Distinction: A Social Critique of the Judgement of Taste* (London: Routledge, Taylor and Francis, 1979, 2013), 70. Most important for this analysis is that as "the product of history, *habitus* produces individual and collective practices, and thus history, in accordance with the schemata engendered by history" and situates the agent in a particular lifework with its own distinctive habits and practices, a set of acquired dispositions that "operate beneath the level of consciousness and discourse," and that these "sets of dispositions vary by social location and trajectory: individuals with different life experiences will have gained varied ways of thinking, feeling, and acting. . . . The socially constituted conative and cognitive structures that make up *habitus* are malleable and transmissible because they result from pedagogical work." Loïc Wacquant, "Habitus as Topic and Tool: Reflections on Becoming a Prizefighter," *Qualitative Research in Psychology* 8 (2011): 81–92; see also Jeffrey J. Sallaz and Jane Zavisca, "Bourdieu in American Sociology, 1980–2004," *Annual Review of Sociology* 33 (2007): 21–41. So for Bourdieu, societies reproduce themselves not because human beings are intrinsically mechanistic/deterministic, but because we are historical beings. The past is always present as habit. For our purposes, this leaves some room for subjectivity and freedom while recognizing that our consciousness is socially determined. In other words, the *habitus*—embodied history, internalized as a second nature and so forgotten as history—is the active presence of the whole past of which it is the product. As such, it is what gives practices their relative autonomy with respect to external determinations of the immediate present. This autonomy is that of the past, . . . which, functioning as accumulated capital, produces history on the basis of history and so ensures the permanence in change that makes the individual agent a world within the world.

Bourdieu, *Logic of Practice*, 56.

41 Fluker, *Ethical Leadership*, 168.

42 Sheila Smith McKoy, "The Limbo Contest: Diaspora Temporality and Its Reflection in *Praise Song to the Widow* and *Daughters of the Dust*," *Callaloo* 22, no. 1 (1999): 208–22, quoted in LeRhonda Manigault-Bryant, *Talking to the Dead: Religion, Music and Lived Memory among Gullah/Geeche Women* (Raleigh: Duke University Press, 2014), 98, 157; see also chap. 5, "Lived Memory," 172–203.

43 John S. Mbiti, *African Religions and Philosophy* (Oxford, UK: Heinemann, 1990), 22. Potential time is the time in-between, and is therefore fluid, malleable, and reconstructable. I am interested here in how potential time as in-between-time allows for the reconstruction or revisability of language as *sound* and improvisation of *mood* and tone. We, through our agency, "make the path" that leads to the river. The river is timeless—before and after time. We are constantly in the stream of the river, which flows in and out, forever ingressing and egressing, depicting two modes of reality—the inner and outer—which are inseparable but experienced as modes of consciousness. Howard Thurman asserts the following: (1) The river is the way to freedom (Deep River, my home is over Jordan) because life is like the river—simple beginnings with a swell of complexity over time, and then it empties itself into the sea "whose far off call the river hears." (2) There is an *intimate relationship* between the river and its banks. The banks have no choice—the river leaves its deposits, and we know the nature of the river by analyzing the sediment that is left; hence "the story of the river is the story of the banks that are touched by it"—a reference to Bourdieu's "embodied knowledge." (3) The flood time of the river brings with it the unexpected, the tragic, "that which has no rational resting place so that as the mind contemplates the experience it finds itself tilted and awry . . . and the answer to the flood time of the river is the larger opening of the sea." Howard Thurman, "Deep River," Louisville Chapel, Louisville Presbyterian Seminary, November 11, 1967.

44 Howard Thurman, "The Negro Spiritual Speaks of Life and Death," in *Deep River and The Negro Spiritual Speaks of Life and Death* (Richmond, IN: Friends United Press, 1975), 18.

45 Jan Assmann, *Moses the Egyptian: The Memory of Egypt in Western Monotheism* (Cambridge: Harvard University Press, 1997), 14–17, quoted in Fluker, *Ethical Leadership*, 50.

46 M. Shawn Copeland, *Enfleshing Freedom: Body, Race, and Being* (Minneapolis: Fortress, 2010). "Enfleshed life" refers to Copeland's argument that we remember and reimagine black women's bodies by reclaiming the body as being made "in the image and likeness of God, . . . having a unique place in the cosmos God created, and . . . made for communion with other living beings" (24). Beginning with narratives of emancipated slaves, Copeland's examination of theological anthropology reframes the marked body of Jesus in relation to race, gender, empire, and sexuality and how bodies are embraced, and a (re)marking of the flesh of the church (57–58, 88). See also Christopher Conway, review of *Enfleshing Freedom: Body, Race, and Being*, by M. Shawn Copeland, *Journal of Interdisciplinary Feminist Thought* 4, no. 1 (2010).

47 Emilie M. Townes, *Womanist Ethics and the Cultural Production of Evil* (New York: Palgrave Macmillan, 2006), 12; see also 18, 159, 165.

48 Eze, *Achieving Our Humanity*, 15; see also Cornel West, "A Genealogy of Modern Racism," in *Prophesy Deliverance!*, 47–68; and Brad Elliott Stone, "Prophetic Pragmatism and the Practices of Freedom: On Cornel West's Foucauldian Methodology," *Foucault Studies*, no. 11 (February 2011): 92–105.

49 Sojourner Truth, *The Narrative of Sojourner Truth*, 3rd ed. (Mineola, NY: Dover, 1997), 46.

50 Amos N. Wilder, "The Rhetoric of Ancient and Modern Apocalyptic," *Interpretation* 25, no. 4 (October 1971): 440.

51 David Walker, "Article 3: Our Wretchedness in Consequence of the Preachers of the Religion of Jesus Christ," in *Appeal to the Coloured Citizens of the World*, available at website of *IPOAA Magazine* (Indigenous People of Africa and America), www.ipoaa.com, accessed July 1, 2015.

52 West, *Prophetic Fragments*, 41 (emphasis in original). See also Peter J. Paris's treatment of the "black Christian tradition as prophetic principle" in *Social Teaching of the Black Churches*; and Robert C. Williams, "Moral Suasion and Militant Aggression in the Theological Perspective of Black Religion," *Journal of Religious Thought* 30, no. 2 (1973–74): 27–50.

53 Evelyn Brooks Higginbotham, *Righteous Discontent: The Women's Movement in the Black Baptist Church, 1880–1920* (Cambridge: Harvard University Press, 1994); Anthea D. Butler, *Women in the Church of God in Christ: Making a Sanctified World* (Chapel Hill: University of North Carolina Press, 2007).

54 Cornel West, "Black Strivings in a Twilight Civilization," in *The Future of the Race*, by Henry Louis Gates Jr. and Cornel West (New York: Knopf, 1996), 78.

55 Warnock, *Divided Mind of the Black Church*; see also Robert Franklin's metaphor of the "strenuous self." Robert Michael Franklin, *Liberating Visions: Human Fulfillment and Social Justice in African-American Thought* (Minneapolis: Fortress, 1990), 44–47.

56 "The ability of a practice to retain its integrity will depend on the way in which the virtues can be and are exercised in sustaining the institutional forms which

are the social bearers of the practice." Alasdair MacIntyre, *After Virtue* (Notre
Dame: University of Notre Dame Press, 2007), 195; see also 190–91, 218–22.

57 Kevin K. Gaines, *Uplifting the Race: Black Leadership, Politics, and Culture in the
Twentieth Century* (Chapel Hill: University of North Carolina Press, 1996), 31.

58 Evelyn Brooks-Higginbotham's discussion of the "politics of respectability" as
being the primary sociopolitical strategy for women of the Negro Club Movement
is helpful. Brooks-Higginbotham, *Righteous Discontent*, 14–15; see also Butler,
Women in the Church of God in Christ; and Cheryl J. Sanders, *Saints in Exile: The
Holiness-Pentecostal Experience in African American Religion and Culture* (New
York: Oxford University Press, 1996).

59 See also C. Eric Lincoln, *Race, Religion, and the Continuing American Dilemma*
(New York: Hill and Wang, 1984); and Victor Anderson, *Beyond Ontological
Blackness: An Essay on African-American Religious and Cultural Criticism* (New
York: Continuum, 1995). See Cornel West's observations on "doubleness" in
"Black Strivings," specifically, its relationship to despair, destruction, and death,
using Du Bois's metaphor.

60 Harold Cruse, *The Crisis of the Negro Intellectual: A Historical Analysis of the
Failure of Black Leadership* (New York: New York Review of Books, 1967), 564,
quoted in Bruce J. Dierenfield and John White, *A History of African-American
Leadership* (New York: Routledge, 2012), 1.

61 Kevin Gaines adds that "education of the freedpeople was often tied to moral
evolution and industrial training rather than citizenship and political independence." Gaines, *Uplifting the Race*, 35.

62 See Walter Earl Fluker, "Recognition, Respectability, and Loyalty: Black Churches
and the Quest for Civility," in *New Day Begun: African American Churches and
Civic Culture in Post–Civil Rights America*, ed. R. Drew Smith (Durham: Duke
University Press, 2003).

63 Walter Earl Fluker, "Dangerous Memories and Redemptive Possibilities:
Reflections on the Life and Work of Howard Thurman," in *Black Leaders and
Ideologies in the South: Resistance and Nonviolence*, ed. Preston King and Walter
Earl Fluker (New York: Routledge, 2005), 147–76. "*Dangerous memories* fund a
community's sense of dignity; they inspire and empower those who challenge
oppression. *Dangerous memories* are a people's history of resistance and struggle,
of dignity and transcendence in the face of struggle." Sharon Welch, "The Beloved
Community," *Spirituality Today* 40 (Winter 1988): 11–12. The German political
theologian Johann Baptist Metz uses this language to identify the Cross as an act
of political resistance. Johann Baptist Metz, *Faith in History and Society: Toward a
Practical Fundamental Society* (New York: Seabury, 1980), 89.

64 Christine M. Smith, *Preaching as Weeping, Confession, and Resistance* (Louisville:
Westminster John Knox, 1992); see also Ann Hinz, *Preaching as Weeping,
Confession, and Resistance: Using Christine Smith's Metaphor of Preaching to
Confront Issues of Individual and Systemic White Racism towards Spanish Speaking*

People in a Local Congregation—Community (San Francisco: San Francisco Theological Seminary, 2002).

65 Thurman, *Deep River and The Negro Spiritual Speaks of Life and Death*, 24–25.

66 Richard Roquemore, "If You Just Hold Out until Tomorrow," in *The Silver Lining*, album, available on www.youtube.com, accessed September 23, 2015.

67 Langston Hughes, "Mother to Son," www.poemhunter.com.

68 I am using *crossing(s)* in three analytically distinct yet interrelated grammatical ways. First, *crossing(s)* represents the act of a person or thing that *crosses and encounters another*; second, it is a site where figures, lines, streets, tracks, etc. cross each other; or a site at which a figure, road, railroad track, river, etc., may be crossed. *Crossing(s)* suggests that it can be pluralized depending on the perspective brought to bear and the many different contexts in which *crossing(s)* occur. *Crossing(s)* in the first sense describes the *act* of a person or thing that crosses—it speaks to agency. In the second sense, *crossing(s)* suggests a *space* where figures and things cross one another as in intersecting lines, as crossroads. In a third sense it represents something or someone there who/that is crossed like a river or a road or a figure. The third sense is also a play on religious and cultural dynamics of trickster analogues that point to the in-between spaces of life and death. See, for instance, Nathaniel Mackey, *Discrepant Engagement: Dissonance, Cross-Culturality and Experimental Writing* (New York: Cambridge University Press, 1993); and Edward M Pavlić, "'Papa Legba, Ouvrier Barriere por Moi Passer': Esu in *Their Eyes* and Zora Neale Hurston's Diasporic Modernism," *African American Review* 38, no. 1 (2004): 61–85. My main purpose in thinking of *crossing(s)* in these ways has to do, therefore, with agency, space, and that/whom we encounter in our passages through history and time for the birthing of consciousness in respect to subjectivity, intersubjectivity, and human and nonhuman flourishing.

69 See the discussions of *crossing(s)* in chapters 6, 7, and 8 as examples where individuals and collectivities experience these phenomena.

70 See a fascinating commentary on the notion of crossings by Robert Cheatham, "Who Goes There?," Public Domain, Inc., www.pd.org, accessed November 14, 2015.

71 Morrison, *Beloved*, 102–4; see also Carl Plasa, ed., *Toni Morrison: Beloved*, Columbia Critical Guides (New York: University of Columbia Press, 1998), chap. 4, "This Is Flesh I'm Talking About: Language, Subjectivity and the Body."

72 See James C. Scott, *Domination and the Arts of Resistance: Hidden Transcripts* (New Haven: Yale University Press, 1990); and Sterling Stuckey, "The Death of Benito Cereno: A Reading of Herman Melville on Slavery," in *Going through the Storm: The Influence of African American Art in History* (New York: Oxford University Press, 1994), 53–70. See also Joshua Leslie and Sterling Stuckey, "The Death of Benito Cereno: A Reading of Herman Melville on Slavery: The Revolt on Board the *Tryal*," *Journal of Negro History* 67, no. 4 (Winter 1982): 287–301.

CHAPTER 3. CULTURAL HAUNTINGS

1 For an example of the many times that Thurman used this phrase, see Howard Thurman's meditation in memory of Jim Reeb in the spring 1965 issue of the *Liberal Context*, a paraphrase from Hermann Hagedorn's "The Boy in Armor":
   We died. And now you fathers who make wars
   Shall do a harder thing than dying is—
   For you shall *think!* And ghosts will drive you on! (italics in original)

2 Walter Earl Fluker, "President-Elect Barack Obama: Race Has Been Haunting This Election," *U.S. News and World Report*, November 5, 2008, www.usnews. com.

3 Kathleen Brogan, *Cultural Haunting: Ghosts and Ethnicity in Recent American Literature* (Charlottesville: University Press of Virginia, 1998), 2.

4 Brendan Fischer, "Verdict in Jordan Davis Case Highlights Continuing Injustice of 'Stand Your Ground,'" February 17, 2014, www.prwatch.org; Lizette Alvarez, "Jury Reaches Partial Verdict in Florida Killing over Loud Music," *New York Times*, February 15, 2014, www.nytimes.com; Ta-Nehisi Coates, "On the Killing of Jordan Davis by Michael Dunn," *Atlantic*, February 15, 2014, www.theatlantic.com; Lauren Williams, "Michael Dunn Was Just Sentenced to Life without Parole for Murdering Jordan Davis," *Mother Jones*, updated October 17, 2014, www.mother-jones.com.

5 See David Eldridge, "Tavis Smiley: Obama's Race Speech 'Weak as Kool-Aid,'" *Washington Times*, July 21, 2013, www.washingtontimes.com. For other statements regarding President Obama's alleged racism, see Scott Keyes, "Top 12 Conservative Freakouts after Obama's Race Speech," *ThinkProgress*, July 19, 2013; Ahiza Garcia, "Larry Klayman: 'Racist in Chief' Obama Siding with 'Black Brothers' in Ferguson," *Talking Points Memo*, August 18, 2014, http://talking-pointsmemo.com; and Larry Klayman, "Obama's Insidious Racism," WND.org, August 15, 2014, www.wnd.com.

6 See chapter 2, note 2 for my definition of black churches.

7 A number of scholars at different poles of the spectrum argue from the vantage point of post-racism, both for and against its reality and effects. See, for example, Jason Riley, *Please Stop Helping Us: How Liberals Make It Harder for Blacks to Succeed* (New York: Encounter Books, 2014); Frederick C. Harris, *The Price of the Ticket: Barack Obama and the Rise and Decline of Black Politics* (New York: Oxford University Press, 2012).

8 Barack Obama, *The Audacity of Hope: Thoughts on Reclaiming the American Dream* (New York: Random House, 2006).

9 "The Rev. Jeremiah Wright Was an Early Concern, Obama Aide Admits," *Los Angeles Times*, March 16, 2008, http://latimesblogs.latimes.com.

10 Michael Eric Dyson, *The Black Presidency: Barack Obama and the Politics of Race in America* (New York: Houghton Mifflin Harcourt, 2016), 80–117; and Roland

Martin, "The Full Story behind Wright's 'God Damn America' Sermon," CNN. com, March 21, 2008, http://ac360.blogs.cnn.com.

11 "Rev. Wright Delivers Remarks at National Press Club," *Washington Post*, April 28, 2008, www.washingtonpost.com.

12 Cornel West, *Black Prophetic Fire*, in dialogue with and edited by Christa Buschendorf (Boston: Beacon, 2014); Manning Marable and Kristen Clarke, eds., *Barack Obama and African American Empowerment: The Rise of Black America's New Leadership* (New York: Palgrave Macmillan, 2009). See Michael Eric Dyson, "The Ghost of Cornel West," *New Republic*, April 19, 2015, www.newrepublic.com; see also Dyson's comments on the same in Michael Eric Dyson, "All Black Lives Matter: Seeing the Humanity of Those I Criticize Is Vital to Every Claim I Make under the Banner of #BlackLivesMatter," *New Republic*, April 24, 2015, www. newrepublic.com. Since the writing of this book, new critiques of this phenomenon have been eloquently addressed by Dyson, *The Black Presidency*; and Glaude, *Democracy in Black*.

13 Gary Dorrien, *The Obama Question: A Progressive Perspective* (Lanham, MD: Rowman and Littlefield, 2012).

14 Fareed Zakaria, *The Post-American World* (New York: Norton, 2008).

15 For history and analysis of the Occupy movement, see Michael A. Gould-Wartofsky, *The Occupiers: The Making of the 99 Percent Movement* (New York: Oxford University Press, 2015); Thomas Jerome Baker, *Black Lives Matter: From Holocaust to Lynching to Liberation* (n.p.: CreateSpace, 2015). For alternative knowledge systems, see David Frum, "Post-Tea-Party Nation," *New York Times Magazine*, November 12, 2010, www.nytimes.com.

16 Robert Reich, *Supercapitalism: The Transformation of Business, Democracy, and Everyday Life* (New York: Knopf, 2007), 167.

17 Michael Mandelbaum, *The Case for Goliath: How America Acts as the World's Government in the Twenty-First Century* (New York: Public Affairs, 2005).

18 Peter Baker, "In Congress, Netanyahu Faults 'Bad Deal' on Iran Nuclear Program," *New York Times*, March 3, 2015, www.nytimes.com. Ralph Ellison, *The Invisible Man* (New York: Vintage, 1995), 3.

19 In *The Obama Question*, Dorrien characterizes Obama as reaching always for "the liberal leaning middle ground" (54); as being conciliatory to a fault (portrayed by his rhetoric of "rightly or wrongly"/ "on the one hand, then on the other"); and his predisposition for finding the middle way, always "balancing" contending forces, especially as it relates to racial politics. Dorrien summarizes Obama's nonpolemical *raced* reasoning this way: "Since white guilt is largely exhausted in America anyway, those who care about racial justice need to talk about common good, not racial justice" (55). Dorrien adds, "To succeed, he believes that he must care more about civility and cooperation than about fighting for a principle" (226). Obama is fearful of losing face and intent on "not making the perfect the enemy of the good" (55, 90).

20 Harris, *Price of the Ticket.*

21 Ibid., 155.

22 Ibid., 182. At another place he writes, "For many black voters the symbolism of a black president and black family in the White House is well worth the price of the ticket."

23 Ibid., 151–55. See also Dyson, *The Black Presidency,* 33–68.

24 Shelby Steele, *A Bound Man: Why We Are Excited about Obama and Why He Can't Win* (New York: Free Press, 2008), quoted in Dorrien, *Obama Question,* 59.

25 During President Obama's second bid for office, at the Republican National Convention in August 2012, the actor and director Clint Eastwood mocked Obama's alleged "invisibility" by speaking to an empty chair. While the Republican faithful found his remarks humorous, many were deeply embarrassed and humiliated by what appeared to be empty ramblings that further exacerbated the Republican image as racist and defeatist. Halimah Abdullah, "Eastwood, the Empty Chair and the Speech Everyone's Talking About," CNN.com, August 31, 2012, www.cnn.com.

26 Noel Sheppard, "Cornel West: MSNBC's Black Commentators 'Sold Their Souls for a Mess of Obama Pottage,'" NewsBusters.org, November 12, 2012, http://newsbusters.org.

27 See also Cornel West, "Last Words on Black Prophetic Fire in the Age of Obama," in *Black Prophetic Fire,* 161–65.

28 Manfred Kets deVries, *The Leadership Mystique: Leading Behavior in the Human Enterprise* (Upper Saddle River, NJ: FT Press, 2006), 5.

29 Irving Goffman, *Presentation of Self in Everyday Life* (New York: Anchor, 1959).

30 See Ronald Takaki, *Iron Cages: Race and Culture in 19th-Century America* (New York: Oxford University Press, 1990), 121.

31 See Langston Hughes, "I, Too," in *The Weary Blues* (New York: Knopf, 1926).

32 Frantz Fanon, *Black Skin, White Masks,* trans. Charles Lam Markmann (New York: Grove, 1967), 17–18.

33 Fluker, *Ethical Leadership,* 87–88.

34 As Dorrien put it, "But the banks that Paulson and Geithner stuffed with taxpayer money had no interest in reforming, and by setting his sights too low, Obama missed a precious opportunity—to reduce Wall Street to the role it had in American society before it fell in love with securitization and derivatives." *Obama Question,* 87.

35 Jeffrey C. Goldfarb, *Civility and Subversion: The Intellectual in Democratic Society* (Cambridge: Cambridge University Press, 1998), 1.

36 Jim Wallis, *God's Politics: Why the Right Gets It Wrong and the Left Doesn't Get It: A New Vision for Faith and Politics in America* (San Francisco: HarperCollins, 2006), chap. 19. On *Face the Nation* on November 27, 2011, Condoleezza Rice said, "It is a birth defect with which this country was born out of slavery; we're never

really going to be race blind." Lucy Madison, "Condi Rice: U.S. Will Never Be 'Race Blind,'" CBSNews.com, November 27, 2011, www.cbsnews.com.

37 See note 26 in chapter 2; also Prendergast, "Derrida's Hamlet."

38 Steven M. Tipton, "Close to the Heart of Humankind: Faith Transformed and Renewed in America Today" (presented at Chautauqua Institution's "Religion: Vanishing and Emerging" conference, August 3, 2015).

39 "Amazing Grace" was published in 1779, with words written by John Newton (1725–1807). See Jonathan Aitken, *John Newton: From Disgrace to Amazing Grace* (Wheaton, IL: Crossway, 2007).

40 Senator Barack Obama, "A More Perfect Union," March 18, 2008, www.politico. com; President Barack Obama, "Remarks by the President in Eulogy for the Honorable Reverend Clementa Pinckney," College of Charleston, Charleston, South Carolina, June 26, 2015, www.whitehouse.gov; see also T. Denean Sharpley-Whiting, ed., *The Speech: Race and Barack Obama's "A More Perfect Union"* (New York: Bloomburg USA, 2009); and Angela D. Sims, F. Douglass Powe Jr., and Johnny Bernard Hill, *Religio-Political Narratives in the United States: From Martin Luther King, Jr. to Jeremiah Wright* (New York: Palgrave Macmillan, 2014).

41 For the full text, see "Remarks as Prepared for Delivery–by President Barack Obama, Address to the People of Africa," *Voice of America*, African Union Headquarters, Addis Ababa, Ethiopia, July 28, 2015, www.voanews.com.

42 Vincent L. Wimbush, "Interpreters—Enslaving/Enslaved/Runagate," *Journal of Biblical Literature* 130, no. 1 (2011): 5–24; West, *Black Prophetic Fire*.

43 Jonathan Walton, *Watch This! The Ethics and Aesthetics of Black Televangelism* (New York: New York University Press, 2009). See also reviews of Walton's book, by Ben Sanders III in *Religious Studies Review* 36, no. 2 (June 2010): 39; Mary D. Hinton in *Journal of American Ethnic History* 30, no. 4 (Summer 2011); and Ryon J. Cobb in *Journal for the Scientific Study of Religion* 49, no. 4 (2010): 771–82.

44 Afe Adogame, *The African Christian Diaspora: New Currents and Emerging Trends in World Christianity* (London: Bloomsbury Academic, 2013); Kwabena Asamoah-Gyadu, *Contemporary Pentecostal Christianity: Interpretations from an African Context*, Regnum Studies in Global Christianity (Eugene, OR: Wipf and Stock, 2013); Nimi Wariboko, *The Pentecostal Principle: Ethical Methodology in New Spirit*, Pentecostal Manifestos (Grand Rapids: Eerdmans, 2012).

PART II. VISION

1 Countee Cullen, "Heritage (For Harold Jackman)," in *American Negro Poetry*, ed. Arna Bontemps (New York: Hill and Wang, 1960), 86.

CHAPTER 4. *TURNING* FROM DILEMMA TO DIASPORA

1 Toni Morrison, "Home," in *The House That Race Built: Black Americans, U.S. Terrain*, ed. Wahneema Lubiano (New York: Pantheon, 1997), 10–11.

2 In the following I borrow largely from Richard A. Jones, "Race and Revisability," *Journal of Black Studies* 35, no. 5 (2005). See also Outlaw, *On Race and Philosophy*; Charles Mills, *Blackness Visible: Essays on Philosophy and Race* (Ithaca: Cornell University Press, 1998); Naomi Zack, "Mixed Black and White Race in Public Policy," in *Race, Class, Gender, and Sexuality: The Big Questions*, ed. Naomi Zack, Laurie Shrage, and Crispin Sartwell (Malden, MA: Wiley-Blackwell, 1998); Eze, *Achieving Our Humanity*; Howard McGary, *The Post-Racial Ideal* (Milwaukee: Marquette University Press, 2012); F. Michael Higginbotham, *Ghosts of Jim Crow: Ending Racism in Post-Racial America* (New York: New York University Press, 2013); Michael Tillotson, *Invisible Jim Crow: Contemporary Ideological Threats to the Internal Security of African Americans* (Trenton, NJ: Africa World Press, 2011); Catina Fritz and John Stone, "A Post-Racial America: Myth or Reality?," *Journal of Ethnic and Racial Studies* 32, no. 6 (2009): 1083–88; David Ikard, *Nation of Cowards: Black Activism in Barak Obama's Post-Racial America* (Bloomington: Indiana University Press, 2012); Devon W. Carbado and Mitu Gulati, *Acting White? Rethinking Race in "Post-Racial" America* (New York: Oxford University Press, 2013).

3 Lyrics from "Glory," produced by John Legend and written and performed in collaboration with Common.

4 See, for example, Kwame Anthony Appiah, "Illusions of Race," in *In My Father's House: Africa in the Philosophy of Culture* (New York: Oxford University Press, 1992), 28–46. Describing the eliminativist thesis as an Enlightenment ideal, Jones writes, "according to the eliminativists, if race is not a scientific fact, it must be a sociohistorical convention that can be eliminated by the construction of a counterconsciousness based on the delivery of the high egalitarian promises of the Enlightenment." Jones, "Race and Revisability," 621, 626.

5 Zack, "Mixed Black and White Race in Public Policy," 83.

6 Dyson, *The Black Presidency*, 65.

7 Toni Morrison's work on race as metaphor also informs my thinking on shape-shifting and, hence, the revisability of race. See Morrison, *Playing in the Dark: Whiteness and the Literary Imagination* (Cambridge: Harvard University Press, 1993), 63.

8 Jones, "Race and Revisability," 627.

9 See earlier discussion on *habitus* in note 40, chapter 2. Bourdieu, *Logic of Practice*. See especially Bourdieu's conception of *habitus* as "a principle of a selective perception of the indices tending to confirm and reinforce it rather than transform it, a matrix generating responses adapted in advance to all objective conditions identical to or homologous with the (past) conditions of its production" (64). In chapter 8, I will return to this notion of *habitus* alongside Orlando Patterson, ed., *The Cultural Matrix: Understanding Black Youth* (Cambridge: Harvard University Press, 2015) as a way of better understanding and negotiating the structure versus culture debate in black life and practices. See also M.

Brewster Smith, *Values, Self, and Society: Toward a Humanist Social Psychology* (New Brunswick, NJ: Transaction, 1991).

10 M. Brewster Smith, "The Metaphorical Basis of Selfhood," in *Culture and Self*, ed. A. J. Marsella et al. (New York: Tavistock, 1985), 58–63.

11 See Fluker, *Ethical Leadership*, 92–99.

12 A. Paul Hare and Herbert H. Blumberg, *Dramaturgical Analysis of Social Interaction* (Westport, CT: Praeger, 1988), 3.

13 Bourdieu, *Logic of Practice*, 19.

14 See Fluker, *Ethical Leadership*; F. LeRon Shults and Steven J. Sandage, *The Faces of Forgiveness: Searching for Salvation and Wholeness* (Grand Rapids: Baker Academic, 2003).

15 Thandeka, *Learning to Be White: Money, Race, and God in America* (New York: Continuum, 1999).

16 See Stuart Hall, "Subjects in History: Making Diasporic Identities," in Lubiano, *House That Race Built*, 299.

17 Willie James Jennings, *The Christian Imagination: Theology and the Origins of Race* (New Haven: Yale University Press, 2010).

18 Hortense J. Spillers, "Mama's Baby, Papa's Maybe: An American Grammar Book," *Diacritics* 17, no. 2 (Summer 1987): 65–81.

19 Giorgio Agamben, *Homo Sacer: Sovereign Power and Bare Life*, trans. Daniel Heller-Roazen (Stanford: Stanford University Press, 1998), 53, 60–62 (italics in original).

20 *Pharmakos (φαρμακός)* in its ancient Greek meaning refers to the slave, the criminal, the deformed, the exile who is ritualistically sacrificed for the safety and order of society. Walter Burkert, *Greek Religion* (Cambridge: Harvard University Press, 1985), 82; Walter Burkert, *Structure and History in Greek Mythology* (Berkeley: University of California Press, 1979), 59–77; René Girard, *The Scapegoat*, trans. Y. Freccero (Baltimore: Johns Hopkins University Press, 1986); and Jacques Derrida, *Dissemination*, trans. Barbara Johnson (Chicago: University of Chicago Press, 1981). *Pharmakon (φάρμακος, οῦ, ὁ)*, on the other hand, is associated with poison (drug) that heals; sometimes referenced as a person who poisons and who heals through skilled uses of herbs and plants, a magician, sorcerer, or conjurer. See my discussion of the use of *conjure* in chapters 7 and 8 of this volume.

21 Stuckey, *Slave Culture*, 18.

22 Babacar M'Baye, *The Trickster Comes West: Pan-African Influence in Early Black Diasporan Narratives* (Jackson: University Press of Mississippi, 2009), 162–67.

23 Stuckey, *Slave Culture*, 19.

24 Ibid., 17–23.

25 Ibid., 23.

26 Michelle M. Wright, *Physics of Blackness: Beyond the Middle Passage Epistemology* (Minneapolis: University of Minnesota Press, 2015).

Epiphenomenal time denotes the current moment, a moment that is *not* directly borne out of another (i.e., causally created). . . . [It] does not preclude any and all causality: only a *direct*, or *linear*, causality. In other words, the current moment, or "now," can certainly correlate with other moments, but one cannot argue that it is always already the effect of a specific, previous moment. (4)

27   Lamentations 3:20–22 NIV.

28   *Sankofa* is the Akan (Ghana) word that means to "reach back and get it" (*san*—to return; *ko*—to go; *fa*—to fetch, to seek and take) and is symbolized by a bird that *turns* its head backwards, pointing to the truth of the past and its necessity for moving into the future and living wisely in the present. I am thinking of it here as an ongoing movement from the long-ago and not-so-long-ago past to the future as vision that beckons for it in a dance that is continuously present.

29   Gunnar Myrdal, *An American Dilemma: The Negro Problem and Modern Democracy* (New York: Harper and Brothers, 1944). See Fluker, *Ethical Leadership*, 100–102; and Fluker, "Recognition, Respectability, and Loyalty."

30   Cruse, *Crisis of the Negro Intellectual*; Gaines, *Uplifting the Race*, 5; Darlene Clark Hines, "Rape and the Inner Lives of Black Women in the Middle West: Preliminary Thoughts on the Culture of Dissemblance," in *Unequal Sisters: A Multicultural Reader in U.S. Women's History*, ed. Ellen DuBois and Vicki L. Ruiz (New York: Routledge, 1990); and Joy James, *Transcending the Talented Tenth: Black Leaders and American Intellectuals* (New York: Routledge, 1997). See also Carl P. Henry, *Culture and African-American Politics* (Bloomington: Indiana University Press, 1990), 10–11.

31   Ralph Luker, *The Social Gospel in Black and White* (Chapel Hill: University of North Carolina Press, 1991); Sidney M. Wilhelm, *Who Needs the Negro?* (New York: Anchor, 1971); and Benjamin Quarles, *The Negro in the Making of America* (New York: Collier, 1964).

32   Victor Turner, "Betwixt and Between: The Liminal Period in *Rites de Passage*," in *The Forest of Symbols* (Ithaca: Cornell University Press, 1967).

33   Romans 7:24.

34   Glaude, *Democracy in Black*; Lubiano, *House That Race Built*; see especially her introduction.

35   See Terrence L. Johnson, *Tragic Soul-Life: W. E. B. Du Bois and the Moral Crisis Facing American Democracy*, Imagining the Americas (New York: Oxford University Press, 2011); Tommie Shelby, *We Who Are Dark: The Philosophical Foundations of Black Solidarity* (Cambridge, MA: Belknap, 2007), 62; T. Owens Moore, "A Fanonian Perspective on Double Consciousness," *Journal of Black Studies* 35, no. 6 (July 2005): 751–62, www.jstor.org; Emmanuel C. Eze, "On Double Consciousness," *Callaloo: A Journal of African-American and African Arts and Letters* 34, no. 3 (Summer 2011): 877–98, 983; Sanders, *Saints in Exile*, 125; Cornel West, *Race Matters* (New York: Vintage, 1994), 98; and Paul Gilroy, *Against*

Race: Imagining Political Culture beyond the Color Line (Cambridge, MA: Belknap, 2002), 77–78.

36 Lincoln, *Race, Religion and the Continuing American Dilemma*; and Anderson, *Beyond Ontological Blackness*. See Cornel West's observations on "doubleness" in "Black Strivings," specifically, its relationship to despair, destruction, and death using Du Bois's metaphor; see also Franklin's discussion on "strenuous life" in *Liberating Visions*.

37 Pinn and Hopkins, *Loving the Body*.

38 Paris, *Social Teaching of the Black Churches*, 29.

39 Neville, *Truth of Broken Symbols*.

40 Jennings, *Christian Imagination*.

41 Dean E. Robinson, *Black Nationalism in American Politics and Thought* (Cambridge: Cambridge University Press, 2001); Stuckey, *Slave Culture*; William Jeremiah Moses, *The Golden Age of Black Nationalism, 1850–1925* (New York: Oxford University Press, 1978); John H. Bracey, *Black Nationalism in America* (Indianapolis: Bobbs-Merrill, 1970).

42 See my treatment of King's *turning* in chapter 7.

43 Lewis V. Baldwin and Paul R. Dekar, eds., *"In an Inescapable Network of Mutuality": Martin Luther King, Jr. and the Globalization of an Ethical Ideal* (Eugene, OR: Cascade, 2013).

44 Tracey E. Hucks, *Yoruba Traditions and African American Religious Nationalism*, with foreword by Charles H. Long (Albuquerque: University of New Mexico Press, 2012, 2014); Walter F. Pitts, *Old Ship of Zion: The Afro-Baptist Ritual in the African Diaspora*, Religion in America Series (New York: Oxford University Press, 1996); Eddie S. Glaude Jr., *Exodus! Religion, Race, and Nation in Early Nineteenth-Century Black America* (Chicago: University of Chicago Press, 2000).

45 Hucks, *Yoruba Traditions*, 14.

46 Paul Gilroy, *The Black Atlantic: Modernity and Double Consciousness* (Cambridge: Harvard University Press, 1993); Walker, *Mothership Connections*; Charles H. Long, *Alpha: The Myths of Creation* (Chico, CA: Scholars Press, 1963); Charles H. Long, *Significations: Signs, Symbols and Images in the Interpretation of Religion* (Philadelphia: Fortress, 1986); Hucks, *Yoruba Traditions*.

47 J. Lorand Matory, *Black Atlantic Religion: Tradition, Transnationalism, and Matriarchy in the Afro-Brazilian Candomblé* (Princeton: Princeton University Press, 2005), 274.

48 Matory, *Black Atlantic Religion*, 280–82; Hucks, *Yoruba Traditions*.

49 "Rhizomatic" from Gilles Deleuze and Felix Guattari, *A Thousand Plateaus: Capitalism and Schizophrenia*, rev. ed., trans. Brian Massumi (New York: Continuum, 2004), 21. See also Awad Ibrahim, *The Rhizome of Blackness: A Critical Ethnography of Hip-Hop Culture, Language, Identity, and the Politics of Becoming*, Black Studies and Critical Thinking Series (New York: Peter Lang, 2014).

50 Matory, *Black Atlantic Religion*, 280.
51 Ibrahim, *Rhizome of Blackness*. Borrowing from Deleuze and Guattari, Ibrahim observes,

> *Line of flight* means a path, line of possibilities. Both in the plural and singular forms, in the end, *line of flight* is about pursuing and following paths where the end result is either unknown (rhizome) or assumed to be known, binary and totalizing (arborescent). As such . . . the rhizome is altogether different from the arborescent. It is more complex, complicated, fluid, multiple, and multiplying, and forever becoming. The rhizome is in constant flow or movement of *deterritorialization*. It is not a point that we reach, and finally say, We are finally here. Rather, it is a way of becoming that we are forever struggling to attain. Being open to the unknown, the rhizome is an uncontainable dimension "or rather directions in motion" that are forever in "between things, interbeing intermezzo." (3, citations deleted)

Thus, becoming and being named as black within diasporas is simultaneously to speak of an unknown destination and identity that signifies on all definitions of blackness as definitive or complete.
52 Quoted in Hucks, *Yoruba Traditions*, 47–48.
53 Outlaw, *On Race and Philosophy*. See especially his essays "African Philosophy? Deconstructive and Reconstructive Challenges" (51–73); "Africana Philosophy" (75–95); and "Life-Worlds, Modernity, and Philosophical Praxis" (159–82).
54 "*Being* as a conscious act of becoming deploys not a fixed entity but a production, a signifier that is already open for signification, a performative category that is never saturated." Deleuze and Guattari, *A Thousand Plateaus*. For instance, Ibrahim borrows from Judith Butler's work in *Gender Trouble: Feminism and the Subversion of Identity* (New York: Routledge, 1999) and *Frames of War: When Is Life Grievable?* (New York: Verso, 2009) the idea of performativity "that does not assume *idées fixes*; quite the opposite, it requires repetitive, parodic and continual acts of becoming."
55 Ibrahim, *Rhizome of Blackness*, 7; Roland Barthes, *The Fashion System*, trans. Matthew Ward and Richard Howard (Oakland: University of California Press, 1990).
56 Morrison, "Home," 10.
57 Keri Day, for instance, writes about the limits of intersectionality and how a "theory of assemblage" might help ground an articulation of affective political communities. Drawing from Jasbir Puar, Day argues that a theory of assemblage suggests a different set of metaphors for identities within the social world such as mosaics, patchwork, heterogeneity, fluidity, and temporary configurations. According to this theory, there is not a fixed, stable ontology for the social world and its multiplicity of identities (as theories of intersectionality assume). Rather, identities (such as race, class, sexuality, gender) are complex, fluid configurations that can properly be characterized as discursive practices and expressions, which

means that identities are social constructions generated by material and linguistic conditions rather than ontological assertions. Keri Day, *Religious Resistance to Neoliberalism: Womanist and Black Feminist Perspectives* (New York: Palgrave Macmillan, 2016), 17, 106, 123–26; Alexander G. Weheliye, *Habeas Viscus: Racializing Assemblages, Biopolitics, and Black Feminist Theories of the Human* (Durham: Duke University Press, 2012); see also Jasbir Puar, "I Would Rather Be a Cyborg Than a Goddess: Intersectionality, Assemblage, and Affective Politics," *PhiloSOPHIA: A Journal of Feminist Philosophy* 2, no. 1 (2012): 49–66, www.jasbirpuar.com; Manuel Delanda, *A New Philosophy of Society: Assemblage Theory and Social Complexity* (London: Continuum, 2006); Daniel Smith and John Protevi, "Gilles Deleuze," in *The Stanford Encyclopedia of Philosophy* (Winter 2015 edition), ed. Edward N. Zalta, http://plato.stanford.edu; and Daniel Little, "Understanding Society: Assemblage Theory," November 15, 2012, http:// understandingsociety.blogspot.com.

58 Walker, *Mothership Connections.*

59 Howard Thurman, "I Will Not Give Up," in *A Strange Freedom: The Best of Howard Thurman on Religious Experience and Public Life*, ed. Walter Earl Fluker and Catherine Tumber (Boston: Beacon, 1998), 308.

60 Rainer Maria Rilke, "I Find You, Lord, in All Things and in All," in *Ahead of All Parting: The Selected Poetry and Prose of Rainer Maria Rilke*, trans. Stephen Mitchell (New York: Random House, 1995), 9.

61 Hall, "Subjects in History," 299.

62 Howard Thurman, *Disciplines of the Spirit* (New York: Harper and Row, 1963; reprint, Richmond, IN: Friends United Press, 1973), 48–55.

63 The problem of spiritual dynamism and its relation to religious and political systems were lifelong concerns for Thurman. See "Howard Thurman to Mordecai Wyatt Johnson," September 20, 1927, Oberlin, Ohio, in *My People Need Me*, vol. 1 of *The Papers of Howard Washington Thurman*, ed. Walter Earl Fluker (Columbia: University of South Carolina Press, 2009), 117. See also Howard Thurman, "Our Underlying Spiritual Unities," in *Christian, Who Calls Me Christian?*, vol. 2 of *The Papers of Howard Washington Thurman* (Columbia: University of South Carolina Press, 2012), 285–88.

64 Anderson, *Beyond Ontological Blackness*, 38–50, 80–81, 159; Anderson, "The Smell of Life: A Pragmatic Theology of Religious Experience," chap. 4 in *Creative Exchange*, esp. 115–35, where he provides similar critiques.

CHAPTER 5. *TURNING* FROM EXODUS TO EXILE

1 Albert J. Raboteau, *A Fire in the Bones: Reflections on African-American Religious History* (Boston: Beacon, 1995), 28.

2 J. W. Johnson and J. R. Johnson, eds., *American Negro Spirituals* (1926), www. negrospirituals.com.

3 Ibid.

4 Best, *Passionately Human, No Less Divine*, 1.

5 Isabel Wilkerson, *The Warmth of Other Suns: The Epic Story of America's Great Migration* (New York: Random House, 2010).

6 Glaude, *Exodus!*; Rhondda Robinson Thomas, *Claiming Exodus: A Cultural History of Afro-Atlantic Identity, 1774–1903* (Waco, TX: Baylor University Press, 2013).

7 Robin D. G. Kelley, *Freedom Dreams: The Black Radical Imagination* (Boston: Beacon, 2002), 35; for a fuller exposition of the Exodus narrative in the African American cultural imaginary, see chap. 1, "Dreams of a New Land," 13–35.

8 Perry Miller, *Errand into the Wilderness* (Cambridge, MA: Belknap, 2000), originally published 1956.

9 Glaude writes, "I refer to Exodus, then, not only for its historical relevance to any account of the emergence of nation language in the United States but also as a metaphor for a particular style of imagining the nation in early nineteenth century black America." *Exodus!*, 6. Reference to "bloody-red waters" is from Henry Highland Garnet's 1843 "Address to the Slaves of the United States of America" in Buffalo, New York. Similarly, Rhondda Robinson Thomas argues, "When Afro-Atlantic authors appealed to Exodus, however, they decentered the narratives by giving different roles to the Europeans and giving new meaning to English and American Exodus experiences." Quoting George Achiele et al., *The Postmodern Bible: The Bible and the Cultural Collective* (New Haven: Yale University Press, 1995), 286, she argues that *decentering* is an "ideological critique [that] serves as an important critical tool for *decentering* the reading subject and the subject matter being read. This means recognizing the privileged identification made between the reader's interest and the narrative and then deliberately shifting the identification to allow for the text to be a text 'for' another and reading experience." *Claiming Exodus*, 5.

10 Glaude, *Exodus!*, 100.

11 Ibid., 141–59.

12 Herbert Robinson Marbury, *Pillars of Cloud and Fire: The Politics of Exodus in African American Biblical Interpretation* (New York: New York University Press, 2015).

13 Ibid., 10.

14 Thomas, *Claiming Exodus*, 4.

15 Stephen Ward Angell, *Bishop Henry McNeal Turner and African-American Religion in the South* (Knoxville: University of Tennessee Press, 1992), 136–37; and Roderick Michael McLean, *The Theology of Marcus Garvey* (Washington, D.C.: University Press of America, 1982), 131, 141.

16 James H. Cone, *God of the Oppressed* (New York: Seabury, 1975).

17 William R. Jones, *Is God a White Racist? A Preamble to Black Theology* (Boston: Beacon, 1998); see also Anthony B. Pinn, *Why, Lord? Suffering and Evil in Black*

Theology (New York: Continuum, 1995), esp. chap. 4, "Alternative Theological Views on Suffering," 91–112.

18 Zakaria, *Post-American World.*

19 See Smith et al., *Contesting Post-Racialism*; Anthony Reddie, "Reconciliation in Christian Theology—A Radical Alternative," *Rethinking Mission* 1 (Winter 2005): 4–10, www.rethinkingmission.org.uk; Anthony G. Reddie, "The Mission of the Black Church in 21st Century" (presentation at Rethinking Mission Biblical Reflection for Partnership for World Mission Conference, November 2008), an excerpt from Reddie, *Working against the Grain.*

20 Battle, *Black Church in America*, xi.

21 Sanders, *Saints in Exile.* Sanders uses the phrase "Sanctified Church" to cover the broad range of Afro-Pentecostal and holiness churches in the United States. She defines the Sanctified Church as an "African American Christian reform movement that seeks to bring its standards of worship, personal morality, and social concern into conformity with a biblical hermeneutic of holiness and spiritual empowerment" (5); see also Cheryl Townsend-Gilkes, "'Together and in Harness': Women's Traditions in the Sanctified Church," *Signs* 10, no. 4 (Summer 1985): 678–99; Butler, *Women in the Church of God in Christ*; and Marion Thomas, "Reflections on the Sanctified Church as Portrayed by Zora Neale Hurston," *Black American Literature Forum* 25, no. 1 (Spring 1991): 35–44, www.jstor.org.

22 Sanders, *Saints in Exile*, 125.

23 Ibid., 132.

24 Paris, *Social Teaching of the Black Churches*, 59.

25 Paul Robeson, "Sometimes I Feel Like a Motherless Child," recording, available on www.youtube.com.

26 See Patterson, *Slavery and Social Death*, 5, quoted in Holland, *Raising the Dead*, 13.

27 See chapter 2 for Sterling Stuckey's discussion of Brer Rabbit in *Slave Culture*, 17–26; and Howard Thurman's discussion in *Deep River and The Negro Spiritual Speaks of Life and Death.*

28 W. E. B. Du Bois, *The Souls of Black Folk* (Chicago: A.C. McClurg, 1903), 157.

29 Thurman, *Deep River and The Negro Spiritual Speaks of Life and Death*, 25–26.

30 Wolfgang Roth, "Between Tradition and Expectation: The Origin and Role of Biblical Apocalyptic," *EXPLOR*, Spring 1978, 9.

31 Wilder, "Rhetoric of Ancient and Modern Apocalyptic."

32 Johnson and Johnson, *American Negro Spirituals*, www.negrospirituals.com.

33 Thomas Merton, *Contemplation in a World of Action* (Garden City, NY: Doubleday, 1971), 16, quoted in Raboteau, *Fire in the Bones*, 176.

34 Luke A. Powery, *Dem Dry Bones: Preaching, Death, and Hope* (Minneapolis: Fortress, 2012), 15–16.

35 Frederick C. Harris, *Something Within: Religion in African-American Political Activism* (New York: Oxford University Press, 1999), 40.

36 Niels Peter Lemche, *The Israelites in History and Tradition* (Louisville, KY: Westminster John Knox Press, 1998). For Lemche, Exile is related to identity— ethnic, national identity; in its foremost ideological reach, it functions as a myth that "disconnects and unites the present and the past"; it is the basis for a yearning to return home to an ancient time that is simultaneously new, blessed in a covenant relationship with God. Exile is foundation myth for Israel; it functions as "the instrument that guarantees that the transgressors are punished because of their sins and never allowed to return, and that their country is cleansed of their sins" (87).

> The myth of the exile was therefore created as a program for the return to the country of God, where a new and ideal nation should be established. . . . If they had not created such a myth of the exile, there would have been no Jewish people, no Jewish society in Palestine, nothing that distinguished a Jew from other people, and no relationship in the form of a new covenant . . . to the God of the land of Israel. (88)

Exodus, on the other hand, is a myth of origin, the beginnings of a nation, an ethnic identity. It is not, however, fixed: "It is always seen as under the perspective of the future exile in Egypt" (89), it is the "origin myth of a religious history of the chosen people, the holy congregation of God, who having sinned passed the judgement in order to reclaim their land and their God" (93). Thomas Dozeman's, Jon Berquist's, and Mario Liverani's monographs are overviews of the interpretation of Exodus, the background of the post-exilic period, and the history of Israel, respectively. See Jon Berquist, *Judaism in Persia's Shadow: A Social and Historical Approach* (Minneapolis: Fortress, 1995); Robert P. Carroll, "The Myth of the Empty Land," *Semeia* 59 (1992): 79–91; and Thomas B. Dozeman, *Exodus*, Eerdmans Critical Commentary, ed. David Noel Friedman (Grand Rapids: Eerdmans, 2009). For a nearly exhaustive overview, see Mario Liverani, *Israel's History and the History of Israel*, ed. Philip R. Davies (London: Equinox, 2005), esp. part 2; Rainer Albertz, "The Controversy about Judean versus Israelite Identity," in *Judah and the Judeans in the Achaemenid Period*, ed. Oded Lipschits, Gary N. Knoppers, and Manfred Oeming (Winona Lake, IN: Eisenbrauns, 2011), 483–504; Bob Becking, "We All Returned as One! Critical Notes on the Myth of the Mass Return," in *Judah and the Judeans in the Persian Period*, ed. Oded Lipschits and Manfred Oeming (Winona Lake, IN: Eisenbrauns, 2006), 3–18; Jon L. Berquist, "Constructions of Identity in Postcolonial Yehud," in Lipschits and Oeming, *Judah and the Judeans in the Persian Period*, 53–66; J. Blenkinsopp, "Temple and Society in Achaemenid Judah," in *Second Temple Studies*, vol. 1, *Persian Period*, ed. Philip R. Davies (Sheffield: Sheffield Academic Press, 1991); T. C. Eskenazi, "The Missions of Ezra and Nehemiah," in Lipschits and Oeming, *Judah and the Judeans in the Persian Period*, 509–30; Norman K. Gottwald, "Social Class and Ideology in Isaiah 40–55: An

Eagletonian Reading," *Semeia* 59 (1992): 43–57; Richard A. Horsley, "Empire, Temple and Community—but No Bourgeoisie! A Response to Blenkinsopp and Petersen," in Davies, *Persian Period*; John Kessler, "Persia's Loyal Yahwists: Power Identity and Ethnicity in Achaemenid Yehud," in Lipschits and Oeming, *Judah and the Judeans in the Persian Period*, 91–121; Carol Newsom, "Response to Norman K. Gottwald, 'Social Class and Ideology in Isaiah 40–55,'" *Semeia* 59 (1992): 73–78; Manfred Oeming, "'See, We Are Serving Today' (Nehemiah 9:36): Nehemiah as a Theological Interpretation of the Persian Period," in Lipschits and Oeming, *Judah and the Judeans in the Persian Period*, 571–88; Joachim Schaper, "Torah and Identity in the Persian Period," in Lipschits, Knoppers, and Oeming, *Judah and the Judeans in the Achaemenid Period*, 27–38; Katherine Southwood, "The Holy Seed: The Significance of Endogamous Boundaries," in Lipschits, Knoppers, and Oeming, *Judah and the Judeans in the Achaemenid Period*, 189–224; Renita Weems, "The Hebrew Women Are Not Like the Egyptian Women: The Ideology of Race, Gender and Sexual Reproduction in Exodus 1," *Semeia* 59 (1992): 25–34.

37 Carroll, "Myth of the Empty Land."

38 Ibid., 89–90.

39 Delores S. Williams, *Sisters in the Wilderness: The Challenge of Womanist God-Talk* (Maryknoll: Orbis, 1993); Carolyn Rouse, *Engaged Surrender: African-American Women and Islam* (Berkeley: University of California Press, 2004); and Diana L. Hayes, *Hagar's Daughters: Womanist Ways of Being in the World*, Madeleva Lecture in Spirituality 1995 (New York: Paulist, 1995).

40 Robert J. Patterson, *Exodus Politics: Civil Rights and Leadership in African American Literature and Culture* (Charlottesville: University of Virginia Press, 2013), 26.

41 See ibid., 26–28.

42 "Then Pharaoh gave this order to all his people: 'Every Hebrew boy that is born you must throw into the Nile, but let every girl live'" (Exodus 1:22 [NIV]). "In the African American Christian and Muslim communities Exodus 1:22 is the legitimate biblical sanction for heterosexism, expressed in terms of 'the endangered black male.' When interpreted through the constraints of African American experience the Exodus narrative tells African American women that only their men's lives matter." Irene Monroe, "When and Where I Enter, Then the Whole Race Enters with Me: Que(e)rying Exodus," in Pinn and Hopkins, *Loving the Body*, 126.

43 Patterson, *Exodus Politics*, 27.

44 Anderson, *Beyond Ontological Blackness*; and Anderson, *Creative Exchange*.

45 The Exodus narrative in which Moses leads the people of Israel out of bondage by the authority of God is the single most important anchor of black religious thought. Martin Luther King Jr.'s final sermon drew on these same themes of leading the people to, but not himself entering, the Promised Land.

46 Homer U. Ashby Jr., *Our Home Is over Jordan: A Black Pastoral Theology* (St. Louis: Chalice, 2003).

47 Ibid., 81.

48 Ibid., 9.

49 David Tracy, *Plurality and Ambiguity: Hermeneutics, Religion, Hope* (San Francisco: Harper and Row, 1987), 106.

50 McRuer, *Crip Theory*; see also Betcher, *Spirit and the Politics of Disablement*; and Betcher, *Spirit and the Obligation of Social Flesh.*

51 Some portions of this section can be found in Walter Earl Fluker, "Voices in the Wilderness," *Focus Magazine* (Boston University School of Theology), Fall 2015.

52 James Baldwin, *The Price of the Ticket: Collected Nonfiction, 1948–1985* (New York: St. Martin's/Marek, 1985), 312.

53 James Baldwin, "Nothing Personal," in *Price of the Ticket*, 393.

54 See "Thor and Loki in the Giants' City," in Padraic Colum, *Nordic Gods and Heroes* (New York: Macmillan, 1920, 1996), 105–19. See also Hurstwic History Articles, "Þór's Journey to Útgarð," www.hurstwic.org, accessed October 8, 2015.

55 Interestingly, Gilroy mentions the "chronotope" only three times in the entire book (pp. 4, 199, and 225, n. 2), though he announces it as his chief methodological schema. The chronotope is defined as "a unit of analysis for studying texts according to the ratio and nature of the temporal and spatial categories represented. . . . The chronotope is an optic for reading texts as x-rays of the forces at work in the culture system from which they spring." M. M. Bakhtin, *The Dialogic Imagination*, ed. and trans. Michael Holquist (Austin: University of Texas Press, 1981), 426.

56 Gilroy, *Black Atlantic*, 205–23.

57 Laurence Mordekhai Thomas, *Vessels of Evil: American Slavery and the Holocaust* (Philadelphia: Temple University Press, 1993); Michael Lerner and Cornel West, *Jews and Blacks: A Dialogue on Race, Religion, and Culture in America* (New York: Plume, 1996).

58 "The Black Atlantic remains surprisingly abstract and indeterminate with respect to the very 'chronotope' the book claims as its analytical 'organizing symbol'— namely 'ships in motion across spaces between Europe, America, Africa, and the Caribbean.'" Houston Baker, *Turning South Again: Re-Thinking Modernism/ Re-Reading Booker T.* (Durham: Duke University Press, 2001), 85.

59 "Once inside plantation protocols and economies, the black situation was one of disciplined immobility and servile labor, whether in heavily surveilled and administered plantation fields or in the strictly governed plantation domestic 'house service.'" Moreover, "penal plantation protocols were the *telos* of the black body's journey through Atlantic incarceration to 'life upon these shores.'" Ibid., 88.

60 Agamben, *Homo Sacer* is an excellent place to conduct such an analysis given the notions of "camp as a biopolitical paradigm for the modern" (part 3) and the

incarceration of young black men and women. "New practices, priorities and intensities are realized partly . . . through constructions and reconstructions of the prophylactic state, . . . which [produces] healthy, self-regulating and self-fashioning citizens." Richard Iton, *In Search of the Black Fantastic: Politics and Popular Culture in the Post–Civil Rights Era* (New York: Oxford University Press, 2008), 131–32, and 302, n. 47.

61 Matthew Lopez, *The Whipping Man* (New York: Samuel French, 2009), 41–42. See also Gilroy, *Black Atlantic*, 205–23; and Thomas, *Vessels of Evil*.

62 Michelle Gonzalez, *Afro-Cuban Theology: Religion, Race, Culture, and Identity* (Gainesville: University Press of Florida, 2006), 6.

63 Ibid., 11.

64 See, for instance, Marcia Y. Riggs and James Samuel Logan, eds., *Ethics That Matter: African, Caribbean and African American Sources* (Minneapolis: Fortress, 2012), esp. part 1, "Moral Dilemmas" (11–62); Anthony G. Reddie, "The Mission of the Black Church in 21st Century," *Rethinking Mission* (December 2008).

65 See my earlier reference to *Epiphenomenal time* in Wright, *Physics of Blackness*.

CHAPTER 6. *TURNING* FROM THE FRYING PAN TO THE FIRE

1 Clifton H. Johnson, *God Struck Me Dead: Religious Conversion Experiences and Autobiographies of Ex-Slaves* (Philadelphia: Pilgrim, 1969), 74, quoted in Raboteau, *Fire in the Bones*, 183.

2 See "Do Jehovah's Witnesses Believe in Annihilation?," Christianity Stack Exchange, October 1, 2012, http://christianity.stackexchange.com.

3 The reference is to William Schweiker, *Dust That Breathes: Christian Faith and the New Humanisms* (Malden, MA: Wiley-Blackwell, 2010), who sees the constructive task of theological humanism as providing a theological and moral anthropology that is open to a larger conversation with science and the multiple contemporary issues facing the globe.

4 "The lake of fire" appears as a place of punishment, of perpetual torment, not of annihilation (Rev 20:10). The beast (Rev 19:20); the pseudo-prophet (Rev 19:20; 20:10); the devil (Rev 20:10); and the wicked of varying description (Rev 20:15; 21:8) are cast into it. When the same is affirmed of death and Hades (Rev 20:14), it is doubtful whether this is meant as a mere figure for the cessation of these two evils personified, or has a more realistic background in the existence of two demon-powers so named (compare Isaiah 25:8; 1 Corinthians 15:26, 54; 2 Esdras 7:31).

The International Standard Bible Encyclopedia, 3:1822. For a treatment of the lake of fire's pre-Christian origins in ancient Egyptian religion, see Richard H. Wilkinson, *Reading Egyptian Art: A Hieroglyphic Guide to Ancient Painting and Sculpture* (London: Thames and Hudson, 1992), 204–5.

5 See www.navigators.org.

6 James Baldwin, "On Being White . . . and Other Lies," *Essence*, April 1984.

7 The original reads, "But if they poison all them none dare eat; what do they gain?"

8 Olive Schreiner, "The Sunlight Lay across My Bed," in *A Track to the Water's Edge*, ed. Howard Thurman (New York: Harper and Row, 1973), 64–66.

9 For an exposition of the "terror of history," see Mircea Eliade, *Cosmos and History* (New York: Harper and Row, 1954), 156–57.

10 Fluker, *Ethical Leadership*, esp. 1–10.

11 Harrison G. Pope Jr., Katharine A. Phillips, and Roberto Olivardia, *The Adonis Complex: The Secret Crisis of Male Body Obsession* (New York: Free Press, 2000); David Coad, *The Metrosexual: Gender, Sexuality, and Sport* (Albany: State University of New York Press, 2008), 145–46.

12 "The nectar that Aphrodite sprinkled on Adonis' wound had turned the droplets of his blood into beautiful red anemones, while the rest of his blood flowed, becoming the river Adonis, which is today known as the river Nahr Ibrahim in coastal Lebanon." See www.greeka.com, accessed May 30, 2015.

13 Jennings, *Christian Imagination*, 35–36.

14 Howard Thurman, *Jesus and the Disinherited* (1949; reprint, Boston: Beacon, 1996), 43–44.

15 Monica A. Coleman, ed., *Ain't I a Womanist, Too? Third-Wave Womanist Religious Thought* (Minneapolis: Fortress, 2013); Norm R. Allen Jr., ed., *African American Humanism: An Anthology* (Buffalo: Prometheus, 1991); Norm R. Allen Jr., *The Black Humanist Experience: An Alternative to Religion* (Buffalo: Prometheus, 2002); Anderson, *Beyond Ontological Blackness*; Anderson, *Creative Exchange*; Dwight N. Hopkins, *Being Human: Race, Culture, and Religion* (Minneapolis: Fortress, 2005); Kelly Brown Douglas, *Sexuality and the Black Church: A Womanist Perspective* (Minneapolis: Fortress, 1999); Kelly Brown Douglas, *What's Faith Got to Do with It? Black Bodies/Christian Souls* (Maryknoll, NY: Orbis, 2005); Mike Featherstone et al., eds., *The Body: Social Process and Cultural Theory* (Newbury Park, CA: Sage, 2001); Pinn, *Understanding and Transforming the Black Church*. A significant literature is emerging on black queer and queried bodies. Among these are Lightsey, *Our Lives Matter*; Kelly Brown Douglas, "Homophobia and Heterosexism in the Black Church and Community," in *Sexuality and the Black Church: A Womanist Perspective* (New York: Orbis, 1999); Roger A. Sneed, "Dark Matter: Liminality and Black Queer Bodies," in Coleman, *Ain't I a Womanist, Too?*, 139–48; Elonda Clay, "Confessions of a Black Theological Bitch," in Coleman, *Ain't I a Womanist, Too?*, 93–106; Monica Miller, "'I Am a Nappy Headed Ho': (Re)Signifying 'Deviance' in the Haraam of Religious Respectability," in Coleman, *Ain't I a Womanist, Too?*, 123–38; Victor Anderson, "The Black Church and the Curious Body of the Black Homosexual," in Pinn and Hopkins, *Loving the Body*, 10; Victor Anderson, "Scholarly Aesthetics and the Religious Critic: Black Experiences as Manifolds of Manifestations and Powers of Presentations," in Coleman, *Ain't I a Womanist, Too?*, 201–16; and Horace Griffin, "Toward a True Black Liberation Theology:

Affirming Homoeroticism, Black Gay Christians and Their Love Relationships," in Pinn and Hopkins, *Loving the Body*.

16 Garth Baker-Fletcher, *Somebodyness: Martin Luther King, Jr., and the Theory of Dignity* (Minneapolis: Fortress, 1993). Baker-Fletcher's book, which bears the imprimatur of *somebodyness*, is based on King's reflection on the "New Negro" involved in the Montgomery campaign. King wrote,

> Once plagued with a tragic sense of inferiority resulting from the crippling effects of slavery and segregation, the Negro has now been driven to re-evaluate himself. He has come to feel that he is somebody. His religion reveals to him that God loves all His children and that the important thing about a man is not "his specificity but his fundamentum"—not the texture of his hair or the color of his skin but his eternal worth to God.

Martin Luther King Jr., *Stride toward Freedom: The Montgomery Story* (1958; New York: Harper and Row, 1964), 167. See also McRuer, *Crip Theory*; Betcher, *Spirit and the Politics of Disablement*; and Betcher, *Spirit and the Obligation of Social Flesh*.

17 Richard Shusterman, "Somaesthetics: A Disciplinary Proposal," *Journal of Aesthetics and Art Criticism* 57, no. 3 (Summer 1999): 57. The Thoreau quote is also found in this article. See also Phillip Brian Harper, *Abstractionist Aesthetics: Artistic Form and Social Critique in African American Culture* (New York: New York University Press, 2015); and Phillip Bryan Harper, *Are We Not Men? Masculine Anxiety and the Problem of African-American Identity* (New York: Oxford University Press, 1996).

18 Michel Foucault, *Discipline and Punish: The Birth of the Prison* (New York: Pantheon, 1977).

19 Pinn, *Understanding and Transforming the Black Church*, 69.

20 Shearer Davis Bowman, *Masters and Lords: Mid-19th Century U.S. Planters and Prussian Junkers* (New York: Oxford University Press, 1993), 172.

21 Howard Thurman, "The Idol of Togetherness," in *A Strange Freedom*, 39.

22 Howard Thurman, "A Strange Freedom," in *The Luminous Darkness: A Personal Interpretation of the Anatomy of Segregation and the Ground of Hope* (1965; repr., Richmond, IN: Friends United Press, 1989), 89–113.

23 Arrested Development, "Tennessee" (1992), quoted in Kelley, *Freedom Dreams*, 33–34.

24 Pinn, introduction to Pinn and Hopkins, *Loving the Body*, 2.

25 See Jeremiah A. Wright Jr., "Faith in a Foreign Land," *Crosscurrents* 57, no. 2 (Summer 2007): 237–51. I am interested in this text because it is an illustration of the Dilemma-Diasporic, Exodus-Exilic tensions described in the earlier chapters; and in this sermon Wright expresses the hesitancy, fear, and trauma of the black body in its exilic existence.

26 *Gesture* illustrates well Gibbs's argument that the "cultural face" of metaphor enables a person to experience and re-experience the metaphor as embodied

action out in the world and not just in one's head. Raymond W. Gibbs Jr., *Intentions in the Experience of Meaning* (New York: Cambridge University Press, 1999), 158. Shore would probably call some gestures conventional "gestural models" (e.g., the American handshake), which have emerged as social institutions, but other gestures he might call "personal models," possibly unique to the individual but probably overlapping with those of others. Any set of gestures a speaker makes would be a mixture of the two. Shore would probably say that gestures fall under the general rubric of "kinesthetic schemas," which are bodily states that are subject to cultural modeling. Bradd Shore, *Culture in Mind: Cognition, Culture, and the Problem of Meaning* (New York: Oxford University Press, 1996), 47–48, 59. See also Mark Johnson, *The Body in the Mind: The Bodily Basis of Meaning, Imagination, and Reason* (Chicago: University of Chicago Press, 1987); James K. A. Smith, *Imagining the Kingdom: How Worship Works* (Grand Rapids: Baker Academic, 2013); Randee Lipson Lawrence, *Bodies of Knowledge: Embodied Learning in Adult Education* (San Francisco: Jossey-Bass, 2012); Celeste Snowber, *Embodied Prayer: Toward Wholeness of Body, Mind, Soul* (Kelowna, B.C.: Northstone, 2004); and Sondra Horton Fraleigh, *Dance and the Lived Body: A Descriptive Aesthetics* (Pittsburgh: University of Pittsburgh Press, 1987). Many thanks to my colleague Professor Courtney Goto for some of these suggestions and insights.

27 See Robert Innis's exploration of Susanne Langer's treatment of gesturing as part of the circle dance as a primordial symbol that invites us into the sacred. Robert E. Innis, *Susanne Langer in Focus: The Symbolic Mind* (Bloomington: Indiana University Press, 2009), 137. For more on the gesturing body as *bricoleur*, see my discussion in chapter 8.

28 Raboteau, *Fire in the Bones*, 190.

29 See Smith, *Imagining the Kingdom*, 13–14; see also Celeste Snowber, "Dance as a Way of Knowing," in Lawrence, *Bodies of Knowledge*, 53–60.

30 Kundera, *Immortality*, 7.

31 Mayra Rivera, *The Touch of Transcendence: A Postcolonial Theology of God* (Louisville, KY: Westminster John Knox, 2007).

32 See Smith, *Imagining the Kingdom*, 5, 12.

33 Anthony Pinn, *Terror and Triumph: The Nature of Black Religion* (Minneapolis: Fortress, 2003), 159–60.

34 Ibid., 173–74.

35 Elie Wiesel, *The Gates of the Forest*, trans. Francis Frenaye (New York: Schocken, 1996), 197.

36 David Patterson, "The Maggid of Sighet: Jewish Contexts for Wiesel's Storytelling," in *Elie Wiesel and the Art of Storytelling*, ed. Rosemary Horowitz McFarland (Jefferson, NC: McFarland, 2006), 119.

37 This notion of "marking one's place" in the world is an important part of the argument in chapter 9. Thurman, "A Strange Freedom," in *The Inward Journey*, 38.

38 Thurman, *The Luminous Darkness*. As is well known, Thurman's favorite passage of scripture was Psalm 139, especially verses 7–12.

39   The meeting involved in genuine dialogue is rare, and is, in a real sense, a meeting of souls. ("The primary word *I-Thou* can be spoken only with the whole being", Buber 1958: 24). The life of dialogue involves "the turning towards the other" (Buber 1947: 22). It is not found by seeking, but by grace. In a very real sense we are called to genuine dialogue, rather than actively searching for it.

"Martin Buber on Education," Infed.org, http://infed.org, accessed May 27, 2015. For reference to weeping, confession, and resistance, see Smith, *Preaching as Weeping*.

40 A "hermeneutics of style" calls our attention to the black-skinned body as a site of exploitation *and* creativity. Pinn argues that since there is a profound connection between the visible movement of black-skinned bodies and modes of exploitation, the "process of struggle for new ontological and existential status unfolds through black bodies." Pinn, *Terror and Triumph*, 140. And because there is almost always dissonance between the "social body" and the "physical body" in African American cultural life, we need to pay attention to style or aesthetics for the ways the body signifies a creative struggle for a new humanity, a new way of experiencing one's body as free and unencumbered by social regiments.

41 "I indeed baptize you with water unto repentance, but he that cometh after me is mightier than I, whose shoes I am not worthy to bear: he shall baptize you with the Holy Ghost, and with fire: Whose fan is in his hand, and he will thoroughly purge his floor, and gather his wheat into the garner; but he will burn up the chaff with unquenchable fire."

42 The leadership theorist Manfred de Vries has suggested that there is an "inner theater" that represents those core themes that affect an individual's personality and leadership style. He writes, "For each of us, our unique mixture of motivational needs determines our character and creates the triangle of our mental life—a tightly interlocked triangle consisting of cognition, affect, and behavior. No one of these dimensions of the triangle can be seen as separate from the other." DeVries, *Leadership Mystique*, 5.

43 See my discussion in chapter 4, where I note the challenge of revisability because ideas, images, symbols, or metaphors that shape human behavior are informed by and performed with a social audience in mind. For references to the "inner theater" and the tripartite construction of cognition, affection, and behavior(s) of leaders, see Fluker, *Ethical Leadership*, 63.

44 Pierre Bourdieu writes, "Only in imaginary experience (in the folk tale, for example), which neutralizes the sense of social realities, does the social world take the form of a universe of *possibles* [sic] equally possible for any possible subject." Bourdieu, *Logic of Practice*, 64.

45 Practices and rituals are embedded in story discourse that is at once personal, social, and historical.

46 Howard Thurman, *Deep Is the Hunger: Meditations for Apostles of Sensitiveness* (New York: Harper and Brothers, 1951), 52. Thurman contends that it is not sufficient simply to remove an evil thing; it must be replaced with something good. He suggests that the dynamic nature of evil is such that it grows with greater intensity and rapidity than goodness. It is paramount, therefore, that those who work toward community realize that goodness must be achieved through careful planning, deliberate effort, and hard work. Thurman, *Deep Is the Hunger*, 51; Howard Thurman, "Exposition of the Book of Habakuk," in *The Interpreter's Bible*, ed. George A. Buttrick (Nashville: Abingdon, 1956), 981; also reprinted in *The Soundless Passion of a Single Mind*, vol. 4 of *The Papers of Howard Washington Thurman*, ed. Walter Earl Fluker (Columbia: University of South Carolina Press, forthcoming 2017).

47 I borrow the terminology of "disruptive ethics" from Traci West, *Disruptive Christian Ethics: When Racism and Women's Lives Matter* (Louisville, KY: Westminster John Knox Press, 2006). See chapter 8 in this volume, which returns to this important theme.

48 See Diana L. Eck, *Encountering God: A Spiritual Journey from Bozeman to Banaras* (Boston: Beacon, 1993), chap. 5, "The Breath of God: The Fire and Freedom of the Spirit," 118–43.

49 See Raboteau, *Fire in the Bones*; Harvey Cox, *Fire from Heaven: The Rise of Pentecostal Spirituality and the Reshaping of Religion in the Twenty-First Century* (Reading, MA: Addison-Wesley, 1995).

50 Amos Yong, *The Spirit Poured Out on All Flesh: Pentecostalism and the Possibility of Global Theology* (Grand Rapids: Baker, 2005); Diana Diakete, *Three Eyes for the Journey: African Dimensions of the Jamaican Religious Experience* (New York: Oxford University Press, 2005).

51 Allan Boesak, *The Fire Within: Sermons from the Edge of Exile* (Cape Town, South Africa: New World Foundation, 2004). See also Wright, "Faith in a Foreign Land" as an example of exilic preaching and claiming one's own voice and style.

52 bell hooks and Amalia Mesa-Bains, *homegrown: engaged cultural criticism* (Cambridge, MA: South End, 2006), 98.

53 Anderson, *Imagined Communities*, 9–36, quoted in Holland, *Raising the Dead*, 22.

54 Amy Chua, *World on Fire: How Exporting Free Market Economy Breeds Ethnic Hatred and Global Instability* (New York: Doubleday, 2003), quoted in Baldwin and Dekar, *"In an Inescapable Network of Mutuality,"* 10.

55 The need of a constantly expanding market for its products chases the bourgeoisie over the entire surface of the globe. . . . In place of the old wants, satisfied by the production of the country, we find new wants, requiring for their satisfaction the products of distant lands and climes. In place of the old

local and national seclusion and self-sufficiency, we have intercourse in every direction, *universal inter-dependence of nations.*
Karl Marx and Friedrich Engels, *Communist Manifesto*, 1848.

56 He writes, "The exclusive focus on the economic aspects of globalization is somewhat fruitless and . . . in order to have a closer understanding of what is new and different about globalization, we need to focus on the *universal inter-dependence of nations.*"

57 Bill Gates calls this phenomenon "business at the speed of thought." William H. Gates III, *Business @ the Speed of Thought: Succeeding in the Digital Economy* (New York: Warner, 1999).

58 Fried writes,

By and large, these four criteria—extension, intensification, velocity and impact—are providing a workable conceptual framework for mapping the transformations that characterize the world-wide interconnectedness that we are part of—from eating McDonald's in Cairo to SARS and the avian flu or the calling center in India to which we are connected when we have a problem with our computer.

59 See UNESCO, *Global Citizenship Education: Preparing Learners for the Challenges of the 21st Century* (Paris: UNESCO, 2014). See also Amartya Sen, *Identity and Violence: The Illusion of Destiny* (New York: Norton, 2006); Kwame Anthony Appiah, *Cosmopolitanism: Ethics in a World of Strangers* (New York: Norton, 2006); Nimi Wariboko, *The Charismatic City and the Public Resurgence of Religion: A Pentecostal Social Ethics of Cosmopolitan Urban Living* (New York: Palgrave Macmillan, 2014). Wariboko examines the impact of global cities and charismatic spirituality on cosmopolitanism and the boundaries of the church through the lens of the various archetypes of cities.

60 "First I think all of us must develop a world perspective if we are to survive. The American dream will not become a reality devoid of the larger dream of a world of brotherhood and peace and good will. The world in which we live is a world of geographical oneness and we are challenged now to make it a spiritual one." Martin Luther King Jr., in *A Testament of Hope: The Essential Writings and Speeches of Martin Luther King, Jr.*, ed. James M. Washington (New York: HarperCollins, 1999), 209.

61 Joel 2:28–29; Acts 2:17–18.

62 Acts 2:1–4.

63 In 2014, Latin America passed Europe as the continent with the most Christians. In 1900, Europe had six times as many Christians as Latin America. Looking ahead to 2025, however, Latin America is likely to be surpassed by Africa with 628 million in the former and more than 700 million in the latter. We also project that by 2050, Asia will surpass Europe in the number of Christians. Each of the three continents in the Global South

could outnumber Europe, together representing nearly 80% of all Christians (from just over 20% in 1900).

Todd M. Johnson and Gina A. Zurlo, "Christianity 2016: Latin America and Projecting Religions to 2050," *International Bulletin of Mission Research* 40, no. 1 (2016): 22. See also Afeosemime U. Adogame, *Who Is Afraid of the Holy Ghost? Pentecostalism and Globalization in Africa and Beyond* (Trenton: Africa World Press, 2011); Martin Lindhardt, ed., *Pentecostalism in Africa: Presence and Impact of Pneumatic Christianity in Postcolonial Societies* (Leiden: Brill, 2014); Ogbu Kalu, Wilhelmina Kalu Nimi Wariboko, and Toyin Falola, *African Pentecostalism: Global Discourses, Migrations, Exchanges, and Connections* (Asmara, Eritrea: Africa World Press, 2010); Dena Freeman, *Pentecostalism and Development: Churches, NGOs and Social Change in Africa* (Basingstoke: Palgrave Macmillan, 2012); and Sturla J. Stålsett, *Spirits of Globalization: The Growth of Pentecostalism and Experiential Spiritualities in a Global Age* (London: SCM Press, 2006).

64 Lamin Sanneh, *Disciples of All Nations: Pillars of World Christianity* (New York: Oxford University Press, 2008), 275; Philip Jenkins, *The New Christendom: The Coming of Global Christianity* (New York: Oxford University Press, 2007), 8–9, quoted in Asamoah-Gyadu, *Contemporary Pentecostal Christianity*, x–xi.

65 Allan Anderson, foreword to Asamoah-Gyadu, *Contemporary Pentecostal Christianity*, xii–xvi. See also Walton, *Watch This!*

66 The "Pentecostal Principle" is an improvisational play upon and critical interrogation of Paul Tillich's famous "Protestant Principle," outlined in his book *The Protestant Era* (Chicago: University of Chicago Press, 1948). See Nimi Wariboko's differentiation of the Protestant Principle and the Pentecostal Principle in *Pentecostal Principle*, 48–50. Wariboko's integration of theological and ethical issues associated with global Pentecostalism and economics is expressed in his recent books, including *Economics in Spirit and Truth: A Moral Philosophy of Finance* (New York: Palgrave Macmillan, 2014); *God and Money: A Theology of Money in a Globalizing World* (Lanham, MD: Lexington, 2008); *Methods of Ethical Analysis: Between Theology, History, and Literature* (Eugene, OR: Wipf and Stock, 2013); *The Principle of Excellence: A Framework for Social Ethics* (Lanham, MD: Lexington, 2009); *Pentecostal Principle*; and *Charismatic City*.

67 Wariboko, *Pentecostal Principle*, 1.

68 Ibid., 3. See also Wariboko, *Principle of Excellence*, 7.

69 On the issue of black bodies, see how Nigerian Pentecostals struggle with spirituality and the weight of blackness, particularly how Nigerian Pentecostals conceptualize their bodies, black bodies, as either holy or defiled. Nimi Wariboko, *Nigerian Pentecostalism* (Rochester, NY: University of Rochester Press, 2014), chap. 9.

70 "From Greek *diaspora* 'dispersion,' from *diaspeirein* 'to scatter about, disperse,' from *dia-* 'about, across' . . . + *speirein* 'to scatter' (sprout). The Greek word was

used in Septuagint in Deut. xxviii: 25." It is also related to the Hebrew word *galuth*, which is interpreted as "exile." *Online Etymology Dictionary*, www.etymonline. com.

71 First, *babel* is a play on the Hebrew word *balal*, which means to "mix" or "confuse." "That is why it was called Babel—because there the Lord confused the language of the whole world. . . . From there the Lord scattered them over the face of the whole earth." Pentecost, in this perspective, is a corrective of the failure and folly of Babel. Scholars tend to agree that Luke intentionally places the birth of the church on the Day of Pentecost, the celebration of the harvest, and as such it came to symbolize the reversal of Babel. In Palestine there were two harvests each year. The early harvest came during the months of May and June; the final harvest came in the fall. Pentecost was the celebration of the beginning of the early wheat harvest, which meant that Pentecost always fell sometime during the middle of May or sometimes in early June. Craig S. Keener, "Why Does Luke Use Tongues as a Sign of the Spirit's Empowerment?," *Journal of Pentecostal Theology* 15, no. 2 (2007): 118; Craig S. Keener, "Power of Pentecost: Luke's Missiology in Acts 1–2," *Asian Journal of Pentecostal Studies* 12, no. 1 (2009): 62. Among the sources Keener cites are C. F. D. Moule, *Christ's Messengers: Studies in the Acts of the Apostles* (London: United Society for Christian Literature, 1957), 23; F. F. Bruce, *The Book of the Acts* (Grand Rapids: Eerdmans, 1988), 64; Justo L. González, *Acts: The Gospel of the Spirit* (Maryknoll, NY: Orbis, 2001), 39; Krister Stendahl, *Paul among Jews and Gentiles and Other Essays* (Minneapolis: Fortress, 1976), 117; Bert B. Dominy, "Spirit, Church, and Mission: Theological Implications of Pentecost," *Southwestern Journal of Theology* 35, no. 2 (1993): 34–39; David I. Smith, "What Hope after Babel? Diversity and Community in Gen 11:1–9; Exod 1:1–14; Zeph 3:1–13 and Acts 2:1–13," *Horizons in Biblical Theology* 18, no. 1 (1995): 169–91; F. Scott Spencer, *Acts* (Sheffield: Sheffield Academic Press, 1997), 32–33; Georgette Chéreau, "De Babel à la Pentecôte: Histoire d'une bénédiction," *Nouvelle Revue Théologique* 122 (2000): 19–36; Alexander Venter, *Doing Reconciliation: Racism, Reconciliation and Transformation in the Church and World* (Cape Town, South Africa: Vineyard International, 2004), 155; Max Turner, "Early Christian Experience and Theology of 'Tongues'—A New Testament Perspective," in *Speaking in Tongues: Multi-Disciplinary Perspectives*, ed. Mark J. Cartledge (Waynesboro, GA: Paternoster, 2006), 32; Cyril of Jerusalem, *Catechetical Lecture*, 17.16–17, *Catholic Encyclopedia*, www.newadvent.org; Richard Hillier, *Arator on the Acts of the Apostles: A Baptismal Commentary* (Oxford: Clarendon, 1993), available on Scholarship Online, www.oxfordscholarship.com; Venerable Bede and Lawrence T. Martin, *The Venerable Bede Commentary on the Acts of the Apostles* (Collegeville, MN: Cistercian Publications,1989); and patristic sources in Daniel Marguerat, *Les Actes des apôtres (1–12)* (Geneva: Labor et Fides, 2015) 81, n. 45.

72 God says to Abraham, "I will surely bless you and make your descendants as numerous as the stars in the sky and as the sand on the seashore. Your

descendants will take possession of the cities of their enemies, and through your offspring all nations on earth will be blessed, because you have obeyed me." Genesis 22: 17–18. In her mercy, God scatters us so that we might become *scatterers*! The Apostle writes, "If you belong to Christ, then you are Abraham's seed, and heirs according to the promise." Galatians 3:29.

73 Charette argues that

> the Pentecost language event signals judgment as well as blessing. The reference to "tongues as of fire" in Luke's description of Pentecost portends judgment. This is consistent both with Luke's use of the image of fire elsewhere and with the very character of Pentecost as an eschatological event. The judgment in view is directed against those who fail to respond appropriately to the word of God present in the redemptive revelation centered in Jesus. The positive response of obedient disciples results in their experience of the baptism with the Holy Spirit. At the same time, the "language of another tongue" that characterizes this experience serves to demonstrate the divine judgment that has come upon the disobedient.

Blaine Charette, "'Tongues as of Fire': Judgment as a Function of Glossolalia in Luke's Thought," *Journal of Pentecostal Theology* 13, no. 2 (2005): 173.

74 Ibid., 179–82. The Parable of the Sower is found in Luke 8:1–15.

75 See Walter Brueggemann, *Genesis* (Atlanta: John Knox Press, 1982), 97–104.

76 Howard Thurman, "Judgment and Hope in the Christian Message," in *The Christian Way in Race Relations*, ed. William Stuart Nelson (New York: Harper and Brothers, 1948), 230.

77 Walter Brueggemann suggests that "the narrative poses important issues about the practice and function of language. It suggests that all human language has become a language of disobedience." *Genesis*, 97. Donald Gowan argues, "The more power they are able to concentrate the more harm they will be able to do to themselves and the world. So we ought to understand God's decision (11.7–8) as not so much the punishment of sin as a preventive act to avert great potential evil." Donald Gowan, "Genesis 1–11: From Eden to Babel," in *The International Theological Commentary* (Grand Rapids: Eerdmans; Edinburgh: Handsel Press, 1988), 119.

78 Fanon, *Black Skin, White Masks*, 17–18. Fanon suggests the relationship between language and citizenship:

> To speak a language is to take on a world, a culture. The Antilles Negro who wants to be white will be the whiter as he gains greater mastery of the cultural tool that language is. Rather more than a year ago in Lyon, I remember, in a lecture I had drawn a parallel between the Negro and European poetry, and a French acquaintance told me enthusiastically, "At the bottom you are a white man." The fact that I had been able to investigate so interesting a problem through the white man's language gave me honorary citizenship. (38)

79 Keener, "Power of Pentecost," 62; Yong, *Spirit Poured Out on All Flesh*, 72–73, also 56–57 on India.

80 The author is aware that this is treacherous territory, given how biblical scholars tend to treat the terms "exile" and "diaspora." While exilic experiences are most certainly a type of dispersion—or, more accurately, a type of dislocation and displacement experience—diaspora as cast in New Testament or early Christian writings is not necessarily an exile or forced displacement. Interpreters often use *diaspora* interchangeably with Hebrew notions of exile, but this is actually misleading. *Galuth* in Hebrew is never translated as *diaspora* in Greek. Or put another way, in the Septuagint (LXX), *diaspora* is never a translation for the HB *galuth* and notions of exile. *Diaspora* is a distinctly Hellenistic Greek term, emerging from Hellenistic military-induced dispersions of people as spoils of war. When it appears in the LXX, diaspora is cast as a theological category, the punitive measure taken by God against an unfaithful people. As such, it is God who remedies diaspora. In the NT, however, the few instances of diaspora language (John 7:35; James 1:1; 1 Peter 1:1; or verb form Acts 8:1, 4; 11:19) do not cast diaspora as a negative and punitive situation. Diaspora is a complex and changing conception across the canonical translations. Many thanks to the Reverend Shively Smith, assistant professor of New Testament at Wesley Theological Seminary, for her careful review and helpful comments on this section.

CHAPTER 7. JUST ABOVE OUR HEADS

1 Manning Marable, *Malcolm X: A Life of Reinvention* (New York: Penguin, 2011); Lewis V. Baldwin, "Malcolm X and Martin Luther King, Jr.: A Reassessment of the Relationship between Malcolm X and Martin Luther King, Jr.," *Western Journal of Black Studies* 13, no. 2 (1989): 103–13; James H. Cone, *Martin and Malcolm and America: A Dream or a Nightmare* (Maryknoll, NY: Orbis, 1991); Franklin, *Liberating Visions*; Robert Michael Franklin, *Harvard Divinity Bulletin* 21, no. 4 (1992); Bruce Perry, *Malcolm: The Life of a Man Who Changed Black America* (Barrytown, NY: Station Hill Press, 1991); Michael Eric Dyson, *Making Malcolm: The Myth and Meaning of Malcolm X* (New York: Oxford University Press, 1995); Michael Eric Dyson, "Who Speaks for Malcolm X? The Writings of Just about Everybody," *New York Times Book Review*, November 29, 1992, 33; Clayborne Carson, "Malcolm X: The Man and the Myth," *San Francisco Examiner*, November 22, 1992, D-9. See womanist interpretations in Linda Wynn, "Beyond Patriarchy," 55–88; Traci West, "Gay Rights and the Misuse of Martin," 141–56, and Cheryl Kirk-Duggan, "Drum Major for Justice or Dilettante of Dishonesty," 100–119, both in *The Domestication of Martin Luther King, Jr: Clarence B. Jones, Right-Wing Conservatism, and the Manipulation of the King Legacy*, ed. Lewis V. Baldwin and Rufus Burrows Jr. (Eugene, OR: Cascade Books, 2013); Gwendolyn Zoharah Simmons, "Martin Luther King Jr. Revisited: A Black Power Feminist

Pays Homage to the King," *Journal of Feminist Studies in Religion* 24, no. 2 (Fall 2008): 189–213; Michael Eric Dyson, *I May Not Get There with You: The True Martin Luther King, Jr.* (New York: Touchstone, 2000), chaps. 8, 10, pp. 155–74, 197–224.

2 In Martin Luther King, Jr. Research and Education Institute, Stanford University, https://kinginstitute.stanford.edu.

3 Marable, *Malcolm X*, 35 (italics added).

4 "The Time Has Come: 1964–1966," *Eyes on the Prize: America at the Racial Crossroads*, produced by Henry Hampton (PBS documentary, 1990).

5 Audre Lorde, "Now That I Am Forever with Child," in *Chosen Poems—Old and New* (New York: Norton, 1992), 13–14.

6 Danita Reed, "Black Madonnas of Europe: Diffusion of the African Isis," in *African Presence in Early Europe*, ed. Ivan Van Sertima (New Brunswick, NJ: Transaction, 1985); Lewis Spence, *Ancient Egyptian Myths and Legends* (New York: Dover, 1990), 3–129; Isha Schwaller De Lubicz, *Her-Bak: The Living Face of Ancient Egypt* (Rochester, VT: Inner Traditions, 1978); Sir Wallis Budge, *Egyptian Religion* (New York: Bell, 1959), 61–107; Ra Un Nefer Amen I, *Metu Neter*, vol. 1 (New York: Khamit, 1990), 125–37.

7 Williams, *Sisters in the Wilderness*, ix, 6.

8 Grace Jantzen, *Becoming Divine: Towards a Feminist Philosophy of Religion* (Bloomington: Indiana University Press, 1999). See Katharine Sarah Moody and Steven Shakespeare, eds., *Intensities: Philosophy, Religion and the Affirmation of Life* (Burlington, VT: Ashgate, 2012).

9 See Sojourner Truth, "Ain't I a Woman?," in online Modern History Sourcebook, Fordham University, http://legacy.fordham.edu, accessed November 6, 2015.

10 Quoted in Barbara Ransby, *Ella Baker and the Black Freedom Movement: A Radical Democratic Vision* (Charlotte: University of North Carolina Press, 2003), 335. For performance and lyrics to "Ella's Song" by Sweet Honey in the Rock, see www.youtube.com.

11 Mills, *This Little Light of Mine*. See also Chana Kai Lee, *For Freedom's Sake: The Life of Fannie Lou Hamer* (Chicago: University of Illinois Press, 1999), 85–102.

12 Author's private journal.

13 "The face of man is the medium through which the invisible in him becomes visible and enters into commerce with us." Emmanuel Levinas, *Difficult Freedom*, trans. Sean Hand (Baltimore: Johns Hopkins University Press, 1990), 140.

14 Fluker, *Ethical Leadership*, 25; Robert Michael Franklin, *Harvard Divinity Bulletin* 21, no. 4 (1992).

15 Baldwin and Dekar, "*In an Inescapable Network of Mutuality*," 9.

16 King, *The Trumpet of Conscience*, chap. 2, "Conscience and the Vietnam War," in Washington, *Testament of Hope*, 640.

17 Martin Luther King Jr., *Where Do We Go from Here? Chaos or Community* (New York: Harper and Row, 1967), 169.

18 King, "I See the Promised Land (3 April 1968)," in Washington, *Testament of Hope*, 280.

19 King, *Where Do We Go from Here*, 167.

20 Ibid., 190.

21 Malcolm X, *The Autobiography of Malcolm X*, with assistance of Alex Haley, intro. M. S. Handler, epilogue by Alex Haley (New York: Grove, 1965), 404, 408. Marable, Dyson, and Cone capture this trope of change in their respective examinations of Malcolm.

22 Malcolm X, *Autobiography of Malcolm X*, 365 (italics added).

23 Christopher Lasch, *The True and Only Heaven: Progress and Its Critics* (New York: Norton, 1991), 81.

24 Roger Mais, "All Men Come to the Hills," in *Yearbook of the Poetry League of Jamaica* (Kingston: New Dawn, 1940); see also *Kyk-Over-Al* 6, no. 20 (1955): 150–52; and John Figueroa, ed., *Caribbean Voices: An Anthology of West Indian Poetry* (London: Evans Brothers, 1970).

25 Malcolm X, *Autobiography of Malcolm X*, 187 (italics added).

26 Ibid., 368–69.

27 Ibid., 369.

28 Lorde, "Now That I Am Forever with Child."

CHAPTER 8. *RETURNING* TO THE LITTLE HOUSE WHERE WE LIVED AND MADE DO

1 Howard Thurman, *With Head and Heart: The Autobiography of Howard Thurman* (New York: Harcourt Brace, 1979), 194–96.

2 Langston Hughes, "American Heartbreak," in *Selected Poems* (New York: Vintage, 1959), 9.

3   O come, O come, Emmanuel,
      And ransom captive Israel,
      That mourns in lonely exile here
      Until the Son of God appear.
    www.cyberhymnal.org, accessed August 22, 2015.

4 Floyd-Thomas et al., *Black Church Studies*, xxiv.

5 See Monica A. Coleman, *Making a Way out of No Way: A Womanist Theology* (Minneapolis: Fortress, 2008).

6 John Jay Chapman, "William Lloyd Garrison," *Twentieth Century Magazine*, May 1912, 3.

7 Malidoma Patrice Somé, *Ritual: Power, Healing, and Community* (Portland, OR: Swan Raven, 1993), 122.

8 Hughes, "American Heartbreak."

9 Walter Earl Fluker, ed., *The Stones That the Builders Rejected: The Development of Ethical Leadership from the Black Church Tradition* (Harrisburg, PA: Trinity Press International, 1998).

10 Morrison, "Memory, Creation, and Writing," 385. Morrison's quote is translated
    from Ragna Stang, *Edvard Munch: Mennesket og Kunstneren* (Oslo: H.
    Aschehoug, 1977), 260.

> An artwork is a crystal—just as the crystal has soul and will, the artwork
> must have them too. *It is not enough that the artwork has proper exterior
> planes and lines. When you throw a rock at a bunch of boys, they scatter in all
> directions. There's a regrouping, an action takes place. That is a composition.
> To reproduce this regrouping with colours, lines and planes is an artistic and
> pictorial motif.* It doesn't have to be "literary." This insult many use for
> paintings which don't present apples on a table cloth or a violin broken in
> two.

J. Gill Holland, "Translations from Edvard Munch," 109 (italics mine), www.
brunel.ac.uk.

11 Frances Ellen Watkins Harper, "We Are All Bound Up Together," Eleventh
    Women's Rights Convention 1866, in Shirley Wilson Logan, *"We Are Coming":
    The Persuasive Discourse of Nineteenth-Century Black Women* (Carbondale:
    Southern Illinois University Press, 1999), 58.

12 Late Middle English: from Latin *congregat-* 'collected (into a flock), united,' from
    the verb *congregare,* from *con-* 'together' + *gregare* (from *grex, greg-* 'a flock').
    Merriam-webster.com.

13 There are clearly contested meanings associated with *repent.* I prefer the sense of
    all those below along with the idea of *repent* meaning to "turn around or turn
    away from" as in *metanoia.*

> The American Heritage Dictionary (Etymology of "Repent") Middle English
> *repenten,* from Old French *repentir:* (*re-*, in response + Latin *pentire,* to be sorry);
> Oxford English Dictionary (Etymology of "Repent") [ad. French. *repentir* (11th
> c.) from re- RE- + Roman **penítre:* Latin. *poenitére:* see PENITENT.] 1. refl.
> To affect (oneself) with contrition or regret for something done, etc. (cf. 3.)
> Also const. of, for, that. Now archaic;
> Merriam-Webster Revised Dictionary (Etymology of "Repent") [? possible
> derivation from Latin *paene* or Greek *poenere* (to suffer, to feel pain)].

L. Kip Wheeler, "Conflicting Sources," Dr. Wheeler's Website, https://web.
cn.edu/kwheeler, accessed July 23, 2015.

14 Warnock, in *The Divided Mind of the Black Church,* outlines four critical
    moments in the history of African American Christian resistance: (1) the
    formation of a liberationist faith (the invisible institution); (2) the founding of a
    liberationist church (independent black church movement); (3) the fomenting of
    a church-led liberationist movement (civil rights movement); and (4) the forging
    of a self-conscious liberationist theology (black theology) (20–21). In his
    conclusion, he calls for a fifth moment, which he refers to as the flowering of a
    self-critical liberationist community that would integrate the preceding moments
    and bring together black academic theologians and black pastors in a broadening

communal space for dialogue, risk taking, and testing reminiscent of the National Conference of Black Churchmen or the Black Theology Project (185–89).

15 The reference here is specifically to the Reverend Al Sharpton's National Action Network and the Reverend Cornell Brooks of NAACP. See Yamiche Alcindor, "Civil Rights Leaders at Odds as Ferguson Protests Grow," *USA Today*, December 28, 2014. See also Randall Kennedy, "Lifting as We Climb: A Progressive Defense of Respectability Politics," *Harpers*, October 2015.

16 See Bryan Stevenson, *Just Mercy: A Story of Justice and Redemption* (New York: Spiegel and Grau, 2014); also see Bryan Stevenson's work with the Equal Justice Initiative (www.eji.org) for timeline associating race, incarceration, and poverty.

17 Kennedy, "Lifting as We Climb."

18 See Barbara Reynolds, "I Was a Civil Rights Activist in the 1960s. But It's Hard for Me to Get behind Black Lives Matter," *Washington Post*, August 24, 2015, www.washingtonpost.com.

19 See Kennedy's discussion of the critiques from Michael Eric Dyson, Melissa Harris-Perry, and Brittney Cooper, who is referenced below. Reynolds lifts up the civil rights icons John Lewis and Andrew Young as exemplars of the effectiveness of respectability.

20 Brittney Cooper, "Stop Poisoning the Race Debate: How 'Respectability Politics' Rears Its Ugly Head—Again," *Salon*, March 18, 2015, www.salon.com; see Jonathan Capehart, "'Hands Up, Don't Shoot' Was Built on a Lie," *Washington Post*, March 16, 2015, www.washingtonpost.com.

21 One of the more interesting features of Occupy was the small representation of African American activists, with the exception of notables like Cornel West. What this phenomenon might mean for the activism of Black Lives Matter can be speculative at best, but running the risk, I suggest that it set the tone in many ways for the strategies and tactics of BLM. Saki Knafo, "Occupy Wall Street, Faces of Zuccotti Park: The Columbia Economics Professor," *Huffington Post*, November 11, 2011, www.huffingtonpost.com; Rosie Gray, "Occupy Wall Street Debuts the New Spokes Council," *Village Voice*, November 8, 2011, blogs.villagevoice.com; Lee Siegel, "Black Friday Is Like Occupy Wall Street," *Daily Beast*, November 26, 2011; Adam Gabbatt, "Occupy Wall Street—Tuesday 25 October 2011," *Guardian*, October 25, 2011, www.guardian.co.uk. See also Ferry Biedermann, "From Europe to the US, Protesters Are Inspired by Arab Spring," *National*, October 5, 2011, www.thenational.ae; Amy Goodman and Cornel West, "Cornel West on Occupy Wall Street: It's the Makings of a U.S. Autumn Responding to the Arab Spring," *Democracy Now!*, September 29, 2011, www.democracynow.org.

22 Walter Earl Fluker, "Now We Must Cross a Sea: Remarks on Transformational Leadership and the Civil Rights Movement," *Boston University Law Review* 95, no. 3 (2015): 1225–32.

23 Greg Lukianoff and Jonathan Haidt, "The Coddling of the American Mind," *Atlantic*, September 2015, www.theatlantic.com.

24 Arthur Schlesinger Jr., *The Disuniting of America: Reflections on a Multicultural Society*, ed. William S. Rukeyser (Knoxville, TN: Whittle Direct Books, 1991), 2. See also Peter Beinart, "Brown University's Campus Liberals vs. Free Speech," *Daily Beast*, October 30, 2013.

25 Howard Gardner, *Truth, Beauty, and Goodness Reframed: Educating for the Virtues in the Twenty-First Century* (New York: Basic Books, 2011). Gardner interrogates these "classical virtues" and raises profound questions related to digitalization, postmodernist critiques, and the asymmetrical relation of the three (beauty is not necessarily good; good is not necessarily true).

26 "What does LGBTQIA Mean?," Tahoe Safe Alliance website, http://tahoesafeal-liance.org, accessed October 9, 2015.

27 I have cited Black Lives Matter as one example of youthful leadership that beckons to the future of the church in respect to mission, but there are others in our communities across the nation. For examples of exciting and promising conversations about LGBTQIA that are taking place in the academy and church, see Christine Y. Wiley and Dennis W. Wiley, Pastors of Covenant Baptist United Church of Christ and co-chairs, DC Clergy United for Marriage Equality, "Christine Y. Wiley and Dennis W. Wiley: Gay Marriage in Our Black Church," http://host.madison.com, accessed October 9, 2015; Pastor Jay Williams, Union United Methodist Church, see http://unionboston.org, accessed October 9, 2015; Lightsey, *Our Lives Matter*; Coleman, *Ain't I a Womanist, Too?*

28 Antonio Negri and Michael Hardt, *Empire* (Cambridge: Harvard University Press, 2000); Michael Hardt and Antonio Negri, *Commonwealth* (Cambridge: Belknap, 2009); Michael Hardt and Antonio Negri, *Multitude: War and Democracy in the Age of Empire* (New York: Penguin, 2004); Reinhold Martin, "Public and Common(s)," *Places Journal*, January 2013, https://placesjournal.org.

29 See Sharon D. Welch, *After Empire: The Art and Ethos of Enduring Peace* (Minneapolis: Fortress, 2004); Mark Lewis Taylor, *Religion, Politics, and the Christian Right: Post 9/11 Powers and American Empire* (Minneapolis: Fortress, 2005). See review of Welch and Taylor by Rebecca Todd Peterson, *Journal of the Society of Christian Ethics* 27, no. 1 (Spring/Summer 2007): 310–13.

30 Mark 9:20–23.

31 See Coleman, *Ain't I a Womanist, Too?* as an example of the continuous turning that is necessary for the revolution of values and priorities as a critique of cultures within African American churchly and theological practices.

32 C. S. Lewis, *Letters to Malcolm, Chiefly on Prayer: Reflections on the Intimate Dialogue between God and Man* (New York: Mariner, 2002), 80.

33 Ed Riddick, foreword to *Your God Is Too White*, by Columbus Salley and Ronald Behm (Oxford: Lion, 1973), 7.

34 See earlier reference to global citizenship; see also Sen, *Identity and Violence*; and Appiah, *Cosmopolitanism*.

35 Iton, *In Search of the Black Fantastic*, 290.

36 Ibid., 14. The difficult question being raised here is in relation to the "house that race built," which is a modernist linguistic construction that is held together by legal (state) and religious/moral ideology. How then might the (black) subject release himself or herself from these iron cages when even the language of "equality" (as in the "radical egalitarian hypothesis") betrays his/her quest for full citizenship?

37 "Middle English (also in the sense 'oblige by oath'): from Old French *conjurer* 'to plot or exorcize,' from Latin *conjurare* 'band together by an oath, conspire' (in medieval Latin 'invoke'), from *con-* 'together' + *jurare* 'swear.'" Google search for "conjure etymology," www.google.com, accessed October 15, 2015. "Magical sense is c. 1300, for 'constraining by spell' a demon to do one's bidding. Related: Conjured; conjuring. Phrase conjure up 'cause to appear in the mind' (as if by magic) attested from 1580s." *Online Etymology Dictionary*, www.etymonline.com, accessed October 15, 2015; see also Dave Harris, "Reading Guide to Derrida," www.arasite.org, accessed October 15, 2015.

38 Anderson, "The Smell of Life," in *Creative Exchange*.

39 See Raboteau, *Slave Religion*, 275–88; see also Sobel, *Trabelin' On*.

40 Theophus Smith, *Conjuring Culture: Biblical Formations of Black America* (New York: Oxford University Press, 1994), 5–6, 58, 146–49, 162–74.

41 Thurman references this internal locus as an "unconscious autonomy." See chapter 9.

42 This can be done in a number of ways using spirituality and forms of cultural imagination (cultural narratives, myths, rituals, and aesthetic triggers) that inform experiential and reflective learning, critical thinking, and moral judgment. In addition to story and ritual, immersion in aesthetic or artistic enterprise is a powerful stimulus to imagining alternatives. After participating in an act of artistic creation, agents view the world differently. They see the world as malleable and open to difference, which triggers consciousness of difference that can be utilized as a learning resource for diversity. Examples of aesthetic triggers are origami, mask making, tai chi, dance, community banner making, spoken word, poetry, fantasy, drawing, photography, painting, song writing, and drama. See Walter Earl Fluker, "Strategies and Resources for Ethical Leadership Education in the Twenty-First Century," in *Educating Ethical Leaders for the Twenty-First Century*, ed. Walter Earl Fluker (Eugene, OR: Cascade Books, 2013), 28–29.

43 Reference to the Apostle is from Romans 10:8 (NIV): "But what does it say? 'The word is near you; it is in your mouth and in your heart,' that is, the message concerning faith that we proclaim." See Gerhard Ebeling, *God and Word* (Philadelphia: Fortress, 1967), 30 for "the word that comes your way."

44 For example, listen to Reverend C. L. Franklin, "The Valley of Dry Bones," on www.youtube.com, accessed October 9, 2015. Ray L. Hart, *Unfinished Man and Imagination: Toward an Ontology and a Rhetoric of Revelation* (Louisville: Westminster John Knox, 2001), 28 (italics in original).

45 See Renita J. Weems, "Preaching from the 'Underside' of the Book of Samuel: David, Jonathan, and Justice" (presentation at "Preaching against the Grain: Recovering the Voices of Those from the Underside of History," Convocation 2008, Second Lyman Beecher Lecture Event, Yale Divinity School, October 14, 2008), http://divinity.yale.edu, accessed October 9, 2015.

46 Jennings, *Christian Imagination*, 60.

47 Thurman's book *The Search for Common Ground* (Richmond, IN: Friends United, 1986) should be understood within this framework. Examples of Thurman's wrestling with the American democratic experiment and fascist tendencies of the state during the World War II era can be found in a number of unpublished sermons preached at the Church for the Fellowship of All Peoples from July 29 to August 26, 1951. In these sermons, Thurman gave a decidedly religious interpretation to the founding principles of democracy, addressing the themes of equality, the right to life, liberty, the pursuit of happiness and their significance for the oppressed. "The Declaration of Independence," Taped Sermon Series, Fellowship Church for All Peoples, San Francisco, July 29, 1951, Thurman Papers, Howard Gotlieb Archival Research Center, Boston University. See also "The American Dream," Taped Sermon, Marsh Chapel, Boston University, July 6, 1958, Thurman Papers, Howard Gotlieb Archival Research Center, Boston University; "America in Search of a Soul," Robbins Lecture Series, University of the Redlands, Redlands, CA, January 20, 1976, Howard Thurman Educational Trust, San Francisco; and "The Fascist Masquerade," in *The Church and Organized Movements*, ed. Randolph Crump Miller (New York: Harper and Row, 1959), 82–100. Some of these documents can be found in Fluker, *Soundless Passion of a Single Mind*.

48 I use the designation *opener of the way* to express the distinctive characterization of Thurman's contribution to leaders in the forefront of the civil rights movement. As a discursive pointer, it also provides a window through which we can examine his understanding of spirituality and how it is wedded to healing and social transformation in Thurman's thought and praxis. This language also highlights Thurman's conscious role as *pedagogue* in teaching and explicating the spiritual and ethical significance of the political, economic, and social arrangements in which these individuals found themselves. Fluker, *Ethical Leadership*, 63.

49 As suggested earlier, Anderson, *Beyond Ontological Blackness*, 38–50, 80–81, 159; and Anderson, "The Smell of Life," in *Creative Exchange*, esp. 115–35, are the best sources on these critiques. For more on "willed creation," see the introduction.

50 Thurman, *Search for Common Ground*, 5.

51 Thurman examines the utopias in Isaiah 11:1–9, Plato's *Republic*, the New Jerusalem of the Apocalypse (Revelation 21), and Sir Thomas More's *Utopia*. Utopias arise, according to Thurman, out of the individual's experience of disharmony in the present. The utopian dream of harmony and order, therefore, is a projection of the ideal of community, which is instinctively a part of the human race. According to Thurman,

> The interesting thing about Utopias is this: they have within their limitations all the elements of community. They do not say anything about whom they are excluding, but theirs is a custom-made projection of dreams of order and harmony which the individual projects and holds at dead center in his soul and mind, seeking thereby to bring to pass in his contemporary experience that which indicates his contemporary experience is under the tutelage of this creative transcendent projection.

Convocation address, Pittsburgh Seminary, Pittsburgh, November 4, 1971, Thurman Papers, Howard Gotlieb Archival Research Center, Boston University, 6.

52 Thurman, *Search for Common Ground*, 22.

53 Jochen Fried, "Rethinking Global Citizenship" (lecture, Leadership Center, Morehouse College, Atlanta, November 19, 2008). "Innocence," says Thurman, "is the state of being which exists without knowledge and responsibility." It is that "which is essentially untried, untested, unchallenged. It is complete and whole within itself because it has known nothing else." Thurman, *Search for Common Ground*, 26–27.

54 Jennings, *Christian Imagination*, 60.

55 Ibid., 27; and Fried, "Rethinking Global Citizenship."

56 For instance, see Paul Gilroy's accounting of Martin Delany's first trip to Africa in 1859. He suggests that "the ambivalence over exile and homecoming conveyed by these remarks has a history that is probably as long as the presence of African slaves in the west." Gilroy, *Black Atlantic*, 23–24.

57 There is a sense of wholeness at the core of man That must abound in all he does; That marks with reverence his ev'ry step; That has its sway when all else fails; That wearies out all evil things; That warms the depth of frozen fears Making friend of foe, Making love of hate, And lasts beyond the living and the dead, Beyond the goals of peace, the ends of war! This man seeks through all his years: To be complete and of one piece, within, without. Thurman, *The Inward Journey*, 96 (italics added).

58 See Howard Thurman, "Knowledge . . . Shall Vanish Away," in *The Inward Journey*, 96.

59 Thurman, "A Strange Freedom," in *The Inward Journey*, 38.

60 *Le point le verge* is an apex, or still point, the "center of our nothingness where one meets God—and is found completely in His mercy." See Merton, *Contemplation in a World of Action*.

61 See Thurman, "I Will Not Give Up."

62 Howard Thurman, "When Knowledge Comes," in *The Inward Journey* (New York: Harper and Brothers, 1961), 16–17, 18.

63 According to Johnson, "Tragic Soul Life explores the clash between religious and political discourse in shaping the unasked question of what does it mean to be a problem. A close examination of the Du Boisian question reveals the subtle ways

moral beliefs inform political life both historically and in contemporary society." *Tragic Soul-Life*, 9.

64 See chapter 3 in this volume. Quoted in Holland, *Raising the Dead*, 13.

65 Ibid., 5. Thurman's meditation "The Inward Sea" is an example of the internal quest for a sense of wholeness and human flourishing:

> There is in everyone an inward sea, and in that sea there is an island and on the island there is an altar and standing before that altar is the "angel with the flaming sword." Nothing can get by that angel to be placed on that altar unless it has the mark of your inner authority. Nothing passes "the angel with the flaming sword" to be placed upon your altar unless it be a part of "the fluid area of your consent." This is your crucial link with the Eternal.

Howard Thurman, "The Inward Sea," in *Meditations of the Heart* (Richmond, IN: Friends United Press, 1976), 15.

66 Ibid., 1.

67 In some shamanistic traditions, an angel or demon tricks and dismembers or slays the initiate who dares to enter; and she or he is reintegrated, remembered, or resurrected into a new being. Mircea Eliade, *Shamanism: Archaic Techniques of Ecstasy* (Princeton: Princeton University Press, 1964), 16.

68 Charles Long, "Howard Thurman and the Meaning of Religion in America," in *The Human Search: Howard Thurman and the Quest for Freedom: Proceedings of the Second Annual Thurman Convocation*, Martin Luther King, Jr. Memorial Studies in Religion, Culture and Social Development, vol. 2, ed. Mozella G. Mitchell (New York: Peter Lang, 1992), 141. For an exposition of the "terror of history," see Eliade, *Cosmos and History*, 156–57. Thurman's early work on the Negro spirituals began as early as 1925 and continued throughout his life to serve as tools of the spirit to inspire hope in the midst of sorrow and despair. Thurman wrote in 1975 that one of the main reasons for his interest in the spirituals was to address "a generation which tended to be ashamed of the Spirituals, or who joined in the degrading and prostituting of the songs as a part of conventional minstrelsy and naïve amusement exploited and capitalized by white entertainers." Howard Thurman, "The Message of the Spirituals," October 1928, *Papers of Howard Washington Thurman*, vol. 1, 126. See also Thurman, *Deep River and The Negro Spiritual Speaks of Life and Death*.

69 Long, "Howard Thurman and the Meaning of Religion in America," 141.

70 Thurman, *Deep River and The Negro Spiritual Speaks of Life and Death*, 135–36; Howard Thurman, "He Looked for a City," Marsh Chapel, Boston University, January 2, 1955, audiocassette, Thurman Collection, Howard Gotlieb Archival Research Center, Boston University.

71 Definition circa 1300: From Latin "conspirare," which means "to agree, unite, plot," and "com," which means "together" + "spirare" meaning "to breathe." So, literally "conspire" means "to breathe together." According to the Online Etymology Dictionary, the word "conspiracy" is from 1386; "conspiracy

theory" is from 1909. Before 1386 the word "conspire" simply meant to breathe together. After the word "conspiracy" was born, the root word "conspire" took on a new meaning—to plot something wrong, evil or illegal. Modern definition of conspire: 1. To agree together, especially secretly, to do something wrong, evil, or illegal; 2. To act or work together toward the same result or goal.

Dictionary.com, 2010, cited in "Conspire," Do as One, http://doasone.com, accessed July 24, 2015.

72 The phrase "black and poor youth" refers to the description of "highly disadvantaged youth" provided by Patterson, *Cultural Matrix*. Patterson writes, "It is safe to assume that nearly all disadvantaged youth live and were brought up in neighborhoods that are highly disadvantaged" (49). The youth (ages sixteen to twenty-four) of these highly disadvantaged neighborhoods represent 46 percent working-class, 34 percent disconnected, and 20 percent ghetto middle-class youth (51). The porous boundaries between these categories of youth tend to result in variation in what Patterson defines as mainstream, proletarian, or street cultures. See Patterson, *Cultural Matrix*, chap. 2, "The Social and Cultural Matrix of Black Youth," 45–135. "While both boys and girls are impacted by neighborhood violence, sociological research suggests that young men in disadvantaged neighborhoods spend more time in public spaces in the neighborhood than do young women." Peter Rosenblatt, Kathryn Edin, and Queenie Zhu, "'I Do Me': Young Black Men and the Struggle to Resist the Street," in Patterson, *Cultural Matrix*, 229.

73 In a study for the Economic Policy Institute examining the condition of public education in America following the desegregation efforts of the 1950s, 1960s, and 1970s, Richard Rothstein found that black students are more isolated in the classroom now than they were forty years ago. See Richard Rothstein, *For Public Schools, Segregation Then, Segregation Since: Education and the Unfinished March* (Washington, D.C.: Economic Policy Institute, 2013). A similar study from the Center on Juvenile and Criminal Justice showed that nationally, nearly 3 million black students attend schools that are 90 percent or more minority. See Randall Shelden, "Two Nations, One Black, One White, Separate and Unequal," Center on Juvenile and Criminal Justice, May 26, 2015, www.cjcj.org. Poverty is another major challenge facing black youth. The U.S. Bureau of the Census's 2010 report on poverty and access to health care indicates that "38.2% of black children under the age of 18 were living in poverty." See U.S. Bureau of the Census, *Income, Poverty, and Health Insurance Coverage in the United States: 2010*, Report P60, n. 238, Table B-2, pp. 68–73. The combination of pervasive poverty and the lack of educational resources results in major health challenges for black youth. The Centers for Disease Control report that black youth "continue to be one of the groups most severely affected by HIV infection in the United States." Young black people represent 57 percent of all new HIV infections among persons aged

thirteen to twenty-four. "Of the nearly 21,000 infections estimated to occur each year among African Americans, one-third (34 percent) are among people aged 13 to 24." See Centers for Disease Control, "HIV among African American Youth Fact Sheet," 2014, www.cdc.gov.

74 According to the NAACP, as of 2001, one out of six black men had been incarcerated. If this incarceration trend continues, one in every three black men born today can expect to be incarcerated in their lifetimes. See NAACP Statistical Fact Sheet, www.naacp.org. Among young people aged thirteen to twenty-four, black males had the highest rate of HIV infection of any race/ethnicity. Black males aged thirteen to twenty-four were eleven times more likely than white men and four times more likely than Hispanic men to contract HIV. Furthermore, black men are highly susceptible to violent crime. In 2007 the U.S. Bureau of Justice Statistics reported that black victims of homicide were most likely to be males (85 percent) between the ages of seventeen and twenty-nine (51 percent). See Erika Harrell, "Black Victims of Violent Crime," Bureau of Justice Statistics, August 2007, www.bjs.gov; see also Justin Wolfers, David Leonhardt, and Kevin Quealy, "1.5 Million Missing Black Men," *New York Times*, April 20, 2015, www.nytimes. com.

CHAPTER 9. CULTURAL ASYLUMS AND THE JUNGLES THEY PLANTED IN THEM

1 Morrison, *Beloved*, 198–99.
2 W. E. B. Du Bois, "Of Our Spiritual Strivings," in *The Souls of Black Folk*, 1.
3 Tupac Shakur, "Black Jesus," *Still I Rise*, on www.youtube.com.
4 See discussion on doubleness in chapter 4.
5 Takaki, *Iron Cages*, 127, 11.
6 These statements were made during speeches in Milwaukee and Madison, Wisconsin, on February 18, 2008. See Evan Thomas, "Michelle Obama's 'Proud' Remarks," *Newsweek*, March 12, 2008, www.newsweek.com.
7 See Douglas Bradburn, *The Citizenship Revolution: Politics and the Creation of the American Union, 1774–1804* (Charlottesville: University of Virginia Press, 2009); and John Park and Shannon Gleeson, eds., *The Nation and Its Peoples: Citizens, Denizens, Migrants* (London: Routledge, 2014).
8 A 2014 report by the Violence Policy Center stated that in 2011, while blacks represented 13 percent of the nation's population, 50 percent of all homicide victims were black. In total, there were 6,309 black homicide victims, and of that total 5,452 (86 percent) were male, and 854 (14 percent) were female. Alarmingly, the homicide rate for black male victims was 31.67 per 100,000. The average age was thirty, and 73 percent were murdered by someone they knew. "In comparison, the overall rate for male homicide victims was 7.13 per 100,000. For white male homicide victims it was 3.85 per 100,000. The homicide rate for female black

victims was 4.54 per 100,000." "Black Homicide Victimization in the United States: An Analysis of 2011 Data," Violence Policy Center, 2014, www.vpc.org.

9 Michel Foucault, "The Birth of the Asylum," in *Madness and Civilization: A History of Insanity in the Age of Reason* (1964; New York: Vintage, 1988), 24.

10 See John Witte Jr., "The Freedom of a Christian: Martin Luther's Reformation of Law and Liberty," *Evangelische Theologie* 74 (2014): 127–35, Emory Legal Studies Research paper No. 14–316, Emory University School of Law.

11 I am fully aware that Morrison's characters, Sethe and Beloved, are female and that my discussion could be interpreted as privileging male agency at the expense of female agency and suffering. I am most interested, however, in Stamp Paid's inner observations and his voyeurism through the window. Moreover, Morrison's comment is helpful in the sense that she includes all black people in her description of the incident. Morrison, *Beloved*, 124.

12 Joy DeGruy, *Post Traumatic Slave Syndrome: America's Legacy of Enduring Injury and Healing* (Portland, OR: Joy DeGruy, 2005).

13 William Julius Wilson, *When Work Disappears: The World of the New Urban Poor* (New York: Vintage, 1996). According to Wilson,

> By social structure I mean the ordering of social positions (or statuses) and networks of social relationships that are based on the arrangement of mutually dependent institutions (economy, polity, family, education) of society. Race, which reflects both an individual's position (in the sense of social status defined by skin color) and network of relationships in society, is a social structural variable. Many liberal explanations of social inequality cite race to the exclusion of other structural variables. (xiii–xiv)

14 See Daniel Patrick Moynihan, *The Negro Family: The Case for National Action* (Washington, D.C.: Office of Planning and Policy Research, Department of Labor, 1965); Oscar Lewis, *The Children of Sanchez* (New York: Random House, 1961); Oscar Lewis, *La Vida: A Puerto Rican Family in the Culture of Poverty* (New York: Random House, 1966); Charles Murray, *Losing Ground: American Social Policy, 1950–1980* (New York: Basic Books, 1984); Richard J. Herrnstein and Charles Murray, *The Bell Curve: Intelligence and Class in American Life* (New York: Free Press, 1994).

15 Titles like John McWhorter, *Losing the Race: Self-Sabotage in Black America* (New York: Free Press, 2000); Juan Williams, *Enough: The Phony Leaders, Dead-End Movements, and Culture of Failure That Are Undermining Black America—and What We Can Do about It* (New York: Crown, 2006); and Shelby Steele, *White Guilt: How Blacks and Whites Together Destroyed the Promise of the Civil Rights Era* (New York: HarperCollins, 2006); and most recently, Shelby Steele, *Shame: How America's Past Sins Have Polarized Our Country*; and Riley, *Please Stop Helping Us* are reflective of the self-critique that abounds with respect to post–civil rights African American leadership.

16 Daniel Bell, *The Coming of Post-Industrial Society: A Venture in Social Forecasting* (New York: Basic Books, 1999), xcix. Bell highlighted several distinct traits that mark a postindustrial society, including the "centrality of theoretical knowledge" and the "creation of a new intellectual technology" (xciv–xcvi). Anoop Nayak defines postindustrialism as a shift toward "deindustrialization that is characterized by more casual forms of work, marked especially by part-time working hours, fixed-term contracts, more 'flexible' patterns of employment and pay scales that can dip below the adult minimum wage." Anoop Nayak, "Displaced Masculinities: Chavs, Youth and Class in the Post-Industrial City," *Sociology* 40, no. 5 (October 2006): 814.

17 Cornel West, "The Political Intellectual," in *The Cornel West Reader* (New York: Basic Books, 1999), 284; bell hooks, "Postmodern Blackness," *Postmodern Culture* 1, no. 1 (September 1990), www.africa.upenn.edu.

18 Wilson, *When Work Disappears.*

19 Robert E. Birt, *The Quest for Community and Identity: Critical Essays in Africana Social Philosophy* (Lanham, MD: Rowman and Littlefield, 2002), 98.

20 Fluker, *Ethical Leadership.*

21 MacIntyre, *After Virtue*, 216.

22 Patterson, *Cultural Matrix*, 29–30.

23 Ibid., 29, 35–44. For Patterson's discussion on the relationship between structuralism and culture and his critique of William Julius Wilson, see pp. 5–6 and 120–25. See also Jennifer A. Glancy, "Early Christianity, Slavery and Women's Bodies," in *Beyond Slavery: Overcoming Its Religious and Sexual Legacies*, ed. Bernadette J. Brooten (New York: Palgrave Macmillan, 2010), 146.

24 The research for this section is indebted to Clinton R. Fluker, Ph.D. candidate, Emory University.

25 See *"Training Day*—King Kong," YouTube, uploaded August 24, 2007, www.youtube.com.

26 After its initial release, the 2005 version of *King Kong* grossed more than half a billion dollars worldwide. The film's great success created a national debate on the presence of race in the movie. One writer, Matt Drudge, performed "a GOOGLE search using the words 'King Kong racism' [and] yielded 490,000 hits." Matt Drudge, "Is 'King Kong' Racist?," *Drudge Report*, December 15, 2005, 1.

27 Bogle quoted in Daniel Bernardi, ed., *Classic Hollywood, Classic Whiteness* (Minneapolis: University of Minnesota Press, 2001), 181.

28 Quoted in ibid.

29 Ibid.

30 Ibid.

31 Ibid., 162–65.

32 Joshua David Bellin, *Framing Monsters: Fantasy Film and Social Alienation* (Carbondale: Southern Illinois University Press, 2005), 26.

33 In his own way, Werner said, West may be doing what Toni Morrison termed "re-memory" in her novel *Beloved*. By invoking Holiday and Simone, he said, West's song is "keeping the voices of ancestors and the awareness of the history alive. Once he's established his dynamic with Murder, Nina and Billie, it's not about the layers, it's about understanding that this is his call, formed in response to the history." Gil Kaufman, "Kanye West's 'Blood on the Leaves' and the History of 'Strange Fruit,'" *MTV News*, June 19, 2013, www.mtv.com. See also "Blood on the Leaves," YouTube, June 13, 2013, www.youtube.com.

34 Bellin, *Framing Monsters*, 27.

35 James H. Cone, *The Cross and the Lynching Tree* (Maryknoll, NY: Orbis, 2013), xv.

36 Brandon Ellington Patterson, "10 Things You Should Know about the Killing of Laquan McDonald by Police," *Mother Jones*, December 1, 2015, www.motherjones.com.

37 John Fountain, "A Song for Laquan," *Chicago Sun-Times*, December 4, 2015, http://chicago.suntimes.com.

38 According to the theologian Shelly Rambo, reading theology and biblical texts through the lens of trauma (time, body, and word) asks the reader to use the site of trauma (*the wound that cries*, that remains in fragmented, distorted, exaggerated, sharp-edged acts of survival) as a way of reading (and listening to) new possibilities inherent in Christian traditions and texts that have historically and at great cost overlooked and not heard the voice(s) from the middle. Therefore, "witness," contrary to proclamation and sacrificial models, is middle activity that sees incompletely, hears somewhat, but never fully, and therefore does not and cannot assume to truly know. At the same time, Rambo argues, "witness" suggests that "a person is positioned to suffering in such a way that she sees truths that often escape articulation, that emerge through cracks in the dominant logic"; and "this tenuous placement also means that witness is subject to the continuous elisions that make it possible to see, but never directly; to hear, but never directly; and to touch, but never directly." Hence various forms of life are imagined in and through that witness. Shelly Rambo, *Spirit and Trauma: A Theology of Remaining* (Louisville: Westminster John Knox, 2010), 40.

39 Foucault, *Madness and Civilization*, 68.

40 Ibid., 69.

41 Ibid.

42 Ibid., 70.

43 Ibid., 69.

44 According to Jose Barchilon's introduction to *Madness and Civilization*, Renaissance men developed a delightful, yet horrible way of dealing with their mad denizens: they were put on a ship and entrusted to mariners because folly, water, and sea, as everyone then "knew," had an affinity for each other. Thus, "Ships of Fools" crisscrossed the sea and canals of Europe with their comic and pathetic cargo of souls. Some of them found pleasure

and even a cure in the changing surroundings, in the isolation of being cast off, while others withdrew further, became worse, or died alone and away from their families. The cities and villages which had thus rid themselves of their crazed and crazy, could now take pleasure in watching the exciting sideshow when a ship full of foreign lunatics would dock at their harbors. (vi–vii)

45 Wright quoted in Bellin, *Framing Monsters*, 29 (italics added).

46 Hussein Bulhan, *Frantz Fanon and the Psychology of Oppression* (New York: Plenum, 1985), 136.

47 Ibid., 137.

48 Michel Foucault, *The Fantasia of the Library* (1967), in *Language, Counter-Memory, Practice: Selected Essays and Interviews*, ed. Donald F. Bouchard (Ithaca: Cornell University Press, 1977).

49 Antonio Gramsci, *Selections from the Prison Notebooks*, trans. and ed. Quintin Hoare and Geoffrey Nowell Smith (New York: International, 1971).

50 Townes, *Womanist Ethics and the Cultural Production of Evil*, 18.

51 Ibid., 3.

52 See partial transcript in "Officer Darren Wilson Describes Michael Brown as a Grunting Aggravated Demon," *Not Allowed To*, November 26, 2014, http://notallowedto.com; aggregated online articles in the *Washington Post* and the *New York Times* summarize the case of Michael Brown: "What Happened in Ferguson?," *Washington Post* online, n.d., www.washingtonpost.com; "What Happened in Ferguson?," *New York Times* online, August 10, 2015, www.nytimes.com; see also Darryl Pinckney, "In Ferguson," *New York Review of Books*, January 8, 2015, www.nybooks.com; and Ben Spielberg, "Ethics, Accuracy and Perspectives on Michael Brown and Ferguson," *Huffington Post*, September 23, 2014, www.huffingtonpost.com.

53 Hardin Coleman, "Culture, Trauma, and Resilience: Psychological Colonization and the Intergenerational Transmission of Trauma" (lecture at Boston University, 2008).

54 DeGruy, *Post-Traumatic Slave Syndrome*.

55 Leon F. Litwack, *Trouble in Mind: Black Southerners in the Age of Jim Crow* (New York: Knopf, 1998); Carlyle Van Thompson, *Black Outlaws: Race, Law, and Male Subjectivity in African American Literature and Culture* (New York: Peter Lang, 2010), esp. conclusion, 198–201; Whet Moser, "American Violence and Southern Culture," *Chicago Magazine*, July 27, 2012, www.chicagomag.com; Patterson, *Cultural Matrix*.

56 Bourdieu, *Logic of Practice*, 54.

57 Townes, *Womanist Ethics and the Cultural Production of Evil*, 3.

58 Ibid., 18.

59 Morrison quoted in ibid., 12.

60 Patterson, *Cultural Matrix*, 41, 92–105.

61 Bourdieu, *Logic of Practice*, 64.

62 Mary E. Goodwin, "Racial Roots and Religion: An Interview with Howard Thurman," *Christian Century*, May 9, 1973, 533–35.

63 West quoted in Fluker, "Dangerous Memories and Redemptive Possibilities," 106.

64 Morrison, *Beloved*.

65 Girard, *Scapegoat*; and Agamben, *Homo Sacer*.

66 See Willie Jennings's excellent work in this regard. His location of the "theological error" in the Christian theological imagination, beginning as early as the fifteenth century in the European colonization of "nonwhite peoples," accounts for much of this diseased theological problem and its reconstruction. Jennings, *Christian Imagination*.

67 Fluker, *Ethical Leadership*, 168.

68 Du Bois, "Of Our Spiritual Strivings."

CHAPTER 10. WAKING UP THE DEAD

1 Normandi Ellis, *Awakening Osiris: The Egyptian Book of the Dead* (Boston: Phanes Press, 2009), chap. 18, "Giving Breath to Osiris," 113.

2 "Basic Black Live: What Is Black Leadership?" *Basic Black*, WGBH, January 18, 2013, www.wgbh.org.

3 Fluker, *Ethical Leadership*, 2009. For the past twenty years, I have engaged African American youth in institutes surrounding these important foci. For a video presentation of this work, see "Educational Docs," Azania Rizing Productions, http://azaniarizing.tumblr.com. Space will not allow a full accounting of the work, but the author is presently engaged in an initiative that will produce online and printed curricula based on this early work for collaboration and training with youth in this country and globally. For a course description, see "Ethical Leadership: Character, Civility, and Community," edX, www.edx.org.

4 See Mary Pattillo-McCoy, *Black Picket Fences: Privilege and Peril among the Black Middle Class* (Chicago: University of Chicago Press, 1999); Mary Patillo, *Black on the Block: The Politics of Race and Class in the City* (Chicago: University of Chicago Press, 2007); and Cathy J. Cohen, *Democracy Remixed: Black Youth and the Future of American Politics* (New York: Oxford University Press, 2010).

5 See Orlando Patterson's treatment of the "street configuration" in *Cultural Matrix*, 78–92.

6 See "Pan African Express," YouTube, March 27, 2013, www.youtube.com.

7 For the Salzburg Global Seminar and Andrew Mellon collaborative, see www.salzburgglobal.org. The TSE Foundation, based in Hong Kong, founded Global Friends; as its name suggests, it is a new initiative exploring pragmatic, holistic models of global social transformation. Its aim is to provide an opportunity to consider global philanthropy's unique ability to lead cross-sector transnational collaboration on a range of twenty-first-century challenges at this pivotal moment for the international community. These are just two examples of the rising

possibilities for global citizenship training and collaboration available for black churches and youth to become engaged. See TSE Foundation, http://tse-foundation.org.

8 This suggestion is not meant to minimize any efforts that may be going on that are similar to these. They are presented here simply as recommendations.

9 Shelly Rambo, "Exiling in America: The American Myth and the Spectral Christ," in *Interpreting Exile: Displacement and Deportation in Biblical and Modern Contexts*, ed. Brad E. Kelle, Frank Ritchel Ames, and Jacob L. Wright (New York: American Council of Learned Societies Humanities E-Book, 2011), 410.

10 Howard Thurman, "Disciplines of the Spirit: The Single Mind," October 16, 1960, taped recording, Howard Gotlieb Archival Research Center, Boston University. Thurman discusses the "fluid characteristic in life, of life" and its relation to commitment. He urges surrender to a higher goal or commitment, citing an example from Rufus Jones of a poor, illiterate farmer who sold his farm to serve as a Quaker missionary in the Middle East.

11 Thurman, "A Strange Freedom," in *The Inward Journey*, 38.

12 See Fluker, *Ethical Leadership*, chap. 7; for reference to self-reading, self-revision, and self-authoring, see 169–70; self-reading, self-revision, and self-authoring are indebted to Ellen Van Veslor and Wilfred H. Draft, "A Life-Long Developmental Perspective on Leadership Development," in *Center for Creative Leadership Handbook on Leadership Development*, 2d ed., ed. C. D. McCauley and Ellen Van Velsor (San Francisco: Jossey-Bass, 2004).

13 The Reverend Traci Blackmon, Christ the King, United Church of Christ in Florissant, MO, the Reverend Dr. R. F. Willis Johnson, Wellspring Church in Ferguson, and the Reverend Dr. Pamela Lightsey, associate dean and professor of ethics at Boston University School of Theology, have worked closely with the Reverend Starsky D. Wilson, president and CEO of Deaconess Foundation, a faith-based grant-making organization devoted to making child well-being a civic priority in the St. Louis region. A small but growing number of conferences, theological consultations, and publications have emerged and more are expected as of this writing. See Francis, *Ferguson and Faith*; Antonia Blumberg and Carol Kuruvilla, "How the Black Lives Matter Movement Changed the Church," *HuffPost Religion*, August 8, 2015, www.huffingtonpost.com; Rev. Dr. Stephanie Buckhanon Crowder, "Not Your Momma's Movement," *HuffPost Black Voices*, August 25, 2015, www.huffingtonpost.com; "Black Scholars National Gathering in Ferguson," *St. Louis Post Dispatch*, http://video.stltoday.com; Cheryl Hoth and Jan Boten, "LSTC Professor Linda Thomas Finds Signs of Hope in Ferguson, Mo.," *Lutheran School of Theology Chicago News*, August 20, 2015, www.lstc.edu.

14 See my discussion in chapter 3 on race and identity.

15 Quoted in Touré, *Who's Afraid of Post-Blackness?*

16 Howard Thurman, "The Sound of the Genuine" (Spelman College Baccalaureate Address, May 4, 1980); Howard Thurman, *The Growing Edge* (New York: Harper

and Row, 1956; Richmond, IN: Friends United Press, 1974), 27–28; preface to *My People Need Me*; Goodwin, "Racial Roots and Religion"; Thurman, *Inward Journey*, 121; Howard Thurman, *Mysticism and the Experience of Love* (Wallington, PA: Pendle Hill, 1961), 21.

17 Anthony Pinn, ed., *Noise and Spirit: The Religious and Spiritual Sensibilities of Rap Music* (New York: New York University Press, 2003), 1.

18 Mark Lewis Taylor, "Bringing Noise, Conjuring Spirit: Rap as Spiritual Practice," in Pinn, *Noise and Spirit*, 108.

19 "Where Shall I Be?" was written by the African American composer Charles P. Jones (1865–1949). See www.hymntime.com, accessed May 8, 2015.

20 James Weldon Johnson, "The Judgment Day," in *God's Trombones: Seven Negro Sermons in Verse* (New York: Viking Penguin, 1927). "The Judgment Day" closes with the refrain "Sinner, oh, sinner, / Where will you stand, / In that great day when God's a-going to rain down fire?"

21 To quote the brilliant philosopher Cornel West, "We're beings toward death, we're . . . two-legged, linguistically-conscious creatures born between urine and feces whose body will one day be the culinary delight of terrestrial worms." Cornel West, *Hope on a Tightrope: Words and Wisdom* (New York: Smiley, 2008), 28.

22 Howard Thurman, "The Growing Edge," in *A Strange Freedom*, 305.

23 Ta-Nehisi Coates, *Between the World and Me* (New York: Random House, 2015).

24 See my essay "Educating Leaders for the Twenty-First Century: Strategies and Resources for Ethical Leadership Education," in Fluker, *Educating Ethical Leaders*, 1–37, for a proposed framework that places methodological emphasis on the nodal concepts of remembering, retelling, and reliving stories. Outlined are concrete strategies that can be customized to address churches and other religious institutions, along with specific communities of discourse and practices in various educational situations.

INDEX

Abraham, and God, 138, 275n72
Adonis, 119, 268n12
affirmative action, 242n21
Africa: African Americans and, 188, 285n56; Diaspora of, 82–83, 112; Thurman and, 188
African American Christianity, 89, 263n21
African American life and practices: Diaspora and, 100–101, 112–13; doubleness in, 78, 199, 200; Exile and, 96–101, 108–9; Exodus and, 93–96, 106. *See also* black cultural practices; *specific topics*
African American pasts, 16; old songs about, 31–32; reliving stories about, 34, 42; remembering stories about, 34, 42; retelling stories about, 34, 42, 74–75
African Americans: Africa and, 188, 285n56; bestiality and, 34; crossing(s) of existence of, 236; Exodus and narratives of, 90–92, 94, 95, 103, 105, 111, 262n9; madness and, 34, 35. *See also* blacks
Agamben, Giorgio, 266n60
agency, moral, 98
America: founding fathers' campaign of terror, 168; political incivility and meanness, 175. *See also* cultural haunting of America; post-racial America
An American Dilemma: The Negro Problem and Modern Democracy (Myrdal), 77
"American Heartbreak" (Hughes), 166
American Idea, 242n19
Anderson, Benedict, 21

Anderson, Victor, 105, 106
Angel with flaming sword, 192, 286n67
apostles, 138–39
Appiah, Kwame Anthony, 68, 134
Arrested Development, 123
artistic creation, 184, 283n42
Ashby, Homer, 104–7
assemblage theory, 85, 260n57
Assmann, Jan, 32
awakening: facing others and, 150–51, 278n13. *See also* waking the dead
Axelrod, David, 48
Azusa Street Revival, 140

Babel story, 138–40, 275n71
Baker, Ella, 147
Baker, Houston, 111
Baldwin, James, 16, 30, 109, 220
Baldwin, Lewis V., 151
baptism: of Fire and Holy Ghost, 123, 129–31, 271n41; in Spirit in black religious practices, 132
Baptist World Center, 122, 123
Barchilon, Jose, 291n44
Battle, Michael, 96
Baumfree, Isabella. *See* Sojourner Truth
Beinart, Peter, 175
Bell, Daniel, 290n16
Beloved (Morrison), 197–98, 202, 289n11, 291n33
bestiality: African Americans and, 34; cultural asylums and, 213; madness and, 213–15
The Birth of a Nation, 210–11

ABOUT THE AUTHOR

Walter Earl Fluker is Martin Luther King, Jr., Professor of Ethical Leadership, editor of the Howard Thurman Papers Project, and Director of the Martin Luther King, Jr., Initiative for the Development of Ethical Leadership (MLK-IDEAL) at Boston University School of Theology.